COMMU[
CITY

COMMUTER CITY

CITY

How the Railways Shaped
London

DAVID WRAGG

Wharncliffe Books

First published in Great Britain in 2010 by
Wharncliffe Local History
an imprint of
Pen & Sword Books Ltd
47 Church Street
Barnsley
South Yorkshire
S70 2AS

ISBN 978 1 84563 109 3

A CIP catalogue record for this book is
available from the British Library

Typeset in Ehrhardt
by S L Menzies-Earl

Printed and bound in England by
MPG Books Group

Pen & Sword Books Ltd incorporates the imprints of
Pen & Sword Aviation, Pen & Sword Maritime,
Pen & Sword Military, Wharncliffe Local History, Pen & Sword Select,
Pen & Sword Military Classics, Leo Cooper, Remember When,
Seaforth Publishing and Frontline Publishing

For a complete list of Pen & Sword titles please contact
PEN & SWORD BOOKS LIMITED
47 Church Street, Barnsley, South Yorkshire, S70 2AS, England
E-mail: enquiries@pen-and-sword.co.uk
Website: www.pen-and-sword.co.uk

Contents

List of Illustrations

Introduction

The slightest addition to the ordinary traffic of the City would make the streets impassable. The mere increase of the metropolis itself must bring about the same result, unless the main thoroughfares should be constantly widened.

The Times, 1863

'I am happy to carry more people for more money,' Sir Herbert Ashcombe Walker, the first general manager of the Southern Railway explained to the then John Elliot, his public relations assistant. 'I don't mind carrying fewer people for more money, but what you are asking me to do is to carry more people for less money, and that's the way to go bankrupt. You will remember that won't you?'

Elliot clearly did remember for, in later years, as Sir John Elliot, chairman of the Railways Executive and of London Transport, he oversaw organisations that were indeed carrying fewer people for more money.

But that is to move on almost 120 years from the early days of the railways in London in the 1830s to the one period when all of London's scheduled passenger transport was in a single ownership, that of the state, whose public persona was that of the British Transport Commission. This was a rare and in fact short-lived period, following the nationalisation of Britain's main line railways in 1948 and long before the break-up of the first British nationalised transport undertaking, London Transport, and the later privatisation of the railways.

We need to go back to the beginning. On the eve of the railway age, London was already the world's largest and most populous city in the world. In 1801, a census of the Greater London area, somewhat larger in size than that of the Greater London Council, which was established in 1965, showed that there were 1,110,000 people living there. By 1841, this had more than doubled to 2,250,000, and the population continued to grow until it reached 6,381,000 in 1901; and eventually 8,187,000 by 1964.

During the early nineteenth century, London was already closely built-up, mainly in and around the twin cities of London and Westminster and the immediate suburbs. West of Marble Arch was open fields. Most of the development was north of the Thames, while south of the river the land was flat and marshy; but already areas such as Southwark contained a tightly-packed overflow from the more expensive, and healthier, accommodation available north of the river. While the Thames was a natural barrier to the south, to the north, some three to five miles back, there were heights such as those around Hampstead Heath, which also helped to define the limits of the old city, much of which dated from the Roman era. The spread of London downstream had already started, with the first enclosed docks built in the previous century.

The West End of London ended at Marble Arch, beyond which were large farms and small villages to the west, one of which was Paddington. Such development as lay to the west was along the banks of the Thames.

Onto this scene emerged the early railways, but at first their impact was hardly noticeable as London's first recorded railway was the Surrey Iron Railway of 1803, which was horse-drawn and used solely for the conveyance of freight to and from the riverside at Wandsworth. Nevertheless, the congested roads and densely-packed property of all types meant that travel within London was difficult and time consuming, as well as often unpleasant. This was the driving force behind the first two London railways: the London & Greenwich, authorised in 1833 and opened between Spa Road and Deptford in February 1836, and then Spa Road to London Bridge that December, with Deptford to Greenwich in December 1838; and the London & Blackwall Railway, authorised in 1836 as the Commercial Railway, and opened after a change of terminus from the Minories to Fenchurch Street and a change of name to the London & Blackwall Railway, in 1840. To minimise the impact on the property along the routes, and overcome the problem of bridging the many streets and narrow lanes crossed by the lines, both railways were built on arches, with the London & Greenwich needing 60 million bricks and running over 878 arches. The LGR used especially low slung carriages to avoid the risk of them falling over the side of the viaduct, despite its walls being 4 ft 6 in high, while the LBR used cable haulage to avoid the risk that sparks from steam locomotives might set fire to the shipping or the cargo in the docks.

These early railways were not without their disruptive effect. They ran through slum areas so displaced many of the poorer sections of society, but did not offend the affluent and influential landowners. Railways could not be built without massive upheaval, not unlike major road schemes today, and the construction of their London termini proved as disruptive in their construction as an airport would be in modern times, and, of course, every new terminus needed its access lines running from the countryside, through the suburbs and through ever more densely-populated areas until at last the end was reached. Like an airport, the passenger terminus was just part of the whole, for there was usually a goods station, although both the London & South Western and the London Brighton & South Coast used their original, somewhat distant, London termini at Nine Elms and Bricklayers' Arms respectively, for this purpose, and there had to be a maintenance area, in short, a locomotive depot, as well as carriage sidings and cleaning facilities.

Just what this all meant can be judged by the fact that, in 1854, the extension of the London & South-Western Railway towards the Thames from Nine Elms to the site of Waterloo meant the demolition of 700 houses for a narrower spread of tracks than exists today, while Waterloo itself was a far smaller terminus, reaching its present size with the addition of a further three stations before complete re-design and re-building between 1910 and 1920. Nevertheless, the attitude of the landowners was to undergo a massive change when the Great Western Railway began its advance towards Paddington and the London & Birmingham started to move towards first Camden and then Euston.

The arrival of the railways cannot be under-estimated. Even in the middle of the nineteenth century, the streets of the capital were so congested that, in 1867, no less than 3.5 million of the 8 million passengers using the terminus at Cannon Street were travelling solely between the City and the West End terminus of the South Eastern Railway at Charing Cross. The new railway was also competitive, charging fares of 6d first class, 4d second class and 2d third class, compared with 3d for the horse bus, while no doubt first class travel compared well with a handsome cab on cost, timing and comfort.

Parliament was determined that railway travel should be for everyone and not just the wealthy. It introduced the so-called Parliamentary Trains, charging a fare of just a penny a mile and exempt from the Railway Passenger Duty levied on fares, but the generosity of Parliament was not always appreciated by those who used them. In 1883, FS Williams wrote in *Our Iron Roads*:

> To start in the darkness of a winter's morning to catch the only third-class train that ran; to sit, after a slender breakfast, in a vehicle the windows of which were compounded of the largest amount of wood and the smallest amount of glass, carefully adjusted to exactly those positions in which the fewest passengers could see out; to stop at every roadside station, however insignificant; and to accomplish a journey of 200 miles in about ten hours – such were the ordinary conditions which Parliament in its bounty provided for the people.

Parliament was increasingly involved in the regulation of the railways, and in London this extended to what might even be regarded as an early interest in town planning. In fact, many of the railways arriving in the capital were adding to rather than solving the congestion and overcrowding. The House of Lords considered forcing the railway companies to build and use a single major terminus, but fortunately this was rejected as impractical and it would have resulted in massive upheaval and no doubt simply unimaginable chaos and congestion on the surrounding streets. Parliament then changed its mind and did an abrupt about turn and decided that any new railway termini would have to be outside the central zone, which left the stations at

Charing Cross, Blackfriars and Cannon Street almost clinging to the banks of the Thames. The construction of Liverpool Street was allowed simply because it approached the City through a tunnel, and even then the Great Eastern had to provide especially low fares for those thought to have been displaced by the construction of the terminus.

The arrival of the underground lines produced a solution to the dispersal of the main termini and to movement around London, and even created a new series of suburbs, famously known as 'Metroland', but this in turn really pointed to further expansion of London. Then, just as the railway map was more or less complete, the electric tram suddenly undermined the railways, taking away a massive share of the inner suburban traffic. The more progressive railways retaliated with electrification, with both the London Brighton & South Coast Railway and the London & South Western Railway having a substantial electrified mileage operational before the First World War.

This is a history of the railway age and its impact on London and the Home Counties, as well as an analysis of the decisions taken by the railway companies, Parliament and local government within London. It shows how in 1906 Golders Green was a muddy country crossroads with hardly a building in sight, but after the Underground reached it the following year, it started to develop into a built-up, but affluent, suburb with a tube depot and a substantial network of bus services operating from the station forecourt and trolleybuses passing close by. It looks at the railways in peace and in war, when occupation by Londoners led to the authorities allowing the deep level tube stations to be used as night time air raid shelters, although as events were to show, these were far less safe than people thought. It looks at the way in which technology has not always come first to London, with the first high speed railway link worthy of the name not finally reaching its terminus at St Pancras until 2007. On the other hand, the popular desire for innovation was not always practical, which is why the Dockland Light Railway was built using 'steel wheel on steel rail', rather than some of the more exciting and exotic solutions proposed before construction began.

The railway network around London is complex, making a spider's web seem logical by comparison. The problems of operating a dense commuter network are equally complex. Many of those travelling in overcrowded peak period trains cannot understand that the train in which they are travelling is losing money due to poor rolling stock utilisation, as much of it lies idle for most of the day, while the commuters can receive discounts of as much as 60 per cent on their season tickets compared to the standard fares.

Yet, while London was not created by the railway, its size and shape and growth during the nineteenth and twentieth centuries was dictated by the railway, and only the railway enables the modern and overcrowded city to function.

Chapter 1

The Great Wen

My fellow-passenger had the highest of all terrestrial
qualities which for me a fellow-passenger
can possess. He was silent.

Jane Carlyle, on travel by coach

London dominates the south of England in a way that no other British city can match with regard to its own particular region. There is nothing new about this, the famous journalist and radical politician William Cobbett castigated London as 'The Great Wen', and today even the *Oxford English Dictionary* in its definition of the word 'wen', goes beyond the archaic 'more or less permanent benign sebaceous tumour on the skin, especially scalp', to 'abnormally large or congested city'.

Cobbett's unflattering appraisal tells us much about London. He died in 1835 at the dawn of the railway age. The fact is that London was not one of those places created by the railway, such as, most famously, Crewe, once a country village, or even enlarged by the railway, such as Derby, but like Bristol was made greater still by the railway. London existed for at least two millennia before the railway. It was selected by the Romans because it was the lowest point at which the River Thames could be crossed. As a natural route between the south and the rest of the country, it had to be protected and fortified. It became the capital of a newly-subjugated Roman province and then eventually of just a part of England after the country divided into a number of independent Anglo-Saxon kingdoms after the fall of Rome. Before this, as the seat of Roman authority, roads radiated out from London, taking the short distances to the east and to the south, the much longer ones to the west, and the even longer routes to the north.

London's importance during the Roman period was relative, as it was simply the capital of a distant colony. Things changed with the establishment of, first a united England, then later the United Kingdom, and then with London as the capital of the world's greatest empire. The emergence of finance as a major industry in its own right, with subsectors such as banking, insurance, stock broking and ship broking, all led to the city establishing a truly global importance that stretched far beyond even Britain's widespread colonial possessions. Even so, after the Norman Conquest in 1066, for the next five centuries, the eastern limit was around the Tower of London while the West End was largely open fields. When it developed, it was the City that was important to commerce while Westminster became important as the centre of government.

London was already a congested and overcrowded, even insanitary city by the Tudor period and by 1801 it had a population of 1,110,000 people, which had more than doubled to 2,250,000 by 1841. By 1901, the population had grown to 6,581,000. The topography varied, but around the Thames it was flat, often marshy, with much property built on reclaimed land, while to the north, the land began to rise, as it did to the south. Beneath the surface, there was thick, heavy clay. To put these figures into some perspective, in 1801, London was well over twice the size of Bristol or Edinburgh today. By 1841, the population matched that of Wales today and was more than a third of Scotland's current population. London in 1801 had a population greater than that of some sovereign states, and that of 1841 even more so. By 1901, the population exceeded that of modern day Denmark or Switzerland, and was roughly three quarters that of Sweden.

The presence of drinkable water in the northern heights ensured that medieval London was viable, which as just as well as the art of building aqueducts, and the controlling hand that ensured that these were built where they were wanted and whenever they were needed, had gone with the Romans and was not to return for some time. The city was already so big that it could no longer feed itself, and it drew in the necessary produce from the surrounding countryside. The so-called 'Home Counties' provided the food that Londoners needed to survive, and in so doing ensured that from the Middle Ages onwards, these areas enjoyed greater prosperity than much of the rest of England.

Old London

It is important not to have a rosy view of old London. Lacking sanitation, it was filthy, and while it is fashionable in this 'green' age to decry the motor car and its internal combustion engine, old London depended on horse power in the most literal sense, and so the streets were wet and smelly as well as noisy. Not for nothing is the crossing-sweeper a recurring character in Dickens, while outside the homes of the well-to-do, if one of the occupants was ill, straw was laid in the street outside to ensure peace. Victorian prints show the major thoroughfares effectively jammed by the sheer weight of horse-drawn traffic. Colourful in retrospect, this was clearly the age when the coachbuilders' craft was at its highest, with even the humble horse-drawn bus being a work of astonishing strength and lightness. Yet, it was smelly and unpleasant, especially in summer. And the horse-drawn bus, we should remember, was no humble convenience as it was very much the mode of transport of the middle classes, who could afford the fares, while the working classes walked.

The one obvious relief to all of this pressure on the streets was the River Thames. This was the main source of many of the supplies needed by London. True, London grew as a great international trading port, and its growth matched that of the British Empire, but much of the cargo handled in London came from elsewhere in England and was intended for the consumption of Londoners and London business. Coal came from Newcastle by sea, and salted fish from ports much closer in East Anglia and Kent. It was not just cargo that came and went using the Thames. If one wanted to travel between London and, say, Edinburgh or Aberdeen, the more comfortable and sometimes safer alternative to the stage and mail coaches was by sea. By sea or by land, travel was expensive and slow. By land, there were the dangers of the highwaymen, but a more persistent danger was that of accident, and this was something that was also ever present when travelling by sea.

The Thames itself was also used on a regular basis for transport. None of this should make one believe that this was an idyllic age afloat anymore than ashore, for the truth was that the river was London's main, and smelliest, sewer. Nevertheless, one could travel by boat from a number of piers along the river, aboard boats that were reasonably frequent, and competitive in time with such other transport as was available to the travelling public.

For all of these problems, in one sense the economy and life of London was better balanced than today. London was not just the seat of government, the centre of finance and commerce; it still had its own extensive manufacturing industry. Shipbuilding continued on the Thames, and there were ironworks. Manufacturing was not something conducted away from London, in the Midlands and the North. Even in comparatively modern times, manufacturing remained in London, with Vauxhall cars taking their name from what would now be regarded as an inner-London suburb, before moving to Luton. Commercial vehicles were built during the mid-twentieth century at Southall, and aircraft at Cricklewood.

Early journeys

People in earlier centuries travelled far less than is the case today. Travel was expensive and often fraught with hazard. This was due in part to the lack of a banking system, so one had to carry all one needed while away from home in the form of hard cash.

At first, even if one lived in a city, one walked or, if one was prosperous enough, rode on horseback. If one couldn't ride, one was at a disadvantage until the introduction of the sedan chair to Britain in 1634 by Sir Richard Dunscombe. The conveyance consisted of a small cabin, smaller than a telephone kiosk but, fortunately, much lighter, which was carried by two men, known as 'chairmen', one in front and one behind, who lifted long poles on which the 'chair' was placed. The conveyance got its name from southern Italy and not from the French town of the same name. Quite why it took so long for such a conveyance to evolve was probably due to the need for something light to be constructed so that just two men were needed, rather than the team that would have been needed to lift a litter. By the eighteenth century, this was the conveyance of choice for those who could afford it, smoother and cheaper than a carriage, not much slower in the congested streets and able to use narrow alleyways and steps, and unlike the humble pedestrian, one was not splashed by horses as they trotted past.

The next development was the short-stage carriage, which ran between points, usually an inn, with the operator having first obtained a licence from the Board of Stamps. This was also expensive and required pre-booking, while the choice of routes was limited. This was the urban version of the stage coach, the town bus as opposed to the inter-city motorway coach. The use of the Commissioners of Stamps as what would today be described in British terms as traffic commissioners was no doubt a reflection of the primitive means of licensing and revenue-raising by the government of the day, when widespread taxation was generally unknown and evasion much easier than today. The operators of stage coaches and of omnibuses paid the stamp duty according to the number of passengers carried plus an annual mileage levy, which was during the early years set at 3d per mile.

When the Metropolitan Police was formed as a result of Robert Peel's Metropolis Police Improvement Act 1829, the police were not concerned with the licensing of vehicles, whether plying for hire or not. The first thousand police officers, or 'Peelers', who started their patrols on the evening of 29 September 1829, had other more pressing matters to attend. Later, the Metropolitan Police was to have an extensive involvement in the licensing of hackney carriages and buses, and even after the Road Traffic Acts of 1930 and 1933, in London they uniquely remained responsible for the licensing of bus drivers and conductors, while elsewhere this was a matter for the traffic commissioners.

The *Public Advertiser*, on 18 January 1772, informed its readers of a 'new contrived coach' which could carry up to fourteen passengers at 6d each (2.5p in today's money, but at the time, fifteen shillings a week was a good wage) and which would run between Charing Cross and the Royal Exchange. This was clearly another development of the short stage as the passengers entered the single enclosed compartment using side doors while the remainder sat outside either alongside the driver or at the back over the parcels and luggage.

The London omnibus

The bus, as we know it, had its origins much later, more than half-a-century in fact, when on 3 April 1829, one George Shillabeer advised John Thornton, Chairman of the Board of Stamps, that he was building 'two vehicles after the manner of the recently established French *omnibus*, which when completed I propose starting on the Paddington Road'. Shillabeer was a coachbuilder by trade, and this no doubt made it easier for him to bring such an innovation to London. Unlike the stage coaches, short or not, his carriage was a long box-structure set high off the ground and entered by three steps and a door at the end. Instead of booking at an inn or a coaching office nearby, fares were collected by a conductor who stood on the steps. Inside, there were longitudinal seats for eighteen passengers, nine on each side. Three horses abreast provided the propulsive effort for this vehicle, described by the *Morning Post* on 7 July 1829 as 'a handsome machine, in the shape of a van with windows on each side, and one at the end'.

While the stage coaches often bore names, the early horse bus was far more practical: along the sides, between the windows, were panels describing the route taken. The sides were half panels, half windows, while below the windows was the single word, in capital letters just eight inches high, 'OMNIBUS'. The route details were important because, far more important than the design of the vehicle, was its means of plying for hire. No longer did intending passengers have to call at a coach office and wait for a departure, but instead they could flag down the omnibus in the street, pay a fare on boarding, and ask to be set down wherever they chose, even after riding for just a short distance. No sooner had George Shillabeer started operations between Paddington Green and the Bank, on 4 July 1829, than the established operators claimed that his action was illegal. It wasn't, as Shillabeer had been careful to ensure that his carriages were licensed, but any doubt was soon removed as the Stage Carriage Act 1832 authorised the operation of omnibus services. Further legislation in 1838 required the licensing of drivers and conductors working within ten miles of the General Post Office, who had to wear numbered badges. In addition, the conditions of the original act of 1832 were tightened up, requiring all buses in London to carry the words 'Metropolitan Stage Carriage', the Stamp Office number and the number of passengers the vehicle was allowed to carry under the conditions of its licence, painted on both the outside and inside. A Registrar of Metropolitan Carriages was appointed by the Home Secretary.

A substantial degree of freedom was still accorded operators. There was no restriction on the number of buses any one operator could have, or where they would operate. As with shipping, which allowed a similar free for all, it soon became obvious to those involved that collaboration was better than all-out competition. It also became obvious that cooperation in this way meant that operators could serve more routes and that improved frequencies could be offered to the passengers. Starting as early as September 1831, operators began to group themselves into associations, each operating a route or a group of routes. Vehicles began to carry the name of the route or of the district served rather than that of the proprietor: this was the start of the practice of bus operators tending towards geographical names rather than the names of the owners, a practice that was largely reserved for tour and private hire coach operators, with a few exceptions.

When the railways arrived later, geographical names, and often ones that were highly descriptive, became the standard, while London and the Thames were important to the very imprecisely-named General Steam Navigation Company, mentioned in Charles Dickens' *Sketches by Boz*.

The earliest use of the abbreviated and meaningless term 'bus' was recorded in 1832.

While Shillabeer's first two vehicles used three horses, his subsequent vehicles and those for other operators were built to be drawn by two horses. At first all passengers were accommodated inside, but gradually the practice grew of having a row of passengers seated first beside and then behind the driver, following stage coach practice. While popular belief has it that the practice of riding on the roof or 'outside' dated from the Great Exhibition of 1851, and the first great influx of visitors to London, it is clear that the practice started much earlier. During the 1840s, many of the newer buses were less box-like and had curved roofs, and at busy periods many male passengers would climb onto the roof and sit back to back, noted by Alfred Crowquill in November 1845 as being '...something after the sitting fashion of a batch of undertaker's men going to a country job'. The next step was to build buses with a clerestory roof to improve headroom and ventilation inside, and this provided a longitudinal seat, with the first of these put into service in April 1847 by the Economic Conveyance Company.

Initially, routes were short and a flat fare was charged, but as longer services were provided, graduated fares became more commonplace, often with a starting fare of just 2d. A variation was that, following stage coach practice, those riding outside paid just half the fare of those riding inside, and soon a fare of 2d per mile inside and 1d per mile outside became standard. Access to the roof was by iron foot rungs, so it was certainly not an option for the Victorian lady with her long flowing dress. But not all bus proprietors welcomed the carriage of passengers 'outside', especially as the new buses were heavier and placed a greater strain on the horses, reducing the number of journeys they could perform daily, while higher stamp duties were also levied and, of course, for much of the time the outside space was not needed. It was no doubt helpful that the stamp duty was reduced from 3d to 1½ d per mile in October 1842. The Great Exhibition persuaded the more conservative omnibus proprietors that using the roof space was an economic necessity and those buses without roof seats had an improvised seat provided by the simple expedient of nailing a plank along the apex of the roof, which promptly became known as the 'knifeboard'.

Life inside was by no means comfortable, with the vehicles riding roughly over cobbled roads. It was not until 1853 that interior lighting was required, and even then it usually consisted of no more than a small colza lamp hung on the door, so that when the door was opened for passengers to board or alight, the interior once again plunged into darkness. The lamps were provided by James Willingham & Company, for a charge of 4d per day, and until 1870, the charge was paid by the conductor.

For those travelling 'outside', there was always the risk of falling off until side rails became commonplace. Fortunately, speeds were slow, and overall journey times were between 4 and 6 mph. This was blessing, for when it rained, the only shelter was one's own umbrella, and this could be put up with no more concern about it being blown inside out than if one was walking.

The Board of Stamps lost its licensing function in October 1847, when this was transferred to the Commissioners of Excise.

Taking to the river

The steamboat arrived before the train, in terms of evolution. The General Steam Navigation Company (later acquired by a much grander shipping line, P&O) boasted that it dated from 1824, before the first steam railways. The

River Thames had been an important thoroughfare in London as the city grew and the roads became more congested. In his diaries, Samuel Pepys and his associates made frequent use of the river, being rowed by boatmen, and no doubt this was a comfortable if expensive means of travel. The steamboat changed this, being larger and cheaper, and capable of coping with high winds and strong spring tides.

In London, during the 1840s, there was a steamboat service between London Bridge and Westminster, with a departure at the staggering frequency of every four minutes. The journey took just fifteen minutes, far less than it would by any form of public transport today, and cost an old penny, far less than the then alternatives. Slower boats served intermediate piers. In all, there were some forty-five riverside piers between Hampton Court and Southend.

This may have been an agreeable form of transport on a fine day, provided that it wasn't too hot as one was travelling along London's main sewer, but in fact, it often wasn't. One expects the popular media and politicians to give every form of transport sharp criticism, ignorant of the practicalities, but the journal, *The Engineer*, with a far more knowledgeable editorial staff, described the Thames steamers as '...shamefully mismanaged, dirty and lubberly handled, to the risk of life and limb'. Matters did not improve with competition from the railways and the horse omnibus, as during the 1860s, by which time these vessels were managing around 12 miles per hour (more than a modern bus in the centre of London), the same journal described the accommodation as being somewhat '...inferior to that of a third-class railway carriage'.

One thing that would not have changed, however, between the late seventeenth century and the late nineteenth century, that would have made river travel hazardous, was the London fog. No radar, not even the comfort of a reassuring signal, for the traveller by river. In fact, the fog of the 1860s would, if anything, have been far worse than that of the 1660s.

Inter-city travel before the train

For us today, it is hard to realise just how important an advance the railway was when it first appeared as a form of public transport, breaking out from its early existence in quarries. Business had been transformed during the previous century by the arrival of the canals, dramatically cutting the costs of moving bulky goods such as coal, but canals were slow and expensive to build, facing considerable problems when forced through steep hills or over deep valleys and always demanding the provision of large quantities of water. That the canal system slashed the costs of bulk commodities such as coal so dramatically only shows just how difficult and costly transport, usually by packhorse, was before the eighteenth century. The railway was easier to build and to operate, and from the outset it was far faster than any form of transport then known.

The railways arrived on the scene at a time when few people made lengthy journeys, with most going no further than the nearest town. The Christmas card glamour of the long distance stagecoach or its rival the mail coach, first introduced in 1784, was in reality so harsh and bleak, as well as being expensive, that it was not to be undertaken lightly. In winter, coaches squelched through mud or could be overwhelmed by snow, or find bridges swept away by rivers in flood, while in summer, the roads were baked hard and the coaches banged from one deep rut to another. Coaches could, and sometimes did, overturn or get blown off an exposed stretch of road. Competition on the busiest routes could see some wild driving with more than one stage coach reduced to matchwood in an accident. The arrival of the turnpike trusts in the early eighteenth century, due to much improved road building and mending techniques, brought a considerable improvement, except that stretches of non-turnpike highway were still to be found between the turnpikes, themselves not wholly popular amongst those who had always used the roads free of any charge or taxation and who were damned if they were going to pay anything now, even for better roads.

Passengers froze in winter despite heavy clothing, blankets and foot warmers, and sweltered in summer, longing for the next stop and liquid refreshment. Those outside fared worst, and even on a good road could not seek solace in sleep because to nod off was to fall off! Another consideration on any journey was one's fellow passengers, especially if travelling inside, for which privilege one paid double.

Meals were served at inns, and at many of them, passengers were treated to rotten food badly prepared by unscrupulous proprietors well aware that they had a captive market. The hungry customers, perhaps on a journey taking as much as sixty hours, paid their money and were often cheated. Passengers had to eat and drink, and relieve themselves, in as little as twenty minutes before being hurried back to their coach. Few were regular travellers. Scolding hot soup would be served, so that customers would not have much time for subsequent courses, for which much of the food, as a result, was often stale. If one was contemplating a journey from, say, Edinburgh or Newcastle to London, it was worth considering going by sea, and coasting voyages were indeed an option. So too was travel by canal barge, on the relatively few routes served, but slow.

In the 1830s, at the dawn of the railway age, a passenger from London to Newcastle on the *Lord Wellington* coach would be charged £3.10s

(£3.50p) for the 274 mile journey, a fare of just over 3d (1.25p) per mile, for an outside seat. Ignoring inflation, this fare was exactly the same per mile as the standard rate for a second class railway ticket in the early 1960s for a journey of up to 200 miles, after which the rate per mile fell. To put these fares into perspective, a footman in a grand house, by no means the most junior member of the servant class, would have been doing well to earn £20 per annum. Looked at another way, £3.10s in 1830 would be the equivalent of almost £200 today.

Drivers and guards were not backwards in seeking a tip: 'I'll be leaving you now sir…your driver who has driven you the past 50 miles.'

All of this was for outside accommodation, exposed to the elements, dirt and dust. For those inside, the fare would have been £5 15s (£5 75p), and in addition to meals, the driver and guard would have expected far higher tips, say 3s (15p) for the former and 3s 9d (18.75p) or even 4s for the latter.

This assumes that the journey was a simple affair. Those living in a village, away from the main coaching routes, would have had to make their way to the coach, and perhaps also to their destination at the end of the journey if that too was off the coaching map. This might mean walking, or perhaps hiring a carriage, at considerable additional expense. Londoners at least had the short stages and then, later, on the eve of the railway age, the omnibus.

Travelling north from London to Newcastle or Edinburgh, the traveller would have been spared changing the time on his watch. For those travelling east or west, it would have been wise to check the time whenever they stopped as there was no conception of, and no need for, a single national time.

There is no doubt that the fares charged by the stagecoach operators were high, but the costs were high, for up to six people inside and eleven outside on a stage coach, with fewer outside on a mail coach as the seats at the back were reserved for the guard, and the rewards were by no means guaranteed. On a run from London to Edinburgh, a single coach would need the services of 400 fine horses. Fewer horses were needed pro rata on the shorter routes, say from London to Portsmouth or Brighton. These were the so-called 'short stages', for which smaller teams of horses were used so that the coach, which with a full team was capable of running at up to 10-12 miles per hour (16-19 kmph) on a good stretch of road, did not deposit its passengers at their destination in the middle of the night.

Parliament saw another opportunity to raise money. Owners of carriages had been taxed as early as 1747, and their horses were taxed as well from 1785. As early as 1775, an annual duty was levied on each stagecoach of £5, followed in 1783 by a duty of ½ d (0.2p) for every mile run, doubled to 1d after a few years and then increased later, when a coach licensed to carry fifteen passengers could pay 3d (1.25p) per mile. There was also a tax on every coach and carriage produced that had to be paid by the carriage builders. Only mail coaches were exempt from taxation, on the grounds that they were employed on state business. On London to Edinburgh, the horses provided by contractors, usually at the inns along the way, would cost another £5, and the turnpikes would charge another £6 15s (£6. 75p). Canal barges were free of taxation, although it had been proposed by William Pitt the Younger who had wanted to tax the carriage of cargo in 1797, but backed down in the face of extremely strong opposition.

Given costs on such a scale for carrying so few people at speeds of around 12 mph, it is not surprising that the new railway made an impact and that entrepreneurs could see that there was money to be made. At the beginning of the steam age, there were a number of attempts at harnessing steam to the stage coach, but none were successful. Steam-powered carriages were heavy and damaged the roads, while the heavily rutted roads in turn produced such a rough ride that that mechanical reliability was seriously compromised. In any case, the costs remained high given the small number of passengers that could be carried.

Chapter 2

The Railway Age Arrives in London

*It is quite a just remark that the Devil, if he travelled,
would go by train...*
Diary of the Seventh Earl of Shaftesbury, 1839

No mode of transport could ignore London. The River Thames had ensured the capital's value as a port, and while it might be an exaggeration to say that all roads led to London, it was nevertheless both the start and the end of a network of major highways. When the canals had arrived, and proved just as significant a step forward in reducing transport costs and improving communications as the railways were to be later, London was on the canal network. The most obvious of these was the Grand Union Canal, linking London with Birmingham, but there were others linking into the docks, then much further upstream than is the case today. For the canal users, the Regent's Canal, completed as late as 1820 and curving around the northern and already heavily built-up suburbs, was a vital link around London, but for the railways, it was another obstacle to be overcome.

Yet, the earliest railways were built away from London and between pairs of towns with local trading interests. In the south of England, Canterbury needed to be linked with the nearby port of Whitstable, while the truly great early railways were in the north, with perhaps the most important being the Liverpool and Manchester. Nevertheless, it was inevitable that lines would be sent into London at an early date. London presented both opportunities and problems for those entrepreneurs anxious to develop the railways. The opportunities included its size and the congestion, the fact that it was a political, legal and financial capital, the largest port, and that it needed fresh food and coal brought to it in vast quantities; the problems were the congestion and the sheer impossibility of fitting anything easily into this dense mass of humanity, housing and industry, and the poor drainage, especially south of the River Thames.

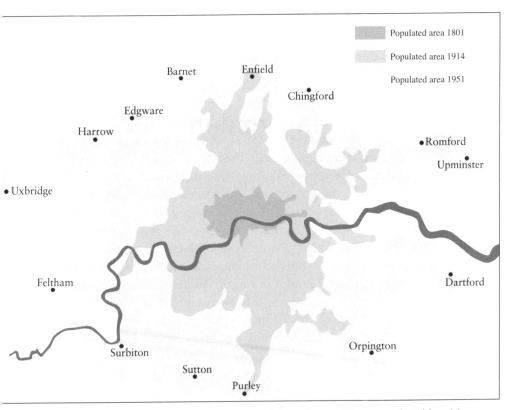

Populated area 1801

Populated area 1914

Populated area 1951

The growth of London after the introduction of the railways. The cross-hatching 1 is the built-up area in 1801, and the hatching at 2 shows the built-up area in 1914, while the stipple at 3 shows the built-up area in 1951.

London's first railway was the Surrey Iron Railway, a horse-drawn tramroad built to carry freight from the Thames, and authorised by Parliament in 1801. When authorised, the Surrey Iron Railway was the world's first public railway and its route ran from the banks of the River Thames at Wandsworth to Croydon, a distance of some 8¼ miles, following the course of the River Wandle. The track consisted of cast-iron plates of L-section fixed to stone blocks, with a gauge of 4ft 2in. Traction was provided by horses, which, because of the lack of any substantial gradient, could move five or six wagons, each weighing 3½ tons fully loaded, at around 2½ mph. The line was supported by the many mills and factories spread along its route, showing that some, at least, of London's urban sprawl pre-dated the arrival of the railways.

Not realising its shortcomings, so obvious to us today with the benefit of hindsight (always 20:20 vision, of course) the promoters of the line had ambitions and were keen to see it extended to Portsmouth, but only succeeded in extending the tracks as far as the quarry at Merstham, a further 8½ miles. All was not lost, however, as part of its route was later to be used by the London Brighton & South Coast Railway.

London's first railways

It was not until the London & Greenwich and London & Blackwall Railways were built in the 1830s that the railway as we know it arrived in London. As elsewhere in Great Britain, once again these were both short distance.

The London & Greenwich Railway was authorised in 1833. The line ran through some of the poorer areas on a brick viaduct 22ft above street level to clear the existing pattern of streets around its terminus at London Bridge and also to avoid periodic flooding around Bermondsey. As London's first railway, raising the necessary capital proved difficult at first and so, like many lines, it opened in stages between early 1836 and late 1838, despite being just 3½ miles in length. An unusual feature was the use of low centre of gravity carriages, with frames just 4 in above the track, to avoid carriages falling off the viaduct, which had 4ft 6 in walls, while as a further safety measure, the line was gas lit at night. Also unusual, and impractical, initially granite sleepers were set into concrete.

However, this costly short line was to prove to be a vital link in the capital's railway network, and in addition to being used by the London & Croydon, it was then used by both the London & Brighton and the South Eastern, initially for a toll of 3d per passenger, although this was increased to 4½ d once the viaduct was widened in 1842 over the 1¾ miles between Corbetts Lane Junction and London Bridge. Three years later, the line was leased by the SER.

The London & Blackwall Railway was originally authorised in 1836 as the Commercial Railway, using a 5ft gauge and linking the Minories, to the east of the City of London, with Blackwall, with the first 2½ miles of the 3½ mile route being on a viaduct 18 ft above street level. An extension to Fenchurch Street was authorised in 1839, the company adopting the London & Blackwall title, and the following year the line opened. The line was worked by cable powered by stationary steam engines to reduce the risk of fire to shipping and cargo in the docks. Each carriage had a brakeman and carriages were slipped and picked up at intermediate stations. It was the first to adopt an even headway service with a train every fifteen minutes. In 1849, the line was converted to standard gauge and steam traction adopted, while the company connected with the Blackwall Extension Railway, which ran from Stepney Junction to Bow, then the

Eastern Counties Railway, and in 1856, the line was linked with the London Tilbury & Southend Railway at Gas Factory Junction. The line was too small to remain independent, even with connections with other companies and running rights, so it was no surprise when, in 1866, the Great Eastern Railway leased the London & Blackwall for 999 years.

These early railways in the London area were of minor importance and built largely on viaducts in poor areas, so that there were few objections even though they displaced many slum dwellers and no doubt added to their misery.

It was the London & Greenwich that built London's first railway terminus, London Bridge, opened in 1836, where it was joined in 1839 by the London & Croydon Railway, which ran over the LGR's lines but had its own parallel station just to the north of the LGR lines. Earlier, the LGR had used a temporary terminus at Bermondsey, opened in February 1836. Longer distance trains arrived in 1841 when the London & Brighton Railway ran over the London & Croydon tracks into London Bridge, and was joined the following year by the South Eastern Railway.

The opening of London Bridge station in December 1836 was a grand affair attended by the Lord Mayor of London, even though strictly it was just outside his jurisdiction, and around 2,000 guests. This was in stark contrast to the reality of the station, which was basically little more than the end of the viaduct, on which the LGR had been built with more than 800 arches, with low platforms and with the railway offices and booking offices below. The railway only ran as far as Deptford and it was not to reach Greenwich until 1838. Plans for a triumphal arch at the entrance to this crude station were never fulfilled. With remarkable foresight the LGR had bought more land than it needed with the London Bridge end of the viaduct able to take eight tracks.

The two early London railways were isolated examples, but not for long. Neither could have created the railway age on their own in London, still less the south of England. This is an important point, because it was not simply the railways *in London* that changed the course of the conurbation's history and development, it was the railways *around London* and feeding into London that made the big difference.

Even this is to risk understating their importance. The railways were not simply a means of transport for London; they were also a business and financial opportunity. The railways played an important part in the development of the British financial system, and it was their insatiable thirst for finance that placed great strains on the banking system, itself still to reach maturity, and which acted as a stimulus to the development of the stock market and the concept of the joint stock company and businesses that limited the liability of shareholders. The railways had an impact on London in other ways as well, for they had to be regulated and, strange as it may seem today when massive public subsidies are poured into the railways, they had to be taxed. Having a railway land on its doorstep was as big a godsend to a hard-pressed local authority in the nineteenth century as having a major airport would be today, but in the case of the railways, central government also saw its opportunity to raise revenue, and took it just as surely as in recent years it has begun to tax travellers by air.

Given that London was the capital of a major empire, and that business did not feel itself constrained to remain within the bounds of that empire, the impact of London as a financial centre on railways was not confined to the British Isles or to the British Empire, but to countries that were independent of it and had no ties of language or culture. British companies were active in Latin America and Asia, developing railways and tramways.

The first trunk lines arrive

It was not just the fact that London was already heavily built-up that was a problem for the new railways as they attempted to get as close as possible to the centres of the City and of the West End, some of the railways had to approach through the better class of area where important property owners held sway.

In driving through the better class areas from the north-west, the London & Birmingham, and from the west, the Great Western, not only had landowners to deal with, but also residents who had a voice and a pen, and knew how to use them. The inhabitants of these areas may well have been renting their properties, but they were a class apart from those affected by the first London railways. Today, with widespread property ownership, it is necessary to remember that in pre-Victorian Britain, and even during the Victorian period, home ownership was very much in the minority, even amongst the upper middle and professional classes.

The Great Western got no further towards the centre of London than Paddington, then a village outside the built-up area and to this day an inconvenient location, while the London & Birmingham was also checked on the outskirts and settled at Euston Square, which was slightly better placed, albeit due in no small part to the subsequent pattern of development of the underground, and especially the deep level tube lines.

It is only with hindsight that we can assess the efforts of the early railway planners. The Great Western wanted to keep costs to the minimum and share Euston with the London & Birmingham. Nevertheless, the ambitions and suspicions of the backers of the railways got in the way and negotiations broke down, forcing the GWR to build its own terminus at Paddington and leaving the London & Birmingham alone at Euston. As both the original termini soon proved too small and had to be expanded, it was a blessing that they were not forced to share the same terminus. In any case, part of the problem at Euston, and some of the other London termini such as King's Cross and Liverpool Street, is on the approaches. These mighty stations have approaches which are literally 'choke' points. Even at this time, it was clear to the GWR's directors that Paddington was not the best site for a terminus, and for many years a number of trains took a roundabout route to reach Victoria.

Running over another company's tracks in return for payment of a toll was another means of raising revenue for the early railway companies. Initially many companies acted as if they were running a turnpike, allowing anyone to use their own locomotives and wagons or carriages in return for a toll, but this proved difficult, and as traffic grew, most railway companies provided their own rolling stock and allowed other companies onto their lines through a variety of agreements. Exceptions were to follow later, with company-owned wagons appearing, mainly owned by colliery companies, but these 'private-owner wagons' were never popular with the railway companies. Later still, the Pullman Car Company and, in the late 1930s the Wagons Lits Company on the Southern Railway, started to run their vehicles on Britain's railways, but these were different as the vehicles were effectively hired in by the railway as a new standard of accommodation for their passengers.

The London & Croydon paid the London & Greenwich the then not inconsiderable sum of 3d per passenger carried. A similar arrangement was proposed for the South Eastern Railway which would effectively extend the London & Croydon to Redhill and Dover.

Such arrangements were necessary because the railways were the most costly and capital-intensive business ventures ever attempted at the time, and even today, governments in many countries, and especially in the United Kingdom, fight shy of enlarging the railway network. Britain's railways were seldom built as a major long-distance through route, but piecemeal. Not only was the initial pressure to build a line local, connecting Liverpool with Manchester being a good example, but raising capital was easier with a succession of related railway schemes than as a single major scheme. It was also important to get the railway up and running as quickly as possible so that at least some revenue could be earned. Of the early schemes, the Great

Western was the most ambitious, with a main line running more than a hundred miles from London to Bristol. The need to start earning meant that it opened in stages, initially between London and Maidenhead, and the first Paddington Station, when it opened in 1838, was a temporary structure, and unlike the later magnificent cathedral to the steam age with its two transepts (cathedrals make do with one), it was thrown together in some haste simply using timber. In this form, it lasted sixteen years.

Euston opened the same year. The London & Birmingham was clearly wealthier than the Great Western, or perhaps it was not burdened by Brunel's fanatical insistence on a 7ft broad gauge, which added significantly to costs so that cost overruns were all too frequent. William Hardwick was commissioned as Euston's architect and the approach to the station portrayed its greatness with a magnificent Doric portico. People travelled to view the new station which seemed to say so much about what was to become known variously as the 'steam age' and the 'Victorian-era', and boded so well for both. It got even better, for by 1849, Euston had acquired a Great Hall and a Shareholders' Room. On the other hand, the train shed that lay beyond this grandeur was a disappointment, for low iron fabrications covered the two platforms, and there was no question that cheapness awaited the traveller after he had purchased his ticket.

The early railway termini differed greatly from those of today. Both Paddington and Euston were typical of their age in having separate arrival and departure platforms. Even as they grew, this system prevailed for many years. Illogical to modern eyes, these spoke of a more leisurely age when a train would arrive, and its carriages would be taken away for cleaning after the passengers had alighted, while the locomotive would reverse and 'run light' in railway parlance to an engine shed to receive water and coal. This system eventually came under scrutiny because of the amount of space required for running roads for carriage workings and locomotive workings, but the death knell really came with the arrival of first electric and the diesel traction, which meant that trains could be driven into the terminus, and while the passengers alighted and the train waited for a fresh passengers boarded, the driver simply walked from a cab at one end of the train to one at the other. Even when diesel locomotives or electric engines were used, a replacement was simply coupled on to the other end of the train, or in railway parlance the 'rake' of passenger carriages, ready to take it on its return journey, leaving that which had worked the train into the terminus to reverse out into a siding, and await its turn to take the next departure. Many of the early stations, even those which are today major termini, would have just one or two arrival platforms and a single departure platform.

At this stage, railway travel was still in its infancy. A dozen departures a day would be commonplace, far less than in even an off-peak hour at a major terminus today.

As a sign of the times, there were facilities for not only loading horses, but also carriages. Indeed, the early first-class carriages often resembled three road coaches combined, but without any outside passengers. Second-class rolling stock consisted of what we today would regard as an open goods wagon, with high sides and simple wooden planks running from one side to the other as seats. Third-class rolling stock was simply a flat goods wagon. This sounds dreadful by modern standards, but at the time, the stagecoach or mail coach was for the comparatively well-off and the poor either walked or, if they could afford it, climbed on to the carrier's wagon, sometimes sitting on its load.

The lack of corridor carriages meant that on approaching a major terminus, the train stopped at a station immediately before it, sometimes one constructed just for that purpose, so that tickets could be inspected. In some cases, street urchins would use this as an opportunity to sneak past the railway officials and board the train for a free ride to the terminus.

After London Bridge, Fenchurch Street, Euston and Paddington, there was a delay before any further terminus was opened in London. The London & South Western had settled quietly at Nine Elms. The delay in building further termini was to have considerable repercussions. Parliament had noted the upheaval that railway expansion into the centre of London was having. The outcome was an attempt to limit this upheaval, yet a failure to do so that only made subsequent upheaval even worse.

Parliament takes an interest

Parliament had a peculiar on-off relationship with the railways. There was no central direction of railway development as in many continental countries. This was no bad thing in many ways as it enabled locally important cross-country links to be built that might otherwise have been neglected or delayed. Yet, Parliament was not without its involvement as new railways had to receive legal authorisation in the form of an Act, and at the committee stage this was open to public scrutiny.

In 1846, a Royal Commission was set up to look at the London termini, since there was a scramble between railway companies to find locations as close to the centre of London as possible and Parliament thought that some order should be brought to bear. Enterprising ideas of some of the railway companies would have seen a north-south link between Charing Cross and

Euston, which would not only have eased the capacity problems at the former, but would have made it far easier to run trains through from the Channel ports to the Midlands and beyond. The disruption being caused by the railways as they gouged routes through the heavily built up inner suburbs of London and as lines, especially south of the River Thames, crossed one another, was another factor that concerned Parliament. The terms of reference for the Royal Commission were:

> '...whether the extension of railways into the centre of the metropolis is calculated to afford such additional convenience or benefit to the public as will compensate for the sacrifice of property, the interruption of important thoroughfares, and the interference with the plans of improvement already suggested.'

The team of commissioners charged with this exercise were the victims of their age. Their brief was well considered by any rational assessment, but no one understood the true nature of the problem and the impact that the railways would have on the travelling and working habits of the population could not be foreseen. Here we have it, the paradox that it was too early to predict the best way forward, and once the matter really could be examined sensibly with the benefit of experience, opportunities had been lost, and the further development of the London area meant that any attempt to alleviate the problem would be prohibitively expensive and the disruption immense.

One could argue that this was no bad thing. For example, one matter considered was the creation of a single large terminus for all of the railway companies. This begs the questions of where and just how large. After all, there were still fewer than 5,000 route miles in the country as a whole, less than a quarter of the eventual total, and there was no such thing as an underground railway network at the time. Fortunately, the commissioners were adamant that there was no advantage in a single terminus since the number of through passengers across the centre of London was negligible, which was true at the time. They also foresaw problems of congestion at and around such a terminus, while its management, divided between what would eventually be twelve companies, would be extremely difficult. The convenience of long distance passengers of a central London terminus seemed of little importance to the commissioners when set against the disruption that it would cause, and the various stage coach departure and arrival points had usually been just outside the centre. If the convenience of long distance passengers took second place to that of those whose lives and property would be disrupted by any extension into the central area, that of short distance passengers weighed still less.

In their final report, the commissioners recommended that no railway should enter the central area on the north side of the River Thames. By 'central area', they meant from Park Lane in the west to the City Road and Moorgate in the east, and from Euston Road in the north to what would now be the Embankment, but additionally this extended south of the Thames to Borough High Street. Any plans to allow the railways to intrude into this box in the future should only be allowed under an overall plan that had been carefully considered and 'sanctioned by the wisdom of Parliament'. Then, as now, property south of the river was less valuable than that to the north of it, and the commissioners also felt that the disruption to highways and to property would be far less. The commissioners were content with the already authorised construction of Waterloo and felt, wrongly as many passengers have found, that London Bridge was convenient for the City, but they were happy to see the lines from Kent extended to Waterloo.

A glance at a street plan for London will see that for lines from north and west, the commissioners' recommendations held good, even though it left many of the main termini, and especially Paddington, not well sited for either the City or the West End, with only Charing Cross and then Marylebone, the last to be built, anywhere near convenient for the latter. Only Cannon Street and Liverpool Street were well sited for the City, the latter having been built as 'an exception to the rule'. The winners were the southern companies, who for the most part were able to forge ahead, cross the river onto the north bank of the Thames, and serve both the City and the West End, effectively breaching the commissioners' ban on termini on the north bank. The one exception was the London & South Western, which had to remain at Waterloo, relatively isolated until relieved by the completion of the Waterloo and City Line in 1898, and as far as access to the West End was concerned, by the opening of the Bakerloo Line in 1906, followed by what was at first known as the Hampstead tube, today's Northern Line.

Parliament's concern was not surprising, taking as an example of the impact that railways had as they approached the centre of London was the extension of the London & South Western Railway from Nine Elms to Waterloo in 1854, which required the demolition of 700 houses for a much narrower spread of tracks than exists today. The Great Eastern extension to Liverpool Street built during 1861-64 was passed by Parliament on condition that it ran workmen's trains from Edmonton and Walthamstow, at a return fare of 2d per day for the journey of 6-8 miles; and was one of the few allowed to pierce what almost amounted to a surface railway exclusion zone because the final leg of the extension was in tunnel.

Chapter 3

Railway Mania and the Great Exhibition

The shares are a penny, and ever so many are taken by
Rothschild and Baring,
And just a few are allotted to you, you wake with a
shudder despairing.

W S Gilbert

A s the 1840s passed, interest in railways grew frantically. Every town wanted to be on the railway system for fear of being left isolated, and every investor wanted to be involved in the railways for fear of missing what was seen as a guaranteed means to fortune. Comparisons have been made with the so-called 'Dot Com' at the dawn of the twenty-first century, but underestimate the impact of the railways. The new railway companies were amongst the still relatively small number of business undertakings in which the public could make an investment. Business activity in the 1840s was small business. The shipping lines were still developing, but these had only developed slowly from trading arrangements in which a merchant would buy a ship with the help of close family or a few associates. Companies seldom had large headquarters, but instead the proprietor would often live above the business, and if it was larger, he would live above the counting house rather than the workshops or warehouses.

That the railways were an uncertain investment became obvious for those with cool heads as early as the 1820s. Even before this, within living memory, there had been the 'canal' of 1791-94, when forty-two new canals had received parliamentary approval. Even earlier, there had been the South Sea Bubble of 1719-20.

Boom and bust

The boom of the 1820s had been created not just by the railways but by changes in the legislation governing companies and limiting the liability of shareholders. No longer could a creditor bankrupt the owners of a business if it was a limited company. Money was readily available and this encouraged many entrepreneurs to float new concerns, including utility companies and mining. Nevertheless, during 1824/25, there were already many railway companies jostling for the support of investors. In the enthusiasm that followed the easing of investment and the arrival of a new mode of transport, no less than seventy railway companies published prospectuses, and of these about forty got as far as Parliament, but only the Liverpool & Manchester, which in fact preceded this first boom in railway shares, was built, and that after its first bill was defeated in the House of Commons in June 1825. Abandoned in the parliamentary waste paper bins lay plans for lines that would have linked the capital with Birmingham, Bristol, Falmouth, Lancashire and South Wales, but for which capital would never be raised.

This list tells us something about the state of Great Britain at the time. Bristol had been an important port for many years, and Birmingham was already established as a centre of industry, as was Lancashire with its cotton mills. South Wales was becoming increasingly important because of iron and coal. Falmouth was a far more important port than today, and indeed when the Cornish Railway was planned, it was to Falmouth, home of the Falmouth Packet Service, carrying mails and dispatches to and from the country's still growing colonial empire as well as other territories and which flourished between 1688 and 1850.

The first boom came to an end in 1825 with a series of banking failures, a poor harvest and the failure of the measure to authorise construction of the Liverpool & Manchester which completely undermined investor confidence. It was not until the line eventually was authorised and opened in 1830 that interest was re-awakened, but even that failed to materialise in a further boom due to the constitutional crisis over the Reform Bill. However, by 1833, interest in railways and confidence in them as investment projects had returned to the extent that several important schemes were authorised, beginning in 1833, and by 1836 an early peak of legislative activity was reached, so that in 1836/37, more than 1,500 route miles, requiring £34.6 million in capital, received parliamentary approval. As today, stock market booms matched that of economic activity generally, so that a downturn led to a recession and falling share prices, while economic recovery saw a surge. Boom and bust alternated as the economy overheated, and even today, smoothing out these phases of the economic cycle has not been mastered by finance ministers and central banks.

The next stage of the cycle was a further upsurge in the economy and

THE RAILWAY CONTRACTOR:
Thomas Brassey, 1805-70

Having started his career as a land agent and surveyor, heavily involved in the development of Birkenhead, in 1834 he turned to contracting, with his first project being the New Chester Road at Bromborough. The following year, his first railway contract was for the Pendridge line on the Grand Junction Railway, working with Joseph Locke. The working relationship between the two men continued for the rest of Brassey's life, throughout Great Britain and the Continent, including the London & South Western Railway; and most of the Paris-Le Havre Railway.

By 1841, Brassey was one of the country's leading contractors. With William Mackenzie and John Stephenson, he built the Lancaster & Carlisle Railway and worked on the Caledonian Railway, but Stephenson died in 1848 and Mackenzie became seriously ill in 1849. One of his most important contracts was on the Great Northern Railway between London and Peterborough. He also became involved with other contractors, including Peto and Betts, including work on the Grand Trunk Railway in Canada. This new partnership financed and built the Victoria Docks on the Thames, and the London Tilbury & Southend Railway, which was one of several also operated by Brassey, a true contractor's line. All in all, he built more than 6,500 miles of railway, including a sixth of the British network. He was one of the few contractors to survive the failure of the bankers Overend Gurney, doubtless because of his own considerable wealth, for he left a fortune of £3.2 million (around £150 million at today's values).

in new railway projects, starting in 1844. As with every such boom, the initial projects were, for the most part, sound and even long overdue as they had been delayed by the poor economic outlook and lack of confidence. As confidence grew, many schemes that were, at best marginal, were promoted. Railway shares soon became everyone's way of sharing in the growing wealth of the nation, and the stock market meant that they could be easily traded, as long as the boom continued. Certainly, many people became wealthy in a very short period as the value of their investments rose and they were able to realise the capital by selling their shares.

What constituted a viable railway project in 1844 and what constituted one even fifty years later, let alone today, is another question. Travel was so difficult in the early and mid-nineteenth century that many lines were built to cover very short distances. The London & Blackwall was one case in point. The poor prospects of many shorter lines was later highlighted by the arrival of the street tram, especially after tramways were electrified, and the inflexibility of the steel rail was then demonstrated when the motor vehicle became a significant force in transport after the First World War.

Despite this, many of the early schemes soon appeared to be over-optimistic and their prospects unrealistic, and to this list was added those that were simply fraudulent. As the poor prospects of many lines and the sheer lack of substance in others became clear, confidence faltered and then faded away altogether. Credit tightened, and those who had bought railway shares were stuck with them, for better or for worse. Even so, between 1844 and 1847, Parliament sanctioned the construction of more than 9,000 route miles of railways and the raising of more than £500 million. The route mileage alone amounted to around 40 per cent of the peak UK network, and some 90 per cent of that today, although there is the important caveat that the figures for the time included what is now the Republic of Ireland. Nevertheless, when reality dawned, more than a third of the route mileage authorised was not built.

The lessons of this time were quickly learnt, and when subsequent booms occurred in the 1850s and 1860s, they were not on the scale of 1844-1847. Another reason for this was that the industry was already maturing and, later in the century, the main developments involved well-established and substantial companies, while cooperation between companies became increasingly commonplace, allowing efficient running of through trains between London and Scotland, reaching a climax in the 1880s with four railway companies: the Great Northern, Midland and North Eastern, joining the North British Railway in construction of the great bridge across the Firth of Forth.

In the meantime, the collapse of confidence in railway shares had left many lines uncompleted. Raising funds proved difficult, even impossible. The early years of the railway age created one prosperous sector, the contractors who built the lines. Faced with the prospect of no work, many of these cash-rich businesses either provided funds to their hard-pressed clients in return for a substantial stake in the company, or simply got on with completing the work. There were many advantages to the contractors in taking this course. They were kept busy, while whenever new opportunities arose, by offering to build the line in return for a substantial share in it, eliminating the need to tender against other contractors. In some cases, they were able to move their skilled labour forces and equipment in its entirety from one project to the next in what became a rolling programme of railway construction. Some railway lines were even taken over by contractors to the extent that 'contractors lines' were operated for an agreed period after completion.

THE MAN BEHIND 'THE TIMES':
Thomas Tilling, 1825-1893

Born in 1825 at Gutter's Hedge Farm, Hendon, Middlesex, then a small village outside London, Thomas Tilling started his business in 1846, buying a horse and carriage for £30. Presumably his early business was private hire work, for in January 1850 he purchased his first horse bus and the licence to work four journeys a day in each direction between Peckham and Oxford Street. In just six years, he had seventy horses, most of which were used for his growing fleet of horse buses, but which also undertook other carriage work.

Until the second half of the nineteenth century, fire brigade provision in London was provided by insurance companies who looked after their own clients' premises, and it was not until 1866 that the Metropolitan Fire Brigade was formed. The new brigade contracted Thomas Tilling to train and supply horses for the fire engines, and the last part of their training was employment on his horse-bus services so that the animals became used to traffic on the busy city streets. Tilling was a successful horse-bus proprietor, running his vehicles to a timetable and using set stops, so that they were regarded as more punctual and reliable than his competitors, something which he capitalised on by using the fleetname of 'TIMES', painted in large letters on the side of his buses, although illustrations survive of buses carrying his own name. His mode of operation was to be the basis for future regulation of bus services.

When Tilling died in 1893, he was the biggest supplier of horses in London with a stable of 4,000 animals and 250 horse buses. He was buried at Nunhead cemetery.

The business passed to his sons, Richard and Edward, and son-in-law, Walter Wolsey. They continued his work, turning the business into a limited company, Thomas Tilling Ltd, in 1897, and in 1904 were the first to put motor buses into service in London. In 1907, they introduced the first longer-distance or commuter motor-bus service, with thirteen buses working a service between Sidcup in Kent and Oxford Circus. In 1909, a pooling agreement with the LGOC enabled the company to remain independent while the 'General' was acquiring many other companies, and as part of this Tilling's routes were integrated into the LGOC's new route-numbering scheme. One consequence of the pooling was that the only scope for expansion was outside the capital.

In the years that followed, the company started to develop bus services in provincial cities, starting with Folkestone in 1914 and followed by Brighton in 1916, with the predecessor of what became Brighton, Hove & District. Between the wars, Tilling collaborated with the railways in developing bus services, especially in rural areas. The London business was nationalised into London Transport in 1933, and the provincial business into the British Transport Commission in 1948. A number of non-transport businesses survived nationalisation. A distinctive feature of the Tilling bus companies was the used of the Tilling-Stevens petrol electric buses for many years, a means of solving the problems of early gearboxes and easing transition from horse-bus driving to motor-bus work.

One of the most prominent amongst such contractors was Thomas Brassey who worked on the Grand Junction Railway and the London & South Western Railway. With partners, he financed and built the Victoria Docks on the Thames, and the London Tilbury & Southend Railway, which was one of several he also operated. Later, he was one of the few contractors to survive the failure of the bankers Overend Gurney, doubtless because of his own considerable wealth, for he left a fortune of £3.2 million (around £150 million at today's values).

Once confidence returned, the contractor was still to be found offering his services in return for a share of the line, as we will see later with the Central London Railway, the predecessor of today's Central Line.

The Great Exhibition

The famous Great Exhibition of 1851 was a defining moment in the history of transport in London. The concept of exhibitions really dates from the Victorian era and the Great Exhibition, for which the Crystal Palace was built in London's Hyde Park, was simply the grandest and most famous of them of all. For the railways and the horse omnibus proprietors, these great events offered considerable business but brought with them substantial logistics problems. Such exhibitions could not have been possible before the railway age as no other means existed of moving so many people. In an age that still knew few public holidays, the excursion trains to the Great Exhibition were the first examples of mass holiday travel. The nearest thing to this before the Great Exhibition had been the more popular racing events, especially in the Home Counties, where they had the huge population of London as a market.

This ability to convey large exhibits more economically and efficiently than any other mode of transport also came into play with the Great Exhibition, and indeed the exhibits included two steam locomotives. Open from 1 May to 15 October 1851, the Great Exhibition saw six million tickets sold. While the site did not have a railway connection and many arrived on foot, the business generated for the railways and bus operators was considerable. It also boosted other businesses as well, with Thomas Cook, founder of the eponymous travel agency, becoming the Midland Railway's agent for the Great Exhibition in London, for which he provided tickets and other arrangements for 165,000 people.

For the railways it showed many of their existing arrangements were far from suitable. On the Great Northern Railway, its London terminus at King's Cross had still to be built, but the temporary station at Maiden Lane was named 'King's Cross' in the timetable, even though it consisted of just two timber platforms, which had to cope with the traffic of 1851, and also was used by Queen Victoria and Prince Albert for their trip to Scotland that August. At London Bridge, the London Brighton & South Coast station was only half complete.

The LBSC was not above making the most of circumstances to grow its business. It was no coincidence that when the Crystal Palace was demolished it was moved to Penge Park, sold by its owner, an LBSCR director to a company associated with the LBSCR, who opened a new branch ready for the official re-opening of the re-erected building by Queen Victoria in 1854. That this was an astute move can be judged by the fact that a single day in 1859 produced 112,000 passengers visiting the Palace.

The remaining conservative horse-bus owners who had resisted placing seats on the rooftops of their vehicles were also forced to accommodate passengers 'on top'. This was done by the simple expedient of placing a plank longitudinally along the curved roof, which acted as a back support and, if all else failed, something to cling to. While the railways offered attractive excursion fares for the exhibition traffic, the bus operators were less generous, seeing a one-off opportunity to raise their fares. When the exhibition traffic was followed by a slump in business for the horse buses, fares had to be reduced, often to levels lower than those prevailing before the exhibition. No doubt many regular travellers had been driven off the buses by the increased fares, and that this was simply profiteering of the most basic kind, but it was not the last time that raising fares would be used as a means of regulating traffic.

A better horse bus

The double-deck bus is seen by many, especially foreign visitors, as an English icon. Yet, more than once, foreign influences have developed the double-deck bus. The London General Omnibus Company itself was not a British undertaking at the outset, being formed in Paris in 1855 as the

Compagnie General des Omnibus de Londres. The aims of the new company, the LGOC, were ambitious, seeking to purchase as many of the existing horse-bus operators as possible prior to reorganising the network in London. For the first time, there was to be a controlling entity with plans for a network of routes. Yet, there was far more to it than coordination and rationalisation of routes. The horse bus had made remarkably little progress over the early years, and, on 1 January 1856, the LGOC advertised in the press for the 'best design and specification for an omnibus that, with the same weight as at present, will afford increased space accommodation and comfort to the public'. A prize of £100 was offered, and, since no doubt most of the designs would have come from body-builders, there was also the prospect of good business. No less than seventy-five entries were received, and these were shown to the press on 16 February at the LGOC's new offices, 454 West Strand, now home to the South African High Commission.

Designing a completely new double-deck horse bus was easier said than done. For something to have been completely new would have required a tremendous leap of the imagination.

Yet the LGOC was disappointed. The winner was a design by RF Miller, from Hammersmith. This was damned with faint praise as it 'contains several improvements in the details of its construction over those at present in use, although in external appearance it does not present much novelty'. The harsh truth was that the judges had not found 'any one design of super eminent merit, or calculated in its present shape to afford that increased amount of comfort and accommodation your company, with praiseworthy foresight, desires to give the public'. In the end, the LGOC decided to opt for a selection of features from several of the more promising designs. Miller's design was essentially an adaptation of the single-deck bus, with a clerestory roof that incorporated a seat for offside passengers only, which in many ways was a backward step as it could carry fewer passengers than earlier horse buses with 'outside' accommodation. The innovations consisted of what were described as 'improved steps', which meant simply that instead of iron rungs the passenger had metal treads and a handrail. Despite advances elsewhere, there were still no brakes and no means of communication between conductor and driver, even though as early as April 1847, a design for a bell for passengers to communicate with the conductor had been patented by Benjamin Browne.

One reason why the pace of technological change accelerated so much during the Victorian age was that news of developments passed around so much more quickly than during earlier periods. Publications such as the *Mechanics' Magazine* ensured that knowledge was disseminated, and the railways in particular had a growing and active press.

Far more promising was a design by TM Clemence of Westminster, with a wider clerestory on which there were back-to-back seats on both sides, and access by a 'winding ladder' with handrails at both ends of the vehicle 'so that with these means a female might with propriety and ease ascend the roof seats. There was also a handrail inside the bus, and this contained a wire to which handles were attached at intervals so that passengers and the conductor could ring a bell near the driver. Yet this was a step too far for the LGOC, whose desire for innovation was stifled by its own innate conservatism.

The LGOC never had a complete monopoly over bus travel in London. Not all of the existing proprietors sold out to it, so by 1857, the company had just 600 buses, of which thirty-three were in reserve, and of these just 450 worked daily, with 5,879 horses, of which 4,451 were required daily. The average daily mileage per horse was just twelve miles against fifty-four miles for each bus. As late as 1880, a group of city-bound commuters from the London & South Western Railway formed the Metropolitan Express Omnibus Company, to operate horse buses between Waterloo and the City. This company was taken over within a year by the Railways & Metropolitan Omnibus Company, but within five years it was operating eighteen twenty-six-seat buses and carrying 2.5 million passengers annually. In 1858, the LGOC finally emigrated from Paris to London, and became a wholly British organisation.

A contemporary and rival for the LGOC was Thomas Tilling, whose empire was founded during the 1850s. Tilling started with just one horse-drawn bus in Peckham, but in due course his interests in buses eventually ranged much further than London, where the company he founded operated a substantial number of services, especially south of the river.

Weight was always a problem for the horse bus, and eventually the practical limit was twenty-six passengers, of whom fourteen sat outside. Even with the advent of the motorbus, height and weight prevented placing a roof over the upper deck until a change in rear axle design allowed a significant lowering of the chassis height in the late 1920s.

Taxation of the horse-bus business continued, but the large numbers of vehicles and operators meant that the Treasury was earning more than anticipated. The government duty was reduced from 1½ d a mile to 1d by an act of July 1855, and from 1d to ¼ d in July 1866. By this time, taxation of railway travel had already begun, dating from 1832, when railway companies were made to pay what was then the not insubstantial duty of ½ d (0.4p) per mile for every four passengers carried, and the relative significance of the railways compared to stagecoach travel at this time can be judged by the fact that in 1835-37 the Treasury collected £13,000 annually from the railways against £750,000 (worth about £42 million today) from the stagecoach operators. As duties go, this 'passenger tax', as it became known, was a clumsy instrument since it made no distinction between the class of passenger, and so bore more heavily on the poorer travellers than the more affluent travelling in second or first class. It was not until 1844 that the first attempt was made to ease this situation. Duties on horse-drawn public transport were not removed until 1869, by which time the number of stagecoaches as opposed to horse buses had dwindled considerably. Proprietors paid the duty once a month at the Inland Revenue offices, in gold coins.

The stagecoach duties were abolished in 1869, and the following year responsibility for horse buses was passed to the Metropolitan Police under the Metropolitan Public Carriage Act. This also removed an earlier anomaly that had allowed the City of London its own jurisdiction over public transport within the 'Square Mile'. The first horse buses could draw across to the other side of the street to pick up a passenger, but the Metropolitan Streets Act 1867 required buses to stop on the nearside of the road, although this stricture initially only applied to a radius of four miles from Charing Cross, increased to six miles in 1885. This seemingly simple change was to have a profound effect on the design of buses as from this time onwards it was only necessary to provide access on one side of the vehicle. The rear entrance had been a restriction on bus design that allowed passengers to board or alight on either side of the vehicle.

By this time, a competitor to the horse bus had arrived in the form of the tram. This was altogether smoother and the reduced friction from running on a rail also meant that the horses could handle a heavier load. The early trams had stronger and less elegant structures than the horse buses, with inclined staircases on the earliest versions, although a half-spiral became the standard later, so that more passengers had the confidence to travel 'outside'. The half-spiral staircases were not adopted by the horse buses until later, but the trams also brought brakes, and that feature was finally adopted by horse-bus proprietors, although some of this may also have been due to the fact that the Metropolitan Police had made a clean sweep of horse buses in 1870, just as soon as the new legislation allowed, and many vehicles were put off the road, some of them for good. The introduction of brakes was not only a safety feature; it also took the burden of stopping away from the horses and transferred it to the vehicle: a considerable improvement as far as the horses were concerned.

Once a rear staircase rather than a ladder was provided, women started to travel outside. To make the move from inside to outside respectable, 'decency boards' were put along the outer sides of the upper deck so that Victorian men would not be aroused by the sight of a feminine ankle – and before long these decency boards were paying their way, carrying advertisements. The closing decades of the century also saw a sharp fall in fares, making bus travel more popular, and no doubt the advertising revenue was very welcome.

The cycle of boom and bust applied as much to the busmen as it did to their counterparts on the railways. In part it was also a case of supply outstripping demand, a situation aggravated by the growth of the tramway networks. By 1890, there were 2,210 horse-drawn buses on London's roads, and of these, about 5 per cent each year were condemned by the Metropolitan Police as unsafe; usually the older vehicles. This period also saw the appearance of a large number of single-deck one-horse buses operating short routes, such as Hampstead Road to Oxford Circus. These had first appeared during the Golden Jubilee of 1887, charging a flat 1d fare to attract passengers, and later this was dropped to ½ d. To cut costs, these buses did not have a conductor and the fare was dropped into a glass box by the driver. These became known as 'ha'penny bumpers'. By 1901, there were no less than 3,736 horse buses licensed to operate in London. While there were a few large forty-eight-seat buses, painted dark green and drawn by three horses and carrying the fleet name of 'Favorites' (sic), these were not allowed in the City after 10 am because of their size. By the turn of the century, while the horse-drawn buses were still generally two-horse and carrying twenty-six passengers, forward-facing garden seats became standard on the upper deck, while brakes were also standard as was a curved staircase. White lights were carried on the offside front under a London County Council Order, improving safety and recognition of a bus as it approached at night. Standing passengers were not allowed, largely because of weight problems, but the vehicle itself was an outstanding example of the coachbuilder's art, not least because so much of the structure was of glass and yet the upper deck bore the weight of fourteen passengers and the driver.

The bus was a mode of transport for the middle classes. To cater for the needs of city workers, four-horse express buses, but still with twenty-six seats, plied the main routes between the suburbs and the city, usually with regular travellers, and some of the bus drivers became well known for their knowledge of the stock market, and their 'tips' were often sought. The bus was light and strong, and it had to be, for it was not pulled by heavy horses such as Shires or Suffolk Punches.

The London bus scene was chaotic, but colourful. London buses weren't 'always red'. The green 'City Paragon' ran between the City and Streatham, costing just 5d; the dark green 'John Bull' ran between Liverpool Street and Lancaster Road, every three minutes, again for 5d; a white bus, whose fleet name seems to have been lost, ran between Liverpool Street and Putney every three minutes for 6d; while others were painted dark brown. These were commuter services, but the peak periods were much longer than today, and most people worked at least a half day on Saturdays. Even running across the centre of London between Charing Cross and Baker Street cost just a penny, less than half today's 'new' penny.

Speculation and the railways

There can be little doubt that many of the tips gleaned from one passenger and then dispensed to others later by the horse-bus drivers concerned the railways. The railways were not just the hot share of the day, they were exceptionally important until the outbreak of the First World War. Today people associate the railways with decline, loss and subsidy, but until 1914 there were many companies that were very profitable. During the nineteenth century, inflation varied but was low by the standards of post-Second World War Britain, and interest rates were low as well. A dividend of 3 per cent was worthwhile when the Post Office paid 2½ per cent. Indeed, one reason why the country could afford to build the railways was the low interest rates charged or expected, and, of course, the low price of agricultural land, plus cheap labour, much of it imported from famine-stricken Ireland. Building and operating a railway was far less capital intensive than today.

The railways were a shock to the national financial system. Their immediate predecessor, the canals, had a total share capital between them of £20 million, but in the first stage of the railway age, between 1820 and 1844, the railways required more than £40 million, and in another six years, in 1850, their total share capital amounted to £187 million. The railways did not simply create employment by being built and operated, they created employment that was not obviously connected with the railways, being the single most important factor in the creation of the stock market. The London Stock Exchange was revolutionised. The stock market required more than just stockbrokers, for at the time there were also people known as stock jobbers, who effectively acted as wholesalers of

THE RAILWAY KING:
George Hudson, 1800-1893

George Hudson was born in 1800 in the small Yorkshire village of Howsham. He moved to York, working in a draper's shop, marrying the owner's daughter and later, in 1827, received the then considerable inheritance of £30,000 (about £1.38 million today), from a distant relative. He was later to maintain that the inheritance was the worst thing that ever happened to him, but it enabled him to become active in local politics, becoming Mayor of York three times, and also to invest in local railway schemes. In 1836, he was elected chairman of the York & North Midland Railway, linking his adopted city with London, albeit by a circuitous route via Derby and Rugby, taking 217 miles, but offering four through trains a day, with the journey from York to London taking ten hours as against around twenty hours by stage coach. The company leased and then later absorbed adjoining lines, as well as building a number of extensions itself. Hudson pressed for a major trunk route up the East Coast to Scotland, but the line being built by the North of England Railway from York to Newcastle was in difficulties and, by 1841, it had exhausted its capital, but still had only managed to reach as far north as Darlington. Hudson was dismayed by this situation, as not only was his vision of a line to Newcastle and beyond compromised, but the Board of Trade had finally started to take an interest in creating strategic routes, and wanting to link London with Scotland, had opted for a route from Carlisle to Edinburgh using a competing route that had already reached as far north as Lancaster. It was left to Hudson to bring the various assorted railway interests involved together.

Believing that the finance needed was unlikely to be raised on the open market, Hudson suggested that each of the companies present should offer shares in the proposed line to their own shareholders, with a guaranteed dividend of 6 per cent. A new company was formed, the Newcastle & Darlington Junction Railway, with Hudson as chairman. It was not until 1842 that the necessary legislation was passed through Parliament, undoubtedly a factor in Hudson deciding to become an MP.

Meanwhile, the YNMR had been doing well, paying a ten per cent dividend at a time of recession, but the North Midland, over which much of its traffic proceeded, was suffering. Hudson headed a committee enquiring into the affairs of this company, and within a week proposed a dramatic reduction in expenses, cutting these from £44,000 weekly to £27,000. This decisive action saved the company, but its neighbours, the Midland Counties and the Birmingham & Derby Junction, were also suffering difficulties. With remarkable clarity of purpose, Hudson proposed a merger of all three companies, one that would achieve still further savings, with the new Midland Railway formed in September 1843.

Hudson forecast that the railway bubble was about to burst and that many of the new and proposed lines would turn out to be unviable, but staunchly maintaining that '...the public would rather (the railways) be in the hands of companies than...government'. Hudson was asked by the directors of the other railway companies to head resistance to Gladstone's Bill, and so it was that when the Parliamentary process was complete, the Railway Act 1844 saw most of the troublesome and unwelcome clauses of the original bill omitted.

On 18 June 1844, the thirty-nine miles of the Newcastle & Darlington Junction Railway opened. The railway journey from York to London had taken ten hours in 1837, but by 1844 the much longer journey from Gateshead to London took just eight hours, a clear indication of progress. Hudson became Conservative MP for Sunderland in 1845, largely because his railway ambitions could be helped by a seat in the House of Commons. While he did much to improve the town's docks, he was also driven by a desire to sabotage the plans for a direct line between York and London, which later became the Great Northern Railway, and in 1846 this drew him into taking over the Eastern Counties Railway. Hudson won over the ECR shareholders by trebling dividends and it soon became clear that he was paying dividends out of capital: unacceptable but a fairly commonplace practice at the time. This raised questions amongst those concerned with his other companies, and it was soon found that the same practice was being applied, so that by the end of 1849, he was forced to resign all of his chairmanships. By this time, the Great Northern route was open and, pragmatic to the end, Hudson decided to use the new route and abandoned his own plans to extend the Eastern Counties line, with the result that, simultaneously, Hudson was under pressure from angry Midland Railway shareholders who objected to the diversion of traffic away from their route and on to the more direct route.

Had the railway boom continued, Hudson could have avoided the problems that beset him over paying dividends out of capital. It was not to be. Claim after claim was lodged against Hudson, who continued to the end to attract warm local support in both Sunderland and Whitby, as the inhabitants of both towns saw him as a local benefactor. Initially, Hudson was able to fight off the threat of bankruptcy by selling his extensive estates, which he had acquired to leave to his sons, and afterwards because as a sitting MP he could not be arrested for bankruptcy. When he lost his parliamentary seat, he was forced to flee to France, and spent many years in and out of exile.

shares, and then of course there were the backroom people, the clerks, struggling to keep track of the business transacted, the solicitors and bankers, all of whose involvement was necessary.

Yet, one did not need reminding that shares can go down in value as well as up. The performance of any particular railway could have a profound effect on its shares, so when serious deficiencies were found in the accounts of the North British, in 1866, the value of its shares plummeted. The outbreak of the Franco-Prussian War in 1870 also forced share prices down.

One of the problems was that obtaining parliamentary authority to build a new railway took a considerable time, and often a substantial financial outlay. Construction was slow, and although companies operating over any real distance would attempt to open the line and start operations in stages to get some revenue, there was a delay before a railway started to pay worthwhile dividends to its shareholders. This was not quite as bad as it seemed, since, in such circumstances, not all of the money had to be raised immediately, and some shareholders were able to provide just 10 or 15 per cent of their overall investment at the outset. On the other hand, there was a clear temptation to cut corners in construction, and a clear incentive to resort to unscrupulous tactics such as paying dividends out of capital invested simply to keep the early shareholders happy.

The story of no one man quite encapsulates the roller coaster ride that was the lot of the early railway entrepreneur better than that of George Hudson, who, at the peak of his powers, was the chairman of four railway companies. By 1850, he controlled a quarter of the nation's railway route mileage, then over 6,000 miles, itself probably equalling the total route mileage in the rest of the world at the time. It was Hudson who brought together several railway companies to create the Midland Railway, which, after using King's Cross for a while as its London terminus, eventually built its own at St Pancras, but that was to be after his fall from grace in 1849.

Hudson's departure coincided with an end to the railway bubble. Such feverish speculation and the desire to build railways meant that the industry was over-capitalised. Far too many lines with modest prospects were built and, contrary to popular opinion, not all of these survived long enough to be recommended for closure by Beeching. As the century progressed, lines were built as extensions by existing companies.

Nevertheless, railway speculation continued and developing a railway remained a high-risk activity, both for the investor and for those responsible for the project who could suddenly find that support faded away. The 1850s had seen further problems, but it was not until 1866 that a major financial crisis ensured, with the collapse of the bankers, Overend Gurney, which was already over-extended and was brought down finally by its exposure to the Mid Wales Railway, a contractor's line. Overend Gurney failed on 10 May 1866 with liabilities of more than £18 million.

Fallout from this banking collapse hit London and the South East of England hard, with one of the casualties being the London, Chatham & Dover Railway, which served both Farringdon and Victoria Stations in London, and which was forced into receivership from which it did not emerge until 1871. The LCDR was itself already impoverished, having been brought about by the resentment of interests in the north of Kent at the southerly route of the South Eastern Railway, which ran from Charing Cross and Cannon Street and which avoided the Medway towns, including Chatham and Rochester. Much of the work on the LCDR was being undertaken by contractors in return for an interest in the company and it was vulnerable to a banking collapse.

The financial system of the day lacked the sophistication with which to deal with a major banking failure and the Bank of England, itself in private ownership, lacked the means for a rescue. Exposing the vulnerability of a significant bank in itself did little to endear railway investment to the many shareholders. Interest in railway shares eventually recovered, and over the half century that followed, no doubt many were pleased that they had remained loyal to the railways. On the other hand, at difficult times they had little choice other than to sell their shares at a considerable loss.

Chapter 4

Regulation Catches up with the Railways

*A tax on the means of locomotion is as bad a tax
as any that can be devised.*
Robert Lowe, Chancellor of the Exchequer, 1869

T he railways managed to develop for more than a decade without
any attempt at oversight by the authorities. In no small part this
was due to the fact that each railway company had its own Act of
Parliament, but the MPs did not have the knowledge to regulate the
railway. Inasmuch as concerns were expressed as a railway measure passed
through the Commons and the Lords, it was over such matters as land
purchase or the desirability or otherwise of having the new mode of
transport, with its smoke and sparks, passing close by. Commercial
considerations, such as the impact on a town or a port, or an improvement
in the movement of raw materials or manufactured goods, mattered far
more than such matters as safety.

All this changed on Christmas Eve 1841, when a Great Western train
was derailed at Sonning, just to the east of Reading, killing eight third-class
passengers who had been travelling in a goods train's low-sided open
wagons. Until this accident, no one had considered such a means of
conveyance as dangerous as it was no more than a development of the
tradition of paying for space in a carrier's wagon. The only problem was
that the carrier's wagon proceeded at a gentle trot, but the railway was
already pushing speeds well above thirty miles per hour.

In the ensuing inquiry, the inspector pointed out the dangers of
travelling in such unsuitable accommodation. This provoked a general
investigation by the Board of Trade's Railway Department into the
provision made for third-class passengers throughout the country, and it
was found that the GWR example was no exception. It was to be many
years before the GWR gained its reputation as being in many ways special,
and superior to other railways, and even longer before this applied to all

classes of passenger. Many trains had no provision at all for third-class passengers. It was apparent that there was much to be done to correct and control the growth of the railways. The European system of central direction was considered and, as President of the Board of Trade, Gladstone was especially keen to overhaul the system. Much of this was necessary, but it was inevitable even then that an ambitious politician would be keen to extend the powers of his department. Gladstone had by this time been an MP since 1832, but more significantly, he was probably one of the better informed members as far as railways were concerned, since his father, Sir John, had been an enthusiastic promoter of the early railways in Scotland, and by 1843 had accumulated £170,000 (£9.4 million today) of railway investments. The only real question had to be just how impartial did this make his son. It could account for the watering down of the early provisions of the Railway Bill that resulted from the committee's deliberations, but shortly after the measure was enacted, Gladstone resigned, largely because he was aware of the conflict of interest between his own family's involvement in railways and his powers as their parliamentary overlord.

Cheap travel for all

More commonly known as 'Gladstone's Act', the Railway Regulation Act of 1844 was significant as much as for what it didn't do as for what it did, as no attempt was made to enforce gauge standardisation, which would have been a practical measure. The most significant provisions were for cheap railway travel, a predecessor of the later 'Cheap Trains' Act, while telegraph companies were enabled to compel railway companies to allow their wires to be carried alongside their lines and, for the first time, the possibility of nationalisation of the railways was enshrined in British law. Gladstone himself felt that the Act had been an opportunity missed, and that the powers contained within it were far too weak, largely due to the power of the railway companies who had many members of both houses of parliament amongst their shareholders and directors.

The importance of the Act should not be underestimated as it authorised the purchase of railway companies by a British government in the future, although it applied only to those companies established after 1 January 1845, and the powers could not be exercised before 1866. The price to the government of a railway company was to be the profits for a twenty-five-year period, averaged out over the preceding three years. As we shall see, by the mid-1860s, many railway companies were passing through a bleak period and no doubt the cost of acquisition at the time would have been low, but the railway system was still incomplete. One cannot help speculate that, had nationalisation occurred at this early stage, would the total mileage have ever reached its ultimate grand total of more than 20,000 miles? Given post-nationalisation experience of the attitude of the Treasury to investment in the railways, it seems unlikely.

The cheap travel provisions of the 1844 Act created what came to be known as 'Parliamentary Trains', establishing certain standards of speed and comfort for these while carrying passengers at very low fares. This resulted from the Act stipulating that all future railways defined as passenger railways, meaning that they earned a third or more of their turnover from passenger fares, would have to provide at least one daily train, including Sundays, that would call at every station and have an overall speed, allowing for stops, of not less than twelve mph, and that the passengers would have to be carried in enclosed carriages provided with seats. It was also stipulated that the fares would not exceed 1d per mile, and for this each passenger would be entitled to carry up to 56lb (25.4 kg) of luggage, more than economy class air travellers are allowed, and much more still than the 33lb of many charter flights. These low fares were exempted from passenger tax, by this time at a rate of 5 per cent, which of course meant that it no longer weighed most heavily on the poorer passengers. On some railways, this became the new third class, whilst others provided both Parliamentary trains and third class trains, so strictly speaking third-class fares were still subject to passenger tax.

This measure was only enforceable on future railways, but most of the railway companies complied with it anyway. This was not simply a gesture of goodwill. The way in which new lines and extensions to existing lines were sanctioned by private Acts of Parliament meant that any other arrangement would have been cumbersome and impractical. Many railways bitterly objected to the new measure on the grounds that many passengers who could afford much more were travelling in the parliamentary trains and thus depriving them, and, of course, the Treasury, of revenue. In another sense, the new measure was itself scarcely a model of common sense, doubtless because the Treasury was anxious to see as few passengers as possible escape paying tax. An ordinary third-class passenger, possibly commuting, although the term was unknown at the time, to a place of employment, was taxed, regardless of his or her circumstances. Then too, while the twelve mph speed was good for a stopping train in 1844, later this became slow and unattractive, but a subsequent court decision in 1874 ruled that a train that did not stop at every station along its route could not be classed as a parliamentary train and had to pay the tax.

The Act swept aside Sunday observance. At the time, many still held that no work should be done on the Sabbath. This was clearly impractical for those charged with the care of animals or the sick, but it was still commonplace for families to have cold meals on a Sunday, even if they had servants.

Safety

Safety had also become an issue. The first legislation concerned with railway safety came in 1840 and was the first of nine so-called 'Railway Regulation Acts' that passed on to the Statute Book between 1840 and 1893. The Act awarded powers to the Board of Trade which had been collecting statistics on the railways since 1832, to regulate the railways, and whose new responsibilities saw its staff rise from thirty to thirty-five! The Act also provided for the punishment of 'railway servants' for safety transgressions. Such legislation was necessary because the Board of Trade almost seems to have acquired its responsibilities for the railways by default rather than by design, and there was to be no such thing as a Ministry of Transport until after the First World War. The BoT had originally developed to oversee the country's overseas trade and through this had assumed responsibility for shipping.

The Railway Regulation Act 1840 required the railway companies to report all accidents, no matter how minor, involving personal injury to passengers, but not employees, to the Board of Trade, which had the duty to appoint inspectors who had the power to enter railway premises and inspect premises, track and rolling stock, but, strangely, did not have the power at this stage to actually investigate an accident. The first railway accident report dates from the year of the act, 1840. Even the subsequent Railway Regulation Act 1842 did not authorise the inspectors, who, with one exception, were all serving or recently retired officers from the Royal Engineers, to investigate all accidents, only serious accidents had to be investigated, meaning those inflicting serious injury to a member of the public. At the time, accidents generally resulted in serious injury, simply because of the circumstances. Frail wooden carriage bodies mounted on brittle iron underframes meant that even a minor collision could be serious, and this was compounded by the use of oil or gas-fired lighting within the carriages, a practice that persisted on some lines into the twentieth century. Modern rolling stock with its integral monocoque construction and couplings or buffers designed to prevent carriages being pushed on top of one another can mean that even a high-speed derailment can occur without causing serious injuries, especially if all steel construction is used in the carriages and no trackside obstacle, such as a bridge or other structure, is hit.

The Railway Regulation Act 1842 also dealt with such matters as the conveyance of troops by train and policing of the railways, the latter being especially important in the early days when much of the role of the railway signaller, as signalmen have become known in these politically correct times, was handled by railway policemen. The need to convey troops by train was brought about largely by concerns on internal security, rather than by any external threat. The Act brought one significant advance: no passenger-carrying railway line could be opened without the approval of an inspector. This meant that if the inspector was not satisfied, opening, and hence revenue-earning, could be delayed. There were also provisions covering the premature opening of a line before an inspector had given his approval, with railway companies liable to a fine of £20 for each day of operation. This was a year's pay for many a working man and the lengths of line were often relatively short. The inspector's powers were not inconsiderable and were used, with one of the most notable early cases being when the London & South Western Railway extended its line from Nine Elms to Waterloo. The inspector was concerned about the safety of one of the bridges and refused to allow the line to open as planned on 1 July, so opening was deferred for ten days.

The army officers on whom the burden of investigation fell were certainly far better qualified to investigate a railway accident than any intelligent layman, but they too had much to learn about the new science, or perhaps it really should be sciences, brought into widespread use by the railways. Metallurgy was almost unknown and non-destructive means of testing, especially on such things as track and boilers, simply not available. The inspectors were helped in the case of boiler explosions by the Board of Trade seconding experts from its Marine Department. Then there was so much to discover about signalling and the management of a busy stretch of railway line, and a number of practices that had to be understood fully before an improvement could be considered. The inspectors were not above criticism, but they have been universally regarded as having been diligent and honest, and they built up a massive body of experience and expertise through their work. The reports were never secret and always presented to Parliament, and after 1860 they could be bought by the public. Yet, the inspectors had no power to compel the railways to adopt their recommendations, which had to remain no more than advice. It was also the case that sometimes a new precautionary device would resolve one danger, and yet introduce a new one that would not be immediately apparent until exposed by a further accident. This was trial and error, simply because so much had to be learnt. The system endured the passage of time, including grouping and nationalisation, so that officers of the Royal Engineers continued in this role until 1982.

Often, technological advances away from the railways came to the rescue. For example, on the early railways, the distance between a train and the one following it was regulated by time alone. This meant that if there was a mishap or the first train failed to maintain the distance between the following one, assuming that the driver of the following train could not always count on being able to see sufficiently far ahead to be able to stop in time, an accident could only be prevented by the guard of the first train setting back along the track to stop the following train. If the guard did not do this quickly enough, a serious accident could occur, and did so on several occasions. The electric telegraph improved communications so that staff at railway stations knew where trains had passed or were being delayed, and led ultimately to the block system, in which trains were kept apart by distance rather than by time. The system was initially expensive and rejected by some companies on the spurious grounds that it would make enginemen and signalmen less alert. Nevertheless, as early as the 1860s, not only the block system but interlocking of points and signals as a further step forward in safety were both possible, and the 1870s saw the spread of both systems throughout the railway network. Anxious that best practice was implemented as quickly and as widely as possible, in 1869, the Board of Trade asked railway companies to provide an annual return showing the extent to which each of them had adopted the block system.

Using time as the basis for maintaining a safe distance between trains was even more dangerous at the time than would be the case today. Until the railways came, and for some time after the early lines were operational, there was no such thing as a standard time across the British Isles, and the actual time varied between one town and another depending on how far east or west they were, instead there was 'railway time', implying that the locals could continue as they pleased. It was not until the Meridian Conference of 1884 that the basis for what became known as Greenwich Mean Time was laid.

'Railway time' or not, at London Bridge, the London Brighton & South Coast clocks told a different time from those of the South Eastern & Chatham Committee, the successor to the London Chatham & Dover and the South Eastern Railway, two deadly rivals who nearly succeeded in bankrupting each other. Many clockmakers and other businesses obtained the Greenwich Mean Time from a lady, Ruth Belville, who took a pocket chronometer to the Royal Observatory at Greenwich every Monday morning, had it checked and adjusted with a certificate to show its accuracy, and then went around London, as we will see later, literally passing the time with business houses who adjusted their clocks by her chronometer. The Post Office* telegraphed the time to its offices, but did not do so commercially, and it was left to a commercial enterprise, the Standard Time Company, to pursue this course, and even take it a stage further by installing a mechanism that corrected clocks when STC transmitted a daily time signal, but there were problems with current supply at this early stage, so many preferred to continue to subscribe to Ruth Belville's service.

Yet, as in more recent times with controversy over the Train Protection and Warning System, accidents continued to occur, and again, as today, many could not have been prevented by the safety measures available.

The need to report all accidents

Despite the steady flow of legislation regulating the railways and requiring accidents to be inspected, one important class of people associated with the railways was overlooked until 1871, those working on the railways. For the first time, the Railway Regulation Act 1871 required the railway companies to notify the Board of Trade of any accident involving death or injury to anyone, meaning that for the first time railway workers, or 'railway servants' as they were known, were also covered by the legislation. This measure was overdue as goods trains and shunting movements could be involved in accidents without any member of the public getting hurt. The period 1874–78 saw an annual average of thirty-five passengers killed in accidents, but an average of 136 railwaymen fatalities. Many of the accidents were due not just to the absence of safety precautions, but to many railwaymen working excessively long hours, and a number of inspectors highlighted this in their reports. This act also gave the BoT the authority to establish a court of inquiry to investigate a major accident if the Board saw fit. The Railway Regulation Act 1873** finally gave the Board of Trade the power to compel railway companies to provide an annual return of the track mileage covered by the block system.

The inspectorate was also able to highlight problems over unrestricted

* In 1868, the first nationalisation appeared in the form of the Government buying out the operators of the telegraph, including the many telegraph lines operated by the railway companies, and the measure was not without benefit to many of them as it released capital for other projects.
** These measures were so successful that the number of railwaymen killed in the ten years between 1879 and 1888 fell to 479.

THE STAPLEHURST DISASTER:
9 June 1865

A witness to the Staplehurst disaster was none other than the distinguished Victorian novelist Charles Dickens, returning from Paris with his mistress, Ellen Ternan, after giving readings of his work in the French capital. He had returned to writing after a gap of some years following publication of *Great Expectations*, and was in fact checking the proofs of his next work, *Our Mutual Friend*, as he travelled towards London. Dickens and Ellen were travelling in the second carriage, which slewed on the embankment with its rear end in a field. Thrown in to a corner, Dickens was uninjured and was able to reassure both Ellen and an elderly lady travelling in their compartment. At that time, many railway companies locked the doors of the carriages, not with public safety in mind as with the remaining 'slam door' rolling stock in the late twentieth century, but to stop fare evasion, forcing Dickens to climb out through a window to seek help, only to see the scene of devastation, of splintered and broken carriages, and broken bodies.

He obtained a key from the guard and set about unlocking all of the compartments in his carriage, releasing the passengers. He then filled his hat with water and, with a flask of water, went around the injured and dying, giving them what comfort he could.

Afterwards, once back home in London, he wrote to the South Eastern Railway asking if anyone had found trinkets that a lady involved in the accident had lost, including a gold seal 'engraved "Ellen"'.

'I was shaken,' he later said, 'not by the beating of the carriage but by the work afterwards of getting out the dying and the dead.' He never really got over the experience and whenever travelling in later years he was frequently overcome by what he described as 'sudden vague rushes of terror'. He even added a postscript about the accident to *Our Mutual Friend*.

competition. Even so, when a Royal Commission was appointed to investigate railway safety in 1874, taking three years and amassing a considerable volume of evidence, it failed to make firm recommendations. Typical of the way in which the Royal Commission worked was the question of the provision of continuous braking to passenger trains, which was now becoming more extensive as speeds rose, but used different and incompatible technologies. In 1876, the Commission members watched trials of the different systems at Newark, but failed to decide on a standard system, largely because it was hard to see any decisive advantage from one system or another. Nevertheless, in 1878, further legislation at last compelled railway companies to provide twice-yearly returns showing the number of passenger carriages fitted for continuous braking, while the absence of adequate braking ensured higher compensation for the victims of accidents and their families.

Many measures that needed legislation were appallingly simple, such as the Railway Employment (Prevention of Accidents) Act 1900, enforcing measures for the safety of permanent way workers and for adequate lighting on stations and in sidings. It took an order under this Act to enforce the provision of handbrakes on both sides of new goods wagons as late as 1907, suggesting that previously brakemen working in sidings either had to be stationed on both sides of wagons, or had to somehow cross over while a train was being shunted; or, most likely, hope that they could brake sufficient wagons on one side of the goods train to stop it running away!

Far away from London, in Ulster, it took the Armagh accident of 12 June 1889 for the Government to take powers, the Regulation of Railways Act 1889, to ensure that the railway inspectors at last could insist that all passenger trains employed continuous braking and all passenger lines operated on the block system with full interlocking of signals and points.

Fortunately, safe working soon became associated with efficient working, and the steady flow of new safety systems provided profitable business for the manufacturers. The block system, for example, worked well when signalmen were conscientious, but a further safety measure was track circuiting, first introduced in the UK in 1901, and an essential ingredient in any automatic signalling system. The enginemen also had to be alert to ensure safety, but of course, often could not see signals in fog, so the next safety device was an audible warning of a distant signal set at caution, available in 1906. Yet, when the Great Western started introducing automatic train control, ATC, which stopped a train passing a signal set at danger, on its main lines from 1929 onwards, it was the only company to do so. The Southern Railway, while not introducing ATC, was to the forefront in the introduction of colour light signalling, which made signals more easily visible in poor visibility.

Accidents in London and the commuter belt

The number of serious accidents on the railways in and around London involving passenger trains over the years has remained low, despite the fact that this is the heaviest-used part of the railway system. One reason for this could be that being so busy and so close to London, head office for all but the Midland Railway, the most up-to-date signalling equipment and the best-staffed signal boxes were in operation, while another could be that the sheer volume of traffic inhibited high speed running. Strangely, the period from the 1930s through to the late 1950s was bad for safety on London's railways, with that at Harrow being amongst the worst.

Some of these accidents are worth noting, if only because the London commuter area, what the statisticians call the London 'travel to work area', is so extensive. Many of them couldn't happen today – thankfully.

The first major accident in the south of England was some distance from London and at a time before Brighton to London became a feasible daily return journey. This was in Clayton Tunnel, on 25 August 1861, on the main line of the London Brighton & South Coast Railway. Signalling was in its infancy and failed at a time when three trains were leaving Brighton for London within a very short period of time. A signalman attempted to stop the second train as it entered the tunnel before the first had cleared it, but the driver had glimpsed the red flag and stopped before setting back to see if all was well. The signalman assumed that both the first two trains had cleared the tunnel and used a white flag, the LB&SCR's signal for 'all clear', for the third train, which entered the tunnel at full speed and collided with the second train as it reversed to the entrance, killing twenty-one passengers and injuring 176.

This was followed by an accident on the South Eastern Railway at Staplehurst in Kent on 9 June 1865. There was little signalling to protect a bridge that was being repaired and the workmen misread the timetable when estimating how much time they had to replace the bridge timbers, not allowing for Channel boat trains that ran as specials due to their timing being influenced by the tides before Dover and Folkestone became usable at all states of the tide. The problems were compounded by negligence on the part of the look out. A boat train from Folkestone hit the bridge at full speed after some of the timbers had been removed. The locomotive and first carriage almost got across, but the coupling between the first and second carriage broke and the frail wooden carriage crashed down into the stream, breaking up, killing ten persons and injuring another forty-nine, the aftermath of which was witnessed by the famous author Charles Dickens, who was a passenger.

It was to be more than half a century, near Sevenoaks, before another serious accident occurred in the south, and this time it was after the grouping of more than a hundred railways companies into the so-called 'Big Four', of which the Southern Railway was the smallest.

Chapter 5

The Mainline System is Completed

*...whether the extension of the railways into the centre of the
Metropolis is calculated to afford such additional convenience or
benefit to the public as will compensate for the sacrifice of property,
the interruption of important thoroughfares, and the interference
with the plans of improvement already suggested.*
Terms of Reference of the Royal Commission on Railway Termini within
or in the immediate vicinity of the Metropolis, 1846

O f course, this is to rush ahead as we have left the mainline railways
with just the termini at Euston and Paddington, London Bridge,
still to emerge in its final form, and Fenchurch Street. Of course,
the London & Blackwall Railway at Fenchurch Street could hardly be
regarded as 'mainline', and nor at this early stage could London Bridge.
The idea of a central terminus for *all* of the mainline railways as they
reached London had been considered and rejected by the House of Lords,
while Parliament had passed a series of acts that gradually brought a
measure of control to the railways, not simply helping to monitor and
improve safety, but also enabling those of modest means to travel from one
end of the country to the other on any day of the week, albeit not by any
train and not in any measure of comfort.

The question of a central terminus for the whole of the capital was not
handled by members directly, for Parliament did what it still does today
when handed something which is too hot to handle, or which members
know little about or, most likely in this case, in which they themselves have
a vested interest: they set up a Royal Commission, known as the Royal
Commission on Railway Termini within or in the immediate vicinity of the
Metropolis, in 1846.

What had happened was that the country was in the midst of one of
those periodic railway booms that so affected not only the development of
the railways, but the judgement of too many of those involved. This

extended to members of both Houses of Parliament many of whom had also invested heavily in the railways, and even if they hadn't, their friends and families had done so. The largest and most ambitious of the railways planned were those that wished to link the most populous and fastest growing regions with the capital. The West and the Midlands already enjoyed this benefit; others did not want to be left behind. The railway entrepreneurs thought in grand terms, always aiming high, so many of the new lines saw themselves reaching into the heart of the City and the West End. There was also the proposal that there should be a grand central terminus on what is now the Victoria Embankment, which in itself seemed not unreasonable except that it was to be connected by lines linking it with Paddington and Fenchurch Street, running right through both Westminster and the City. This made even the reconstruction after the Great Fire of London seem modest, and the government of the day was terrified at the disruption and inconvenience that would be caused. There would, of course, have had to be lines later connecting with Waterloo and London Bridge, requiring at least one more major bridge over the River Thames, and the connections to the London & North Western, as the London & Birmingham had become, and King's Cross, as well as the later arrival of St Pancras, and Liverpool Street, hardly bears thinking about. Each of these would have required at least four running lines, perhaps six for Waterloo, and even if King's Cross and St Pancras shared a route, it would needed widening as hardly any of the termini remained at the size at which they were first built.

London's mainline termini

We have seen the arrival of the Great Western at Paddington and the London & Birmingham at Euston, but these were only the first of several mainline railways to reach the capital. London was not only a prestigious objective, it was a major traffic generator, and so much so that the Midland Railway and the Great Central made strenuous efforts to reach the capital. It was not just that the alternative of using the lines of other companies was expensive and unsatisfactory, the growth of the railways once built meant that, on the most promising and strategically important lines, the London termini and their approaches were under pressure within a few years of opening.

The first of the next wave of termini to be opened was that at Waterloo, four years after the Royal Commission on London's termini, yet the station suffered from being remote from the destinations of most of the travellers arriving off its trains. On the other hand, despite its location, it was a

OLD WATERLOO

The old Waterloo Station, with its through lines to the South Eastern, was chaotic, and matters were not helped by the narrow wooden bridge that crossed the through lines and was the cause of many a missed train. *Punch* carried a cartoon of a Dorsetshire farmer and his wife struggling through the crowds on the bridge and saying: 'Mary, no wonder the French lost here!'

The surrounding area, as with so many of the London termini, became crowded with cheap hotels and many disreputable establishments, so that the station was sometimes referred to as 'Whoreterloo'.

reminder of the disruption that extending a main line railway closer to the centre of London could bring. It was designed to replace an earlier and even less satisfactory terminus at Nine Elms. Once again, we find a station that was to grow piecemeal, with four separate stages of construction. Unusually, however, Waterloo was extended to provide through running, with the creation of a station just outside, to the east, at Waterloo Junction, on the line from London Bridge to Charing Cross, so it was also used by two railway companies. Waterloo could have been a mess, something akin to the shambles that was Euston Station before its major reconstruction in the late 1960s, but it was completely rebuilt by the London & South Western Railway's last general manager, the vigorous and relatively young, Herbert Walker, between 1910 and 1920, becoming a dignified and cohesive whole, and the first British terminus designed for electric trains.

The predecessor of Waterloo, Nine Elms, was chosen as the terminus for the new London & Southampton Railway, first mooted in 1831, largely because it meant that costly disturbance to business and residential property would be minimal. Its position, close to the southern end of Vauxhall Bridge, mean that passengers could make their way to the West End, while boat services were envisaged for those travelling to the City. It opened on 21 May 1838, when the London & Southampton had reached Woking. The following year, the London & Southampton unveiled its ambitions with a new name, the London & South Western Railway, although it did not reach its original objective until 11 May 1840. The first train, carrying guests, took three hours for the journey of just under eighty miles between Nine Elms and Southampton.

Despite its ambitious title, the LSWR soon found that its heaviest traffic was between what would now be the outer suburbs and London. Many of the station names of the early LSWR differ from those of today, with the original Kingston now being Surbiton. The first branch line was opened on 27 July 1846 from Clapham Junction to Richmond, and soon provided a quarter of the company's traffic. Yet the remote location of Nine Elms meant that road coaches had survived between Chertsey and the City. The original promoters of the branch to Richmond had also proposed a line from Nine Elms to a supposed 'West End' terminus near Hungerford Bridge. Having taken over the Richmond branch before its completion, the LSWR obtained powers in 1845 for a new terminus in York Road, close to the southern end of Waterloo Bridge; and a further act in 1847 increased the number of lines to the new terminus to four and also the size of the site. This meant disruption on a grand scale, with the extension to Waterloo, then requiring far fewer tracks than exist today, required the demolition of 700 houses and the crossing of twenty-one roads, despite the 1¾ mile railway using viaduct with more than 200 arches for most of its length. Obstacles that affected the alignment included Lambeth Palace, Vauxhall Gardens and a gas works. An intermediate station was built at Vauxhall, while a bridge over Westminster Road had to be built on the skew with the then unprecedented span of 90ft. The LSWR was encouraged to think on such a grand scale because of the possibility of sharing the new terminus with the London Brighton & South Coast Railway, but this came to nothing, fortunately, as Waterloo soon proved to be too small for even the LSWR's needs.

Strangely, despite its inconvenient location, Robert Stephenson told the Royal Commission that there was 'no point on the South side of the Thames so good for a large railway station, as the south end of Waterloo Bridge'.

The original Waterloo Station opened on 11 July 1848, after Nine Elms closed the previous day, although remaining for VIP use, including visiting royalty and, much later, the departure of the British Army's horses to the Boer War. With some foresight, Waterloo was designed as a through station and under a two-span 280ft iron and glass roof were six tracks and six 300 ft platform faces, although the length of these was soon doubled, while a spur towards the river suggested that the LSWR was attempting to keep every option open. The catchment area for the new terminus continued to grow, with an extension of the Richmond branch to Windsor on 1 December 1849, by which time an additional up line had been installed.

The LSWR was not content with Waterloo, but wanted to get closer to the City. Already, there was no room for goods traffic, and this was important for many of the London termini in the early years before the demands of passenger traffic moved all but parcels and newspaper traffic down the line to a specially-built goods depots.

Another indication of the pressure that London's growth was placing on some of the more essential services was the lack of cemetery space for the enlarged population. A solution came in 1854 when the London Necropolis & National Mausoleum Company opened a private cemetery at Brookwood, conveniently on the LSWR mainline west of Woking, and a private necropolis station was built at Waterloo for the special trains with their hearse carriages.

Expansion continued at Waterloo as the LSWR network grew. Four additional platform faces were built in 1860, in what was to become known as the Windsor Station, and separated from the original station, now known as the 'Main Station' by its own cab road. The opening of the South Eastern's Charing Cross extension in 1864 was accompanied by a short spur into Waterloo, and this could have enabled passenger trains to work through to London Bridge and, later, to Cannon Street, thus providing the long sought after City extension of the LSWR, but instead it was rarely used by passenger trains. As traffic developed, this was just as well as there would have been many conflicting movements at Waterloo Junction. Through traffic was discouraged by passengers interchanging between the two companies having to rebook, and only later were through fares offered for those attempting to reach the City.

Yet another Waterloo station was added in 1878, opening on 16 December, but on this occasion, new offices were opened and a refreshment room, with a cab yard under a new 300ft frontage on Waterloo Road. In 1885, a further final extension was added, with the North station built as an extension of the Windsor Station and opened in November, with six new platform faces, so that by now Waterloo had a total of eighteen; and unusually for the day, all of them suitable for arrivals and departures, but still served by just four approach tracks, which were the cause of much delay as by this time Waterloo was handling 700 trains daily. The original Waterloo was an open station, with tickets being checked at Vauxhall, and this no doubt added to the delays. The station itself was a mess, not least because of an eccentric platform numbering system that meant that many platforms used the same number for two faces, and this, with a paucity of departure information, meant that even if the intending passenger found the right platform, there was a 50 per cent risk of boarding the wrong train.

Between 1886 and 1892, a further two approach tracks were added and, once again, there was massive destruction of housing, so that the LSWR had to provide new property in 1890 for more than a thousand people.

Passengers for the City were growing in numbers, and were also people of considerable influence. The LSWR itself calculated that of the 50,000 daily arrivals at Waterloo, a quarter of them were heading for the City, divided equally between the buses and the SER. As early as 1882, plans were considered for an overhead railway, but rejected as too costly, and no doubt hazardous given the technology of the day, and these were revived in 1891, but still considered too costly.

Relief was eventually found in the Waterloo and City tube line, authorised in 1893. The LSWR provided much of the capital and five of the eight directors, and agreed to operate the line for 55 per cent of the gross receipts after payment of a 3 per cent dividend. The line opened in 1898, providing a direct non-stop link between a station not strictly deep underground but in Waterloo's basement and a point just across the road from the Bank of England, appropriately enough known as Bank. Open air carriage sidings were constructed at the Waterloo end, and rolling stock could be moved using a hoist. In 1907, the company took over the line completely.

Next came Victoria, the main station for the London Brighton & South Coast Railway, which had acquired the London & Croydon and also used that company's terminus at London Bridge. Victoria and London Bridge were far enough apart to serve different markets, with Victoria being close to, but not actually part of, the West End, while London Bridge was across the river from the City.

The truth was that no one terminus could ever have been sufficient for London, even if the Royal Commission had decided differently. The City would have needed its own station, so that perhaps London Bridge, Broad Street, Cannon Street, Fenchurch Street and Liverpool Street would have been merged into one large city terminus located somewhere in the 'Square Mile'– but where?

As it was, the London Brighton & South Coast Railway was unhappy with its shared terminus with the South Eastern Railway at London Bridge, with friction breaking out between the two companies from time to time. The location was not that convenient for the City, and far too remote for the West End. A new company was established, the Victoria Station and Pimlico Railway, claiming that it would be building a terminus not only for the LBSCR, but also for the South Eastern, the East Kent Railway (the predecessor of the London, Chatham & Dover) and the London & South Western. Despite its poverty, the LCDR realised that the new arrangement still left it at the mercy of other companies, and in 1860 obtained the necessary powers to build its own new routes to both the West End and the City of London, with the former achieved through a new line from Beckenham to Battersea.

Such were the changing fortunes and ambitions of the railway companies, that the Victoria Station and Pimlico Railway found itself building a major terminus for the LBSCR and the LCDR plus the Great Western, which meant that the line from Longhedge Junction, Battersea, where the GWR would approach over the West London Extension Railway, had to be of mixed gauge to accommodate the broad gauge GWR trains. The LBSCR provided two-thirds of the Victoria Station and Pimlico's capital and secured its own terminus and access lines, taking 8½ acres of the 14 acre site, so that despite the magnificent façade of the Grosvenor Hotel, Victoria was really to be two stations in one!

The London & Brighton approach to Victoria from Clapham Junction required both a tight curve and a steep climb, with the bridge over the river built high enough to allow passage of the largest ships likely to use the Thames, which meant that it was unrealistically high as already larger ships were being handled at new docks downriver. This approach had to be shared with the GWR despite that company's connection with the LCDR. On crossing the bridge, the line then had a steep descent to the station as it had been decided that an approach on a viaduct to an elevated station would have been unacceptable to the wealthy landowners in the area. Other concessions to this element included extending the train shed beyond the platforms and the early sleepers, of longitudinal design, were also mounted on rubber to minimise vibration.

The new station opened for LBSCR trains on 1 October 1860, built on a generous scale, being 800ft long and 230ft wide, with a ridge and furrow roof having 50ft spans covering ten tracks and six platform faces. There was a cab road from Eccleston Bridge with an exit into Terminus Place. The Grosvenor Hotel was constructed independently despite its obvious attachment to the terminus as the presence of several railway companies convinced the promoters of its success, and was completed in 1861, but the original hotel was along the west side of the stations and could not conceal the distinctly unattractive, even primitive, start to the station, with offices in a series of wooden huts, for while the LCDR was indeed poverty stricken, even the more affluent LBSCR had found the cost of the move into the centre of London expensive. Matters were not improved when, during February 1884, the Fenian Brotherhood deposited a bomb in a bag in the left luggage office, which also wrecked the LBSCR's cloakroom and ticket office, although fortunately the police were able to prevent similar outrages at Charing Cross and Paddington.

The joint LCDR and GWR station was not completed until 25 August 1862, although the LCDR had made use of a temporary station since December 1860. The LCDR made use of a modest side entrance into the station, which had nine tracks on its smaller acreage, with four of them mixed gauge. The GWR started services to and from Victoria on 1 April 1863, with what was essentially a suburban feeder service from Southall where connections could be made with its main line services. Trains running through to Reading, Slough, Uxbridge and Windsor were also provided at times over the years that followed, and finally, between 1910 and 1912, a daily train in each direction between Birmingham and Wolverhampton and Victoria. Wartime restrictions saw the end of the Southall service in 1915, and in any case, such a service was really superfluous after the opening of the Circle Line in 1884.

Several other railway companies operated into Victoria, including the Great Northern Railway, operating from Barnet via Ludgate Hill from 1 March 1868, and the Midland Railway from South Tottenham and Hendon via Ludgate Hill from 1 July 1875, both of which used the LCDR station. Even London & North Western trains operated from Broad Street via Willesden Junction and the West London Railway from 1 January 1869 into the LBSC station; and survived the longest as an occasional service was still operated between Willesden Junction and Victoria until 1917.

Another new station at Grosvenor Road was too close to Victoria to be of much commercial value, but was used by the LBSCR for up trains to stop for ticket inspection.

By 1890, with all of its lines completed, the LBSCR was producing a steady return on its capital, with the annual dividend running at 6 or 7 per cent. It was time to give Victoria a complete overhaul. Starting in 1892, the LBSCR acquired the houses on the west side of the station and also bought the freehold of the Grosvenor Hotel when the owners refused to sell houses owned by them. The LBSCR let the hotel to a new operator and built an impressive 150-room wing across the front of the station. The initial development of the station during the 1890s produced another 90 ft in width, but only at the southern end of the station between Eccleston Bridge and the hotel. Even this was judged, rightly, to be insufficient. Unable to expand further west due to Buckingham Palace Road, or east because of the LCDR station, the only solution was to extend the station towards the river, and for this the powers were obtained in 1899, so that the station could increase from ten roads and eight platform faces to thirteen roads with nine faces, several of which could be used by two trains at once. Work started in 1901.

Clinging to the north bank

The next two termini arrived at much the same time, with the South Eastern Railway opening what was the West End of London's only terminus at Charing Cross in 1864, followed by the London Chatham & Dover Railway opening its first station at Blackfriars, *but* on the south side of the river, later that year. These stations were to show the full impact of Parliament's rulings.

Despite its cramped location, no London mainline station is as well situated for the traveller as Charing Cross, at the end of The Strand. The substantial forecourt and the impressive façade of the Charing Cross Hotel combine to disguise the fact that the station is smaller than many in medium-sized provincial cities.

A railway terminus was first planned in 1846, when the South Eastern Railway promoted a bill for an extension from Bricklayer's Arms to Hungerford Bridge, but it was unsuccessful. After the SER managed to obtain the approval of the London Brighton & South Coast Railway for a line from London Bridge to the West End, in 1857 the SER settled on the Hungerford Market as the ideal site, with the prospect of a link to the LSWR at Waterloo.

The Charing Cross Railway Company Act 1859 authorised the construction of a line one mile and sixty-eight chains in length, mainly on viaduct except for Hungerford Bridge which took it across the Thames and into the terminus. Once again the CCRC was separate from the SER in theory, but clearly linked to it, with the SER providing £300,000 of the initial £800,000 capital, and later raising this investment to £650,000 as land purchase costs proved to be far heavier than anticipated. Much of the money was spent south of the river, with the governors of St Thomas Hospital exacting the heavy price of £296,000, and then, despite the poverty of the area at the time, the many slum landlords also managed to follow this example. In addition, the SER itself had to pay for the reconstruction of Borough Market as well as a 404ft iron viaduct over it, all the time while taking care to avoid Southwark Cathedral. It was not just the living who had to be accommodated, as the SER had to oversee the removal of more than 7,000 corpses from the College Burial Ground of St Mary, Lambeth, and their removal and re-interment at Brookwood. Later, in June 1878, a new junction was opened to provide a link, Metropolitan Junction, with the LCDR line to Blackfriars.

The new line required the removal and scrapping of Brunel's original Hungerford Bridge, but nothing was wasted as the bridge and iron work was used for the construction of Clifton Suspension Bridge at Bristol. As at Cannon Street, the bridge included a pedestrian walkway, in this case on the eastern side, for which a toll of a ½ d (0.2p) was charged until 1878, when the Metropolitan Board of Works paid the SER £98,000 for pedestrians to enjoy free access.

Charing Cross opened on 11 January 1864, initially with just a limited service of trains to Greenwich and Mid Kent, but on 1 April, trains from the north of the county started to use the new station, and on 1 May, main line services followed.

The six platforms were all built in wood, ranged in length up to 690 feet and extended on to the bridge. The Charing Cross Hotel was designed by the architect EM Barry, with 250 bedrooms and almost wrapped itself around the station by extending down Villiers Street, and later had an annex across the street reached by a covered footbridge.

Powers were obtained in 1864 in the North Western & Charing Cross Railway Act, to provide an underground line running just below the surface for goods and passenger trains from Charing Cross to Euston. The LNWR and SER both gave guarantees to raise 5 per cent of the capital, but this was not enough to encourage investors and the scheme was abandoned in the financial crisis of 1866 that pushed the LCDR into Chancery. The Euston link surfaced again in 1885, with the two railway companies prepared to provide a third of the capital each, but floundered again. Had either line been built, they could have undermined financial backing for the Hampstead tube, but on the other hand, could also have provided the basis for a modern day regional express across the centre of London.

The SER started buying the freehold of property on either side of the station in readiness for much needed expansion. In 1900, powers were obtained to widen Hungerford Bridge on the east side and also to enlarge the terminus. Having got this far, the SER was then discouraged from any further move by the plans to replace the station and bridge with a road bridge.

Meanwhile, Blackfriars opened on 1 June 1864, on the south bank of the River Thames, at the junction of today's Southwark Street and the approach to Blackfriars Bridge. It served as a terminus for just a little over six months until the railway bridge over the Thames was completed, allowing trains to stop at a temporary station at Little Earl Street on the north bank from 21 December 1864. A station on the north bank, Ludgate Hill, opened on 1 June 1865, it too becoming a terminus until the Metropolitan Extension was completed to Farringdon Street on 1 January 1866. The LCDR had persuaded both the Great Northern and London & South Western Railways to subscribe more than £300,000 apiece towards the cost of the extension with the promise of through running powers, which they soon exercised, along with the Midland Railway, which started running trains through to Victoria in 1875. The LCDR itself sent trains from Herne Hill through to King's Cross and then as far as Barnet.

From its opening in 1886, until 1937, the station now known as Blackfriars was known as St Paul's.

The construction of Blackfriars, or St Paul's, was brought about by the success of the London, Chatham & Dover's extension towards London. The LCDR had been allowed to extend to London by its Metropolitan Extension Act of 1860, which gave it powers to reach Victoria and, more ambitious still, to a junction with the Metropolitan Railway at Farringdon Street, offering considerable long-term potential that was not to be realised for many years. The new station at Ludgate Hill and the extension through the City was a considerable success. Unfortunately, a shortage of space meant that Ludgate Hill offered just two island platforms, which soon proved insufficient for the traffic on offer and, as expansion was out of the question given the high cost of property and the LCDR's over-stretched finances, an additional station was built on a spur off the Metropolitan Extension, and it was this that was named St Paul's when it opened on 10 May 1886, despite the fact that the name Blackfriars was already in use as the name of the adjacent District and Circle Line station. It was a necessity forced on the railway and was built as cheaply as possible, even having a wooden booking office. It was as mean a structure as has ever been devised for a terminus in a capital city as the cramped surroundings and the presence of the Metropolitan District Railway immediately under the station meant that there was no forecourt and no cab access to the tar-coated wooden platforms, which were reached by a dark and drab staircase. Only two of the platforms were given numbers, simply 1 and 2, between the eastern siding and the up and down loops. Yet, in incised letters on the stones surrounding the doors, the names were given of fifty-four destinations that could be reached from the station, including St Petersburg and Vienna, with nothing to suggest that the intrepid traveller could expect to make several changes along the way.

Trains running to Holborn Viaduct generally stopped at Blackfriars, while it also took the City portions of trains from the new Gravesend branch, opened on the same day as the new terminus, and which were later joined by those from the Greenwich Park branch, opened in October 1888. The new station was the only one operated by the LCDR with direct access to the underground network. Ludgate Hill continued to prove inadequate for the traffic on offer and became the butt of much press criticism as it was the most convenient station for Fleet Street, then the home of almost all the national newspapers and of the London offices of many provincial dailies.

The other station in this unhappy trio, Holborn Viaduct, was generally regarded as being useless, largely because it was inconveniently sited. Despite these criticisms, it was not until well after the formation of the South Eastern & Chatham that any attempt was made to remedy the situation, with a minor reconstruction of Ludgate Hill between 1907 and 1912. The irony of the situation was that Holborn Viaduct had been built by the LCDR to relieve the pressure on Ludgate Hill, using the £100,000 (around £5 million today) paid by the Post Office for its telegraph system when the telegraph systems were nationalised to provide a cohesive nationwide telegraph system.

In the meantime, for those travelling to London from the south, a terminus in the City at Cannon Street was opened in 1866 for the South Eastern Railway, which had previously decanted its passengers at London Bridge, on the wrong side of the Thames. Earlier plans had been to provide two other stations on the extension line running to Charing Cross, but when the London, Chatham & Dover Railway was authorised to provide an extension to Ludgate Hill, the SER realised that it also needed a terminus on the north bank of the River Thames. It was even felt that there could be local traffic between Cannon Street and Charing Cross from those anxious to avoid the heavy congestion on the streets of London.

This was to prove to be no flight of fancy. From the time it first opened, on 1 September 1866, Cannon Street fulfilled its promise of being served by all trains proceeding to and from Charing Cross, including boat trains, and with these and a shuttle service between the two stations, there was a five minute frequency service between the West End and the City, taking seven minutes, and costing 6d first class, 4d second class and 2d third class, compared with 3d for the horse bus. The local traffic was considerable, with 3.5 million of the 8 million passengers using Cannon Street in 1867 travelling solely between the City and the West End. This continued until the opening of the District Railway between Westminster and Blackfriars in May 1870, and which reached Mansion House in July 1871, while the completion of the Circle Line, on 6 October 1884, saw a station opened under the forecourt of Cannon Street.

One kind of specialised traffic had already disappeared before this. The seven minute run had proved a great draw to certain ladies who found that it combined with the comfort of a first-class compartment to provide the ideal environment for the entertainment of their clients. Once a stop was introduced at Waterloo, from 1 January 1869, the number of drawn blinds on trains running into and out of Charing Cross dropped dramatically!

The extension to Cannon Street had been authorised by an Act of 1861, with a bridge across the Thames and a triangular junction on viaducts with the line between London Bridge and Charing Cross. At first, and for many years, all trains running to and from Charing Cross called at Cannon Street. There were five tracks, four running roads and an engine road, on the bridge, which had pedestrian walkways on either side, with the one on the east reserved for railway personnel, while that on the west was available to the public on payment of a ½d toll. The station itself abutted immediately onto the bridge, with nine roads, and was a handsome building offering stunning views over the Thames, and with a hotel fronting the street. The roof was a single span of 190ft over 100ft above the rails and glazed over two-thirds of its surface, surmounted by a 22ft-wide lantern running almost the whole 680ft length. The two longest platforms extended beyond the roof and on to the bridge, giving commanding views of the river.

The hotel, the City Terminus, was operated by an independent company and opened in May 1867, but was later acquired by the SER, and later renamed The Cannon Street Hotel. It managed, for reasons that remain obscure and can be nothing more than a coincidence, to become the venue for the creation of the Communist Party of Great Britain in July 1920. Cannon Street remained the exclusive preserve of the SER, except during late 1867 and until the end of July, 1868, when the London Brighton & South Coast Railway operated two up morning and two down evening trains to and from Brighton.

Across the City, at Broad Street, another terminus was in hand. In 1863, at the height of a renewed, and very short-lived, railway boom, the House of Lords Select Committee on Metropolitan Railway Communications looked once again at the concept of a large central terminus for all of the railways. Once again the outcome was a report against it. The Committee concluded that any new lines within the central area would have to be underground, with the limits placed by the original Royal Commission of 1846 being extended still further out. The concept of an 'inner circle' north of the Thames to link the termini was first mooted, and this was endorsed by the Parliamentary Joint Committee on Railway Schemes (Metropolis). Thus, the basis of the Circle Line were laid and assured of political support. It might have been even better if the line had managed to touch Euston rather than simply dump passengers with heavy luggage nearby, and also stray south of the Thames to include Waterloo, whose passengers at the time were the most inconvenienced, stuck south of the River Thames.

There was a major accident at Charing Cross shortly after the turn of the century. During the afternoon of 5 December 1905, workmen were busy on a programme of roof maintenance work. At 15.45, there was a sudden noise; passengers and railwaymen looking up saw the workmen rushing to safety, and fortunately followed their example. Shortly afterwards, at 15.57, there was a deafening roar as 70ft of the roof at the outer end of the station collapsed into the station, while pushing outwards the western wall onto the Avenue Theatre in Craven Street. Inside the station, three men were killed, as rubble, iron work and glass crashed on to the 15.50 express to Hastings, while at the Avenue Theatre, three men out of a hundred who, by unhappy coincidence, were also working on renovations to that building, were crushed under the rubble.

The SECR closed Charing Cross at once, and traffic on Hungerford Bridge was stopped, and then the trains set back, one at a time, to Waterloo Junction.

Investigation soon showed that a weakness in a wrought-iron tie rod next to the windscreen at the southern end of the roof was the main cause. The weakness was due to a fault that doubtless had occurred at the time of manufacture, and had grown worse over the years as it expanded and contracted as weather conditions changed. Despite claims by engineers that the remaining roof would be safe for another forty years, the SECR decided to take no chances, rebuilding the roof and walls at a reduced height and dispensing with the single span. Meanwhile, trains were diverted to Cannon Street and Charing Cross could not re-open to traffic until 19 March 1906. The closure did have one benefit, allowing the Charing Cross Euston & Hampstead Railway, precursor of today's Northern Line, to dig down through the forecourt, something which the SECR had prohibited for fear of causing difficulty and inconvenience to their passengers, and press ahead with building The Strand underground station.

Reaching into the City

Travellers from the south were not the only substantial group of city workers, with many coming from the eastern counties, and indeed from around the north of London. The one terminus that was built largely for a suburban clientele was Broad Street, built as the City terminus for the North London Railway, which opened in 1850 as the East & West India

Docks and Birmingham Junction Railway, which was largely controlled by the London & North Western Railway. The name of the original company showed that goods traffic was the aim, but by the time the simpler title of the North London Railway was adopted in 1853, it was clear that passenger traffic was of growing importance. At first the NLR used Fenchurch Street on the London & Blackwall Railway, but this involved a four-mile detour around East London.

The LNWR agreed to meet most of the cost as it needed a goods station in the City, which at the time required large quantities of coal for office heating. The small NLR would not have been able to afford a terminus on its own, no matter what the prospects for passenger traffic. Already, parliamentary approval could not be taken for granted, especially as the extension required demolition of many homes. To overcome this hurdle, the NLR promised to provide workmen's trains from Dalston for a return fare of just one penny. Three tracks connected the station with the rest of the NLR network. The platforms were approached by an external staircase on the eastern side of the station frontage, itself showing a mixture of styles and there is no record of an architect.

The relationship between the NLR and LNWR was not so close that they could operate as a single entity, and so Broad Street operated as a joint station with two booking halls. At platform level, there were two train sheds, initially having just four tracks between them. Opened on 1 November 1865, the initial service was a train every fifteen minutes to Bow, and another to Chalk Farm, as well as a service every half-hour to Kew via Hampstead Heath. In 1866, a service to Watford was introduced and in 1879, some Chalk Farm workings were extended to Willesden, but were cut back again in 1917. The LNWR goods yard was below the passenger platforms and wagons were raised and lowered by hydraulic lifts, but the goods sidings were to the west of the passenger station.

Both the NLR and Broad Street proved to be a great success. The NLR's traffic doubled and increased still further when from January 1875, trains ran through to Broad Street from Great Northern Railway suburban stations. At one time, Broad Street was amongst the busiest of the London termini, handling 712 trains daily with 80,000 passengers in 1906. An indication of the intensity of suburban working was that each pair of platforms shared a coaling stage.

Further massive disruption and demolition of housing was required for St Pancras when it was built for the Midland Railway's extension to London after the original arrangement that saw trains running from Hitchin to King's Cross starting in early 1858, had proved expensive. The heavy excursion traffic for the Great Exhibition of 1862 also showed the limitations on capacity at King's Cross, even before the growth in the Great Northern Railway's traffic in the years that followed. It was clear the MR needed its own terminus and its own approach route.

The MR already had its own goods yard in London at Agar Town, between the North London Railway and the Regent's Canal. It was decided to extend this line to the Euston Road, at the boundary set by the Royal Commission on London's Termini, which effectively barred further incursions by railways into the centre of London. A 4½ acre site was found for the terminus. Once again, the extension required the demolition of thousands of slum dwellings in Agar Town and Somers Town, with some 10,000 people evicted without compensation. Even the dead were not spared the upheaval of railway expansions as the line infringed the cemetery of St Pancras Church, with successive layers of corpses having to be removed and re-interred: unfortunately it took complaints in the press for this to be done with any sense of reverence. The disruption to the cemetery was largely due to a double track link being constructed to the Metropolitan Railway on the east side of the extension, with a tunnel inside which there was a gradient of 1 in 75. Despite these problems, the line to the terminus itself had to pass over the Regent's Canal which meant both a falling gradient towards the terminus and a platform level some twenty feet above street level. Ironically, the widening of the Metropolitan (City Widened Lines) did not go further west than King's Cross and so was of more use for GNR trains than those of the Midland until further widening in 1926, but the spur from the Midland main line was closed in 1935!

Initially, when William Barlow designed the station, he proposed filling the space under the tracks and platforms with soil excavated from the tunnels, but James Allport, the MR's general manager, saw the potential for storage space, especially for beer from Burton-on-Trent. This led Barlow to design a single span trainshed, which not only allowed greater freedom in planning the storage space beneath the station, but also meant that the layout of the tracks and platforms could be altered as needed in the years to come. A large Gothic hotel was constructed in front of the station, giving it the most impressive frontage of any London terminus. While trains from Bedford to Moorgate started using the tunnel under the terminus from 13 July 1868, the terminus itself was opened to traffic on 1 October 1868, without any ceremony.

The Midland Grand Hotel was still at foundation level when the station opened, but this was intended to be the most luxurious of its kind, and a monument to its architect, Sir Gilbert Scott.

The approaches consisted of four tracks, although further out these became an up line and two down lines. After Cambridge Street Junction, the line became simple double track until St Paul's Road Junction, where the lines from the Metropolitan surfaced. The main locomotive depot was at Kentish Town, 1½ miles from the terminus. Despite not being as busy as Waterloo, Victoria or Liverpool Street, the approaches were congested, almost from the beginning, and difficult to operate, especially when working empty stock to and from the station. Improvements in 1907-08 helped, but the problem was never resolved during the age of steam, although in later years diesel multiple unit working with trains turned around in the station helped considerably.

The station was meant to serve the MR's long distance ambitions. The company saw its main market as the East Midlands, but while that was the basis of its traffic, its services to Scotland that started in the 1870s were also important. Despite having a local platform, there was almost no suburban traffic for many years with the MR's suburban trains, never plentiful, working through to Moorgate. Even in 1903, there were just fourteen suburban arrivals between 5 am and 10 am. It was not until 1910 that the Midland Railway began to encourage suburban traffic at St Pancras. The MR needed running powers into the London Docks over the Great Eastern, and in return the GER was able to claim that St Pancras was its West End terminus, which required some stretch of the imagination, and ran trains from Norfolk and Suffolk into the station. The GER trains were eventually suspended in 1917 as a First World War economy measure, and with the exception of a daily train to Hunstanton during the summers of 1922 and 1923, never reinstated. Nevertheless, it was St Pancras that was used by the Royal Family when travelling to and from Sandringham.

From 1894, the London Tilbury & Southend Railway ran boat trains for passengers catching ships at Tilbury to Scandinavia and Australia. These services survived nationalisation and did not revert to Liverpool Street until 1963.

Finally, the largest terminus within the City of London, Liverpool Street, was built to replace the Shoreditch terminus of the Eastern Counties Railway. When the ECR was absorbed into the Great Eastern Railway in 1862, the question arose again of terminus in central London, coupled with the building of additional suburban lines and the conversion of Shoreditch to a goods station. A number of locations were considered, including Finsbury Circus, and for the track to continue from Bishopsgate on viaduct. Parliament approved the scheme in 1864, mainly because the line approached Liverpool Street in tunnel so that the demolition of London's housing stock would be kept to the minimum, but also because it was beside Broad Street.

The plan was that the lines should leave the existing high level route at Tapp Street, just west of Bethnal Green, and fall to below street level, and then run in tunnel under Commercial Street and Shoreditch High Street before turning to enter the terminus, which would be built on what had been the gardens of the Bethlehem Hospital. Some demolition was inevitable, including the City of London Theatre and the City of London Gasworks, and 450 tenement dwellings housing around 7,000 people. The GER was bound under the terms of the Act to run a 2d daily return train between Edmonton and Liverpool Street, and another between the terminus and Walthamstow. Later claims by the GER to pay between 30 and 50 shillings as compensation to displaced tenants can be discounted as the payments at the time would have been much lower.

The terminus was built below street level, much to the consternation of many of the directors, but Samuel Swarbrick, the GER's general manager, was concerned to cut costs, despite the fact that departing trains would be faced with a tunnel through which the track climbed steeply. The new station opened in stages, with the first being on 2 February 1874, handling just the suburban services to Enfield and Walthamstow, and the station was not fully open until 1 November 1875, when the old Bishopsgate terminus was handed over to be converted for goods traffic.

Liverpool Street occupied ten acres in the heart of the City and had ten platforms, numbered from west to east. Platforms 1 and 2 ran under the station building and the street to a junction with the Metropolitan Railway, to the west of its Liverpool Street underground station, known until 1909 as Bishopsgate. The street front of the new station consisted of three blocks, with the main one 90 feet high and running along Liverpool Street itself, and a second running from its western then running into one at its northern end set at right angles to it, 67 feet high. In the space left by the blocks were four roadways for pedestrians and vehicles. The roof was perhaps the best feature of the building, set high and with a delicate appearance, with four glazed spans. There was a clock tower on the outside of the building, on the roof of the north block: inside train shed, the roof later had two four-faced clocks suspended from it.

Behind the north block, was the suburban station with eight tracks and ten platform faces, while the mainline platforms were to the east of the middle block. Later, the suburban platforms were numbered 1 to 8, with platform 9 used by both suburban and long distance services.

Costs for building a terminus in the heart of the City of London were high, and while compensation for the displaced tenants was poor, the landowners received far higher compensation, so that the cost of Liverpool Street eventually mounted to £2 million (£120 million by today's prices), and to allow for this, an Act of 1869 allowed the GER to charge the two-mile fare for the 1¼ mile extension. This was, incidentally, unusual in the British Isles, but a common practice in Europe to charge extra for a railway line involving heavy engineering works.

The opening of Liverpool Street encouraged the GER to build a set of three suburban branch lines north of Bethnal Green, serving Hackney Downs and Tottenham, Edmonton, with a junction with the original Enfield branch, and from Hackney Downs through Clapton to a junction with the Cambridge line and the still new branch to Walthamstow. The latter was extended to Chingford in 1873, and the line to Tottenham and Edmonton was extended to Palace Gates at Wood Green in 1878. Some of these lines were open before Liverpool Street was ready, so a new station, Bishopsgate Low Level, was opened on the new extension to Liverpool Street in November 1872. The low level station was under the existing terminus, and with no room for smoke and steam to escape, the tank engines used were equipped with condensing apparatus, which was also seen as necessary for the projected through running onto the MR. It was eventually closed as a wartime economy measure in 1916.

Added to the GER's own branches were services running from the East London Railway, completed in April 1876. In July of that year, the London Brighton & South Coast Railway introduced a service from East Croydon, while the South Eastern Railway, later South Eastern & Chatham, started a service from Addiscombe in April 1880, which lasted until March 1884. At the beginning of 1886, the GER took over the LBSCR services, although from 1911 they terminated at New Cross and were withdrawn when the ELR was electrified in 1913.

These suburban developments and the continued growth on the earlier lines and a growing business to and from the holiday resorts and market towns of East Anglia, meant that by 1884 it was realised that the traffic at Liverpool Street itself would soon outgrow the station. Fortunately, the GER had been steadily acquiring land to the east of the station, and had eventually land up to Bishopsgate 188-ft wide and six acres in extent. Clearance began and on 1890 work began on what was to become the East Side Station. A sign of social change was that Parliament insisted that alternative accommodation be found for the tenants in the properties cleared away, and indeed that they be rehoused at low rents.

Accommodation could only be found for 137 tenants in existing property, so another 600 were housed in tenements built by the GER.

It was not enough simply to expand the station: the approach lines had to be expanded as well to avoid congestion. A third pair of approach tracks was built between Bethnal Green and Liverpool Street, enabling the westernmost set of tracks to be reserved entirely for the Enfield and Walthamstow services, so from 1891, these were known as the suburban lines, the middle set became the local lines and the easternmost, the through lines. The four tracks continued as far as Romford.

The new Liverpool Street was the largest London terminus until the rebuilt Victoria re-opened in 1908. By the number of passengers handled daily, it remained the busiest terminus even after 1908. In a typical day, it handled 851 passenger arrivals and departures, as well as 224 empty carriage trains, ten goods trains and five light engine movements.

The new East Side frontage was taken by the Great Eastern Hotel, completed in May 1884, and the largest hotel in the City. Beneath the hotel, an area known as the 'backs' included an extension of the tracks from platforms 9 and 10. This was used by a nightly goods train that brought in coal for the hotel and the engine docks, as well as small consignments for the offices and the hotel, while taking away the hotel's refuse and ashes from the engine docks. The eastward extension also meant that these two platforms split the station in two, and so a footbridge was built right across the station, although on two levels and too narrow to accommodate the numbers needing to use it at peak times.

Meanwhile, other suburban branch lines had been added to the GER network, although the first of these, the line to Southend, completed in 1889, would not have been regarded as even outer suburban at the time! It was joined by a line from Edmonton to Cheshunt, known as the Churchbury Loop, in 1891, and between Ilford and Woodford, known as the Hainault Loop, in 1903. The former closed in 1909 due to disappointing traffic, and that to Hainault was not much more successful, so it must have been a relief when an eastwards extension of the Central Line took it over some years later.

The last terminus to be built in London, the Great Central Railway's station at Marylebone, had an especially difficult time as the company's extension to London ran through St John's Wood, the residents of which objected, and past Lords, the cricket ground, having burrowed under Hampstead. Despite its late arrival, Marylebone has always resembled a small provincial terminus. The Manchester Sheffield & Lincolnshire Railway, had been a cross-county operation whose main line ran from

Grimsby to Manchester, and without a London route of its own, it lost this growing traffic to first the Great Northern Railway and, later, the Midland Railway. Opposition to Parliamentary approval was strong, especially from the cricketing fraternity as the line would run close to Lords. There was also opposition from the artists of St John's Wood. Eventually, the extension from near Nottingham to London was authorised in 1893.

The MSLR was not allowed to use the Metropolitan lines, but was able to use the same alignment: the Metropolitan was already very busy with its own suburban traffic. Fresh powers had to be obtained so that new lines could be laid. It was also considered expedient to change the company's somewhat provincial title to the more impressive Great Central Railway, and this was done on 1 August 1897.

Marylebone needed more than fifty acres, including coal and goods depots, and 4,448 persons were evicted during the slum clearance that followed, with many moved to homes nearby, but as a sign of changing times and more enlightened attitudes, more than half, 2,690, were moved to six five-storey locks of flats, built by the company and known as Wharncliffe Gardens after the new chairman of the GCR. This disruption was despite much of the approach being in tunnel or cut and covered construction passing under the streets of St John's Wood. The gradient was kept to 1 in 100. To allow for possible future quadrupling, not one but two tunnels were excavated under Hampstead.

Approaching the terminus, the seven tracks expanded to fourteen as the line passed over the Regent's Canal, which included a second span for the proposed and authorised, but never built, Regent's Canal, City & Docks Railway. Coal and goods depots were built on both sides of Lisson Grove.

The feeble resources of the GCR were stretched almost to breaking point by its expansion southwards. In its best year, 1864, its predecessor, the MSLR had achieved a dividend of just 3.5 per cent. An architect for the station was beyond the company's resources, while the terminus was a modest affair, albeit conveniently at street level, and the Great Central Hotel was left to others to develop. A three storey office block was provided, with provision for additional floors when required, but most of the accommodation remained unused until the GCR moved its headquarters from Manchester in 1905. The concourse, intended for a terminus twice the size with five double-faced platforms, stretched beyond the nine tracks and four built at its eastern end. Even the Great Central Hotel, with its 700 bedrooms, was over-ambitious, and in 1916 it was requisitioned by the government as a convalescent home for wounded officers. In the end, after being purchased as offices by the London & North Eastern Railway after the Second World War, it became 222 Marylebone Road, headquarters of the British Transport Commission, and when that was dissolved, the British Railways Board.

On 9 March 1899, a ceremonial opening was performed by the President of the Board of Trade. Public traffic started on 15 March. For the first month, only two platforms were used. By summer, there were eleven trains daily each way, of which seven were Manchester expresses. Where the GCR did score was in the comfort of its new carriages, all of which were corridor stock with electric lighting.

The problem was that the GCR route to Manchester was longer than that of the LNWR, and that to Sheffield longer than that of the Great Northern. The GCR was best for Leicester and Nottingham, neither of which matched the other cities for traffic. Even so, the Marylebone to Manchester journey time was down to 3 hrs 50 min by 1904, and Sheffield was three hours.

Much of these improved timings were due to a new general manager, Sam (later Sir Sam) Fay, who understood the need for good publicity and high standards of service. Timings were reduced, through services introduced to Bradford and Huddersfield, and to Stratford-upon-Avon using the Stratford-upon-Avon & Midland Junction Railway. Buses were laid on to carry arriving passengers to the West End, for which Marylebone was well placed, and to the City, for which it was not.

Before Fay joined the GCR, the Metropolitan Railway had completed quadrupling its lines as far as Harrow, and later, in 1906, its lines to Chesham, Brill and Verney Junction were leased to a new joint operating company of the GCR and MR, with the companies taking turns every five years to manage and staff the line. The agreement was that the GCR should not take local traffic between Marylebone and Harrow, but it was allowed to develop suburban traffic on the joint lines. The GCR soon took advantage of this, introducing local trains to Chesham and Aylesbury from March 1906. A year later, the opening of the Bakerloo tube line meant that Marylebone had good quick connections throughout the West End and to Waterloo and Charing Cross.

Despite the new found alliance between the GCR and the MR, the former still wanted a new route of its own. The MR line was more steeply graded than the GCR wanted for its planned express network, and also the curves were too severe for high speed running, especially at Aylesbury, which had a severe reverse curve. The answer lay in using the Great

Western's new line from Paddington to Birmingham, with a connecting line from near Quinton Road to Ashendon, and then from Neasden to Northolt. The shared section of the main line was managed jointly by a committee of the GCR and GWR. In return for its generosity, the GWR had the GCR abandon its own plans for a route to Birmingham.

The railways undoubtedly contributed much to the further growth and prosperity of London, and without them, the capital would not have been able to expand to its present extent, and by the end of the nineteenth century London was pulling in workers from as far afield as the Sussex Coast.

Chapter 6

Making Roads Down to Hell – the Underground

A few wooden houses on wheels made their appearance, and planted themselves by the gutter; then came some wagons loaded with timber and accompanied by sundry gravel-coloured men with picks and shovels. A day or two afterwards, a few hundred yards of roadway were enclosed, the ordinary traffic being, of course, driven into the side streets...The exact operations could be but dimly seen or heard from the street by the curious observer who gazed between the tall boards that shut him out; but paterfamilias, from his hard by, could look down on an indefinite chaos of timber, shaft holes...one morning he found workmen had been kindly shoring up his family abode with huge timbers to make it safer...but at last, after much labour and many vicissitudes, even the Underground Railway was completed.

Frederick S Williams

If the centre of London had been completely built-up even before the dawn of the railway age, it was even more densely populated as the nineteenth century wore on. The massive upheaval and disturbance caused by the extension of the South Eastern from London Bridge to Cannon Street and Charing Cross, or of the Midland to St Pancras and of the London & South Western to Waterloo, and then later the Great Central to Marylebone, all told of a city bursting at the seams. Yet, travel within the area remained as slow, difficult and expensive as ever. The river offered one way of avoiding the crush, but despite the meandering of the Thames through London, it could serve only a small part of the growing metropolis.

The only solution was to take the railways underground.

The idea of an underground railway in London surfaced, if that is the right word, as early as 1830, with a scheme for a line from King's Cross to Snow Hill in the City. At around the same time, a proposal arose to put the

London terminus of the London & Birmingham Railway on the banks of the Thames. Neither of these projects made any progress, but the concept appealed to both Charles Pearson and John Stevens, who were the City of London's solicitor and surveyor respectively. Together, over the next quarter century they pressed for an underground railway in London.

Pearson even wrote a pamphlet advocating an underground railway running down the Fleet Valley and using atmospheric propulsion at a time when this technology seemed to offer clean and silent motive power. These plans were brought to an abrupt end when Brunel's experiment on the South Devon Railway failed, at some considerable expense to the shareholders. Before this sharp dose of reality, a Windsor, Staines, Brentford & London Atmospheric Railway was proposed, running to Knightsbridge and doubtless anticipating Royal patronage as it claimed that it would offer 'ample accommodation for transit' between Buckingham Palace and Windsor Castle.

At the time, the thought of digging a deep tunnel was daunting, so the decision was taken to construct a railway that would run under the streets, with construction using the 'cut and cover' method. This meant that a large trench was dug under the streets, and walls constructed that would not only protect the sides of the trench, but also bear the weight of a replacement roadway constructed above. Tracks were then laid in the trench, and stations built at intervals. No doubt this work entailed massive upheaval as traffic on the already congested streets was diverted onto adjoining streets. Even so, such a modest depth of railway was described by the ultra-conservative critics as 'making roads down to hell', and they confidently forecast that buildings would collapse into the workings.

One of Pearson's proposals was a 'Railway Terminus and City Improvement Plan', which was considered by a special committee set up in 1851. The plan called for a 100ft-wide road to be built from Holborn Hill, reached by the newly-built Farringdon Street from Fleet Street in 1830, to King's Cross. This road would be supported on arches, creating a tunnel wide enough for six standard gauge lines and two of the Great Western's broad gauge. No one seems to have considered how the GWR would reach King's Cross, or where it would go once at Holborn Hill.

The Metropolitan Railway

A rather more practical solution was the idea for a Bayswater, Paddington & Holborn Bridge Railway, linking Paddington with King's Cross and then with Pearson's line to Farringdon. This would follow the New Road, wide and reasonably straight, and was estimated to cost less than half Pearson's project. This was also seen as a safer bet financially, as the GWR needed to gain access to the City and demand had already been demonstrated by the success of the bus operators along the route.

This project so inspired the imagination of those involved with railways at the time that contractors Peto & Betts were attracted and John Fowler, who had replaced Brunel on another railway project in the Midlands, was appointed as engineer. One William Malins was appointed chairman, and then spent much time and no small amount of money in trying to prove that he had the idea first, and claim compensation. In preparation for the new line, renamed the North Metropolitan, local authorities were courted for their backing and after making some amendments to accommodate local opinion, a bill was presented to Parliament in 1853, which was eventually enacted.

Unfortunately, the corresponding measure for Pearson's project did not even reach the committee stage. This was a major disappointment for the North Metropolitan backers as without Pearson's line, their project was doomed. Rather than give up, they took over Pearson's project and set about improving it. The route was changed to include the General Post Office and gain the Postmaster General's support, but Pearson's plan for a city terminus of twenty acres was dropped. When the project was taken back to Parliament, despite opposition, it eventually reached the Statute Book in 1854 as the 'North Metropolitan Railway: Paddington to the Post Office, Extensions to Paddington and the Great Western Railway, the General Post Office, the London & North Western Railway, and the Great Northern Railway.'

All this occurred at the height of the Crimean War, and raising money was difficult. Nevertheless, the Corporation of the City of London agreed to subscribe for shares of the value of £200,000, while the promoters agreed to cut the cost of the line to £950,000 by not building the branch from Cowcross Street to the GPO, while the commercial prospects were improved by agreeing to build a line to link the Great Northern with the cattle market at Smithfield for cattle slaughtered at Islington's Copenhagen cattle market. The most obvious beneficiary from the new railway was to be the Great Western, and it also contributed generously by paying £175,000 for shares.

By this time, the title of the Metropolitan Railway had been adopted. Cut and cover was not always as easy as it was meant to be. West of Euston Square, it ran largely through gravel, but at Baker Street it had to have a culvert built for the Tybourne River, essentially a sewer. East of Euston

Square, much of the length was easy going in open cutting, but a 728 yard tunnel had to be built at Clerkenwell and the meandering Fleet River had to be crossed no less than three times. In contrast to the surface mainlines as they approached London, every effort was made to minimise disturbance to property by constructing as much of the line as possible along existing roads, including Praed Street, Marylebone Road, Euston Road, King's Cross Road and Farringdon Road. Nevertheless, this did not mean that this was a quick and easy form of construction, as even at that time London's utilities were well-established and running under the streets, so these, including water, sewerage and gas as well as telegraph wires, had to be diverted before the real work of building a railway could start.

When it opened on 10 January 1863, between Paddington and Farringdon Street, the Metropolitan Railway was the world's first passenger underground railway. Not surprisingly, given that it passed Paddington and was sponsored in part by the GWR, it was laid as mixed 7ft gauge with the lines laid to standard gauge but with an outer rail to provide the broad gauge necessary to enable the GWR's passengers to reach the City of London. This added to costs, as it had with the GWR's own lines, as the trench had to be 28½ft wide instead of the 25ft used on later extensions. On the other hand, there was a certain amount of cheapness in the work, for if one regards the road surface or a building straddling the line as the top of a box, with the trench sides, the box had no bottom and the sides also lacked foundations. No doubt this accounts for the problems visited upon the line by ever heavier commercial vehicles and the speed restrictions of later years on the line itself.

Despite the importance of City traffic and hence of the Metropolitan Railway to the GWR, the relationship between the two railways was unhappy and was finally severed in 1867, when the line changed to standard gauge. The opportunity was taken during this work to increase the depth of the platforms, which originally were just ten feet deep.

Once opened, the line was immediately popular, despite being less than four miles in length. The novelty of travelling 'underground' meant that on the day of opening there were queues at most of the stations and well over £850 was taken in fares on the first day alone. No less than 26,500 passengers a day used it for the first six months. Yet, this was no pleasant form of transport, for it was operated by steam locomotives and the smoke and steam lingered in the cut and cover sections, relieved only by the sections in cutting. Encouraged by this early success, a programme of expansion followed, reaching Hammersmith in 1864, Harrow-on-the-Hill between 1868 and 1880, and, using the East London Railway, New Cross in 1884, by which time the intention was one of creating a railway circle around central London with the Metropolitan District Railway that would link the major termini north of the Thames. Known as the 'City Widened Lines', the original Metropolitan was also intended to provide access to the City for the Midland Railway, Great Northern Railway and London, Chatham & Dover Railway.

The idea of a circular railway was one raised by the House of Lords when they looked again at the idea of a single terminus for London in 1866. Earlier, in 1859, invasion fears led to a proposal for a circular line around London for armoured trains containing artillery to defend the capital, but nothing came of this 'iron road M25', which might have been useful today, especially if it could have connected the three busiest London airports and the main trunk railway lines radiating from the capital.

Further expansion saw the Metropolitan Railway reach out into the countryside, reaching Aylesbury, from Harrow, in 1892, with connections to the Great Central Railway, which gained its original access to London over the Metropolitan in 1899, and the two companies ran the line north of Harrow jointly after 1906. Uxbridge was reached in 1904, Watford in 1925 and Stanmore in 1932, while it acquired the Great Northern & City tube line, in 1913, but the two lines were never linked.

Largely as a result of this expansion, more than any other railway in London, the Metropolitan was popularly associated with the expansion of the suburbs, and even had a country estates subsidiary while its catchment area became known as 'Metroland'. The Metropolitan had managed to obtain an act of Parliament to free it from the restriction that forced railway companies to return land not required for railway purposes to the original owners within seven years of construction being completed, and gained the power to buy land for residential development. In 1915, the Metropolitan produced the *Metro-land* slogan to promote some ten estates built by a subsidiary close to its stations. However, in general use, the term applied to any of the new suburbs growing up within easy reach of one of the company's stations.

The impact of this was that the company earned twice as much per third-class seat during the 1920s as the three largest main line companies, while the Metropolitan Railway Country Estates subsidiary produced an 8 per cent dividend during these otherwise lean years.

Uniquely amongst the London underground railways, it provided three classes for its passengers, and even operated two Pullman cars, but second class was abandoned in 1905 and first, with the Pullman cars, disappeared under the wartime restrictions on suburban railways in 1941. Goods and parcels traffic was also handled. Electrification of the underground section was introduced in 1905, using electric locomotives and the third and fourth rail dc system, initially with trains switching to steam at Harrow, but electrification was later extended to Rickmansworth after the Second World War.

The reason for third class surviving on the Metropolitan and on the Midland when it would have been more logical to have offered first and second classes was due to the legal need to provide third class accommodation.

South of the river, and around the Circle

There could be no mistaking the success of the Metropolitan, which was anxious to see its success repeated elsewhere in London, encouraged by the prospect that a second significant line would make it easier to fulfil a recommendation by a House of Lords Committee that there should be a circular railway serving central London. As with so many other railway projects, despite a close relationship between the Metropolitan and what was known officially as the Metropolitan District (but universally simply as the 'District'), for financial reasons the two companies were promoted separately. The irony was that, when eventually the Inner Circle, or 'Circle Line', was finally completed in 1884, the two companies had moved apart rather than merged and the operation of the jointly-owned Circle was the result of continuous disputes.

When it opened in 1868, the 'District' was still only the second underground passenger railway in the world. Despite using the same cut and cover construction techniques as the Metropolitan, the District was difficult to build, even though disturbance to roads and property was kept to a minimum as it was able to use much of the Thames Embankment, then under construction. When the section between South Kensington and Westminster Bridge opened in 1868, it was worked by the Metropolitan until it withdrew in 1871. The line was completed between West Brompton and Mansion House by 1874, after which it began to expand south of the Thames, once again often using lines built by companies that were nominally independent, to help raise capital. By 1889, it operated to Ealing Broadway, Hounslow, Richmond and Wimbledon in the south-west, including operation over London & South Western Railway metals, to Whitechapel in the east, and over the East London Railway to New Cross. Initially, the District followed the example of the Metropolitan and provided three classes of accommodation. Using the London Tilbury &

Southend Railway, it reached Barking in 1908, and in 1932, went further
east to Upminster on what had become the London Midland & Scottish
Railway.

Yet, for various reasons, the District was never able to fully repeat the
success of the original Metropolitan and, despite its expansion, the line was
seldom profitable. In an attempt to stimulate exhibition traffic, the big
exhibition hall at Earl's Court was built on its property. One reason for its
lack of success could have been that it did not perform the same vital
service in linking remote termini to the City as the Metropolitan had done.
If one travelled on the lines from Kent, one could take a train to the City
or the West End by simply choosing to alight at a different terminus. After
all, the SER served both Cannon Street and Charing Cross, while the
LCDR actually operated into the western districts of the City. Commuters
from the Brighton line could opt for London Bridge rather than Victoria,
and those from the LSWR at Waterloo had to use a horse bus or, later, the
Waterloo & City Railway. This in fact was the crux of the problem. The
House of Lords wanted a circular line that would connect all of the major
termini, but even when the Inner Circle opened, it failed to achieve this.
Had the District strayed south of the river between London Bridge and
Waterloo, turning sharply north to Charing Cross and then on to Victoria,
it might have been a great success.

The extent of the disagreements between the Metropolitan and the
Metropolitan District delayed electrification from the mid-1890s and in
the end the method of electrification had to go to arbitration, but South
Harrow was electrified in 1903 and all trains were electrically worked in the
sub-surface sections by 1905.

The first deep level tubes

The extent of London and the density of building meant that the cut and
cover method of underground railway construction had its limitations. It
was already clear that it by no means always easy to build a new railway in
this manner. It was also clear that in an old city, straight modern
thoroughfares ideal for railway construction were few and far between.
While there were other stretches of reasonably straight or even gently
curved streets, such as Oxford Street, Regent Street and Piccadilly, these
soon ran into a maze of narrower streets and were isolated examples, unlike
the series of loosely connected new streets that the Metropolitan had been
able to use, while the District was built more or less at the same time as the
Thames Embankment.

The only way forward was to dig deep. This was no easy option. It was not just a case of the problems of digging so far underground, and the dangers of unknown streams or substrata of soft earth or sand, but of getting the equipment and workers down to the construction site. There may also have been another difficulty lingering at the back of the minds of the backers – that of getting passengers to travel so far below ground, both in the psychological sense and the physical sense of getting them to and from the depths. Even today, with efficient modern escalators, the time taken to get to and from a deep level tube line means that sometimes it is quicker to walk if the journey is short and one knows one's way around London.

In fact, many of these fears were unfounded. In 1868, a tube tunnel was constructed under the River Thames by the Tower Subway Company.

Operations began the following year, although the formal opening was not until 2 August 1870, using a tunnel 1,350ft long between Tower Hill and Vine Street in Southwark. This was a single line in a single tunnel, which must have been claustrophobic with an internal diameter of just 6ft 7ins, while the track gauge was just 2ft 6ins. At each end, there were steam-driven lifts. Plans for the single 10ft long car to be propelled by manpower were abandoned, and cable haulage was used using two 4 hp stationary steam engines. There were two flat fares of 1d and 2d, but the higher fare did not entitle the traveller to a better standard of travel, instead the greater outlay simply ensured priority in the lift cages.

This bold venture was doomed to failure, however, as the construction and operating costs were very high, yet passenger capacity was too low to cover these costs. In addition, the equipment was unreliable. A few months after the official opening, the service was abandoned, the car removed and the track lifted, and the lifts replaced by a spiral wooden staircase at each end of the tunnel while a footway was built along the tunnel. In this form, the promoters of the Tower Subway Company became not railwaymen, but the proprietors of a toll subway charging pedestrians ½ d for the privilege of using it. Nevertheless, this was a useful link in London's transport provision until the Tower Bridge opened in 1894 and pedestrians then had the pleasure of walking over the river rather than under it. The tunnel was not closed, however, as it was used first for the pipes of the London Hydraulic Power Company, and later carried water mains.

This was the prototype for all tube railways and those that followed learnt much from its success and its failure. Electric traction was seen as the most efficient and reliable means of propulsion as, so deep down, there was nowhere for the steam and smoke of a 'conventional' railway to go.

This is to move ahead as it was not until the Berlin Exhibition of 1879 that Dr Werner von Siemens demonstrated the first electric railway. The promoters of underground railways in London were not backward in embracing the new technology. In 1882, the Charing Cross & Waterloo Railway received parliamentary approval, intended to run between Waterloo and Trafalgar Square using twin tubes under the Thames. A further measure intended to extend this line to Oxford Street and the GPO at St Martins-le-Grand was put before Parliament in 1884, but turned down on the grounds that members first wished to be able to judge the success of the original line. Their caution, while understandable, was the death of the original project, as the promoters saw early expansion unlikely, and without it they doubted their ability to obtain a decent return. The difficulty was that the first stage from Waterloo to Trafalgar Square was already served by trains of the SER running into Charing Cross with a stop at Waterloo.

The next venture was the City of London & Southwark Railway Company: short railways frequently rejoiced in long titles. This was clearly meant to be a deep level tube line, with Greathead, who had perfected the shield that bore his name and which was designed for cutting tunnels, as chief engineer. He had two of the great names of the railway age as consultants, Sir Benjamin Baker and Sir John Fowler. Raising capital was another problem, and when the company was incorporated in 1884, the prospectus promised dividends of 12 per cent, and this at a time when the rate of interest on deposits was around 2.5 per cent.

An indication of the uncertainty that remained with the first of the new deep level tubes was that these also tended to follow the lines of major thoroughfares, with the promoters and engineers anxious to avoid any legal arguments or demands for compensation. The consequences of this were that the City terminus at 46 King William Street, at the junction with what was then known as Arthur Street, but is now Monument Street, had to be built to lie roughly east-west, leaving the line to curve round to the south shortly after leaving the terminus as it headed for the river. Arthur Street was so narrow that the two tunnels had to be placed one above the other to keep within the breadth of the street, and again at Swan Lane. After passing under the river, the line passed under Borough High Street and Newington Causeway to the Elephant & Castle. This gave the line a total route mileage of just 1¼ miles, with intermediate stations at Denman Street and Great Dover Street, now known as Borough.

Work did not begin until October 1886, although preparations had commenced earlier, in May. While standard gauge track was laid, the tunnels on the first section were just 10ft 2in in diameter, but when an extension to Stockwell was authorised in 1887, the tunnel diameters were eased to 10ft 6ins, largely because the gradients on this stretch, of just over 1¾ miles, were much easier. Intermediate stations, Kennington and the Oval, were built between Elephant & Castle and Stockwell.

The line was built to be worked by cable, with an engine house at Elephant & Castle, and with the trains drawn at 10 mph on the section between the City and the Elephant, and 12 mph on the southern stretch between the Elephant and Stockwell. Cable haulage invariably means stopping to switch cable lengths, so having to change cables to change speed was not a serious drawback. Nevertheless, electric traction was increasingly being seen as viable, and it had already been used by Magnus Volk for his promenade electric railway in Brighton, opened in 1883. The CLS's chairman, Charles Mott, sought professional advice, and in August 1888, shareholders were advised that experiments were to be made with electric traction. The advice came from CE Spagnoletti, whose reputation rested on his expertise as a signal engineer, which seems strange today when specialisation is everything, but engineers covered a far broader field even in the late nineteenth century.

The decision was taken to use electricity. Unfortunately, it was too late and much of the infrastructure was already completed. At King William Street, for example, the terminus had a single track with a platform on either side, which suited cable working but was far from ideal for electric operation. Despite the use of electricity for the trains, the stations were gas lit. The platforms were reached by hydraulic lifts. It was not until 1895 that the station was modified to have two tracks with a single platform between them.

At the southern end, a steep 1 in 3½ gradient led from the Stockwell terminus to a rolling stock depot alongside the Clapham Road, and for this cable working was essential.

So novel was the new railway that experimental running began in December 1889 using an electric engine and two carriages. As the generating station at Stockwell was not ready, power was taken from a temporary generating station at Borough and a third rail was laid for the current to reach the engine. A second engine, this time geared to provide better acceleration, joined the trials in February 1890.

The trials clearly went very well for, on 7 March, the CLS took the Lord Mayor of London and other important guests from the City to the Elephant & Castle, intending to bring them back for a celebratory luncheon. Unfortunately, the company supplying water to the power station was unaware of these arrangements, or of the needs of a steam-driven generating station, and cut the water supply to allow work on its mains. The power station was closed down quickly to avoid damage to the boilers. But the VIP party did get back to the City an hour late, using the CLS after the water company realised what was happening.

Renamed the City & South London Railway, it was opened formally by the Prince of Wales on 4 November 1890. As was usual, due ceremony was accorded with the Royal Party being taken on a special train, pulled by an electric engine painted grey and cream for the occasion and named *Prince of Wales*, to the Oval to inspect the works and then to Stockwell for luncheon, and speeches, held in a marquee in the rolling stock depot. Meanwhile, an extension to Clapham had been approved, but staff had still to be trained, so it was not until Thursday, 18 December that the line could open for business. It was an instant success, carrying 15,000 passengers daily. Indeed, it was a victim of its own success, being overwhelmed by the traffic. The problem was that the King William Street terminus was too small and congested, while the two-car trains were inadequate for the traffic that presented itself. Despite the trains having just two cars, the locomotives were under-powered and the current supply unreliable, while the 10ft 2in diameter of the tunnels was too restrictive.

However, despite these problems, the CSLR was both safe and a modest financial success, although the dividend never reached 12 per cent. Greater financial success would have followed but for the fact that the limited passenger-carrying capacity restricted the revenue that could be earned on what was an expensive line to operate. It was soon extended north and south, reaching Moorgate in the City and Clapham Common in 1900 and then Angel in 1901, before reaching Euston in 1907.

Travel on the CSLR was far quicker than surface travel and clearly far better in bad weather. It also lacked the steam, smoke, soot and cinders of the Hammersmith & City and the Metropolitan Railways, but it was by no means a pleasant journey or a quick one. The time taken to reach the platform using the hydraulic lifts had to be added to the overall journey time, as had the return to the surface, while the trains broke no speed records. Passengers travelled in carriages which were without windows, known as the 'padded cells', facing each other from longitudinal seats on either side. There were doors at the ends of each carriage, with a platform and a sliding gate for passengers wishing to board or alight, operated by an attendant.

Despite its shortcomings, many of which can be attributed to its role as a pioneer, with longer trains and a branch or diversion to carry passengers from the termini south of the river to King's Cross and Euston, the line could have been a true financial success. New and rapidly growing suburbs such as Stockwell and Clapham were much sought-after middle class districts, although later they were to become far less attractive before eventually recovering in recent years as gentrification took place. Yet, south of the river was to be a vast area that was to be chronically underserved by the underground system. To the west, the District reached out, often running over London & South Western, later Southern Railway, metals, while the Bakerloo and much later the Victoria lines ventured a short distance. Only what was to become the Northern line went really far, reaching Morden. The explanation was always that the mainline railways had such a dense network to the south, that the underground railways did not see it as promising territory. Yet, as we will see later, the Southern Railway had to build a new branch line to serve a London County Council estate between the wars, showing that the existing surface network was by no means completely adequate for a growing market.

Another reason for the denser underground network north of the Thames was that of topography. The steep hills and densely populated northern suburbs combined to make railway construction more expensive, although parts of the Northern Line were extended over what had been Great Northern suburban lines and the Central Line was later extended over former Great Eastern metals. Building deep level tube lines meant that some of the problems of steep gradients were solved, albeit by having some variation in the depth of the platforms below ground level, and in the time it took to travel between the booking hall and the platforms.

Chapter 7

Victorian Dynamism

*We do not want to raise our citizens under forcing-frames and
grow aldermen like cucumbers. We must protest against being disturbed
in our slumbers by a whistle and a roar overhead, as if the powers
of darkness were engaged in a tournament.*

The Daily Telegraph, 1855

Looking back over more than a century during which it has often
appeared that the United Kingdom has been in decline and all too often
been overtaken by the United States and Germany, and as far as
railways are concerned, France and Japan, it is difficult to envisage just how
dynamic our Victorian forefathers were. While there were railways before
Queen Victoria acceded to the throne, and the network was not completely
finished at her death, the fact remains that more than 90 per cent of a railway
network that was at its peak twice the size of that today, was completed during
her reign. All of this was achieved without the intervention of central
government or the application of taxpayers' money. Indeed, in some places,
such as Carlisle, the city imposed its ancient right to charge a duty on
everything entering its boundaries, and then again on everything leaving.

Local authority rates were another matter, and the railways were rated
very heavily for the amount of land that they occupied, as local authorities
saw the railway as a cash cow to be milked. One of the best examples of this
was at Huyton, near Liverpool, where in 1849 the London & North
Western Railway provided 35 per cent of the rates paid to the parish
council, despite occupying less than 1 per cent of the land.

The system of rating for the railways had to evolve, and it took case law
to decide on a fair basis, with the rental value of stations and other premises
used as a basis for the rates, but for the actual length of line, the local
authorities based their charges on the companies' receipts, making it more
of a local tax or duty than rates. In the end, the railways paid more than
twenty times as much per employee as any other kind of business, and this
was only affected to a degree by the Local Government Act 1858 that
limited rating assessments for railway property to a quarter of the net

value. Even so, this did not stop local authority valuers arguing that a major through line was worth more than a secondary route because it carried a greater volume of traffic and earned the railway greater revenue, but usually this approach was unsuccessful on appeal.

While one can deplore the boom and bust fluctuations that caused so much difficulty, one can see that they would have been difficult to avoid. Everyone felt that they should share in the boom, no one saw the dangers. The country in return gained a massive railway network without public expense, so much so that during the Second World War, even though on occasions the London termini were closed by bombing, routes created in the days of competition were always available between London and the Channel coast. Today, despite the massive cuts of the post-war period, many of which pre-dated the famous, or infamous, Dr (later Lord) Beeching, and the UK having only 44 per cent of the land area of France, it still has seven per cent more railway miles, even after the closure of half the system, and 24 per cent more railway than Japan, despite that country being 54 per cent larger.

Expanding the tube network

The City & South London might not have met the dividend promises of its prospectus, but it was a success by every other measure. It was clear that the deep level tube railway was the way to ease the congestion on the streets of the capital, and provide sheltered all-weather transport at a time when the bus and the tram were still open top, and the former would remain so for some decades to come. It was also a case of this proving to be the best means of ending the isolation of those main line termini that were not fortunate enough to be in the City or the West End, or at least on the fringes. Paddington and King's Cross had already been relieved by the Metropolitan, while London Bridge had the lines to Cannon Street and Charing Cross for the onward conveyance of those arriving there on the Brighton line. The station in most need of relief at this time was, of course, Waterloo, whose shortcomings for the City-bound commuter had already, as we have seen, caused the creation of a new horse omnibus operator.

Once again, we find the Victorian attitude in evidence: a belief that everything could be resolved and that within every problem lay an opportunity.

A City connection for Waterloo came with the building of the Waterloo & City Line, running from the main line terminus to a station outside the Bank of England and the Royal Exchange, appropriately named 'Bank'.

The line opened in 1898 and, although independently-owned, it was worked by the London & South Western Railway, which finally acquired it in 1907. Initially, specially-built four-car trains were used. The line ran for 1½ miles under the Thames without intermediate stations. An electric hoist at Waterloo enabled vehicles to be removed for overhaul.

The legislation authorising the Waterloo & City allowed either cable working or electric traction, and the latter was chosen. This was in fact one of the few underground lines in London on which cable working would have been practical, because of its short length, and it was in any case a unique line having nothing in common with the rest of the LSWR or later SR system, other than the use of third rail traction. The only tube line to be shorter was the Aldwych branch of the Piccadilly Line.

At least twice in its history, once during the Second World War, the line has had to be closed due to flooding from burst or damaged water mains. This was a cruel trick of fate as the line had already become known to its regular users as the 'Drain'.

Next was the Central London Railway, which also ran to the Bank, and was authorised in 1892. When opened in 1900, it linked Shepherd's Bush with the Bank, a distance of 5¾ miles, running under London's West End to the City. Initially, trains were drawn by electric locomotives, but there were complaints from those living or working in buildings along the line about vibration and in 1903, the locomotives and trailer carriages were replaced by the more practical self-propelled trains, the first multiple unit trains in the United Kingdom. The stations were slightly higher than the running tube, so that braking was assisted by trains climbing a short slope to the platforms, and acceleration helped by the corresponding downward slope.

Until 1907, a flat fare of 2d was charged.

In 1908, the western end of the line was extended by a loop to Wood Lane, close to the exhibition centre at White City, and then extended eastwards to Liverpool Street in 1912. The line was badly affected by competition from motor buses after 1910, and in 1913, it was acquired by the Underground Group. A further westward extension followed in 1920, running over Great Western tracks to Ealing Broadway.

One line that avoided the Bank altogether, but which nevertheless provided a vital cross-London link, was the Great Northern Piccadilly & Brompton Railway. When opened in 1906, this was the longest deep level tube line in London, running 8½ miles from Finsbury Park to Hammersmith, with no less than 7¾ miles of it below ground. Its origins lay in a deep level scheme planned by the Metropolitan District, the

Brompton & Piccadilly Circus and the Great Northern & Strand Railways, which were merged in 1902. Rolling stock was bought from France and from Hungary, believed to have been the only Hungarian stock used on Britain's railways. One innovation that never saw public service was a double spiral escalator installed at Holloway Road in 1906, but the company provided London's first railway escalator, also in 1906, at Earl's Court, linking the Piccadilly platforms with those of the Metropolitan District, while those installed later at Leicester Square remain the longest on the London underground system. The GNPB became the London Electric Railway in 1910 on acquiring both the Bakerloo and Hampstead tube railways.

The other cross-London route in the first stage of tube development was the Baker Street & Waterloo Railway. Incorporated in 1893, little happened until 1897 when Whitaker Wright's London & Globe Finance Corporation took over the project. While work began in 1898 with a tunnel under the River Thames, the project stopped when LGFC collapsed in 1901, but the following year the American CT Yerkes Underground Electric Railways Group took over, and the line eventually opened in 1906, going beyond Waterloo to Elephant & Castle, over 3.6 route miles. Initially, there was a flat fare of just 2d. The Baker Street & Waterloo Railway was nicknamed the 'Bakerloo' by the journalist GHF Nichols because it linked the two, but there was some dismay when the title was adopted officially. The *Railway Magazine* sniffly declared that '…for a railway itself to adopt its gutter title is not what we expect from a railway company'.

In 1910, the company passed to the recently formed London Electric Railway, along with the Charing Cross Euston & Hampstead Railway, predecessor of the Northern Line. Steady extension then followed, with the line reaching Paddington in 1913, and in 1915 it reached Queen's Park where it connected to the London & North Western Railway, and in 1917 used the LNWR tracks to reach Watford.

The final deep level tube line to be built until the Victoria Line opened in the 1960s was the Charing Cross Euston & Hampstead Railway, more usually known as the 'Hampstead Line' or the 'Hampstead & Highgate'. This replaced an ambition once held by the South Eastern Railway and the London & North Western Railway to have a link between Charing Cross and Euston. It is highly unlikely that Parliament would have authorised the Charing Cross and Euston line as this would have called for considerable heavy engineering works at both termini and space was short at both, but especially at Charing Cross. While the CCEHR was seen as the answer, and engineering works were far less as the line was already deep underground, the lack of a second mainline link across the centre of London has been a weakness. The ability to run trains through from Kent, and even Sussex, to the Midlands and the North would have been one advantage, but it could also have enabled regional expresses to ease some of the pressure on the existing termini and on the underground system. That said, the approaches to Charing Cross and Euston are amongst the most congested today and substantial widening would have been required. The revitalised link, Thameslink, between Blackfriars and King's Cross shows what could be done, but even this suffers under the strain of meeting demand.

The CCEHR was authorised in 1893, and after many variations opened in 1907 as part of the Underground Electric Railway tube lines. At the time, it was known as 'The Last Link'. It was to run from Charing Cross to Hampstead via Euston, with a branch to the Midland Railway's suburban station at Kentish Town but before opening it was extended to Golders Green, then nothing more than a muddy country cross roads, and Highgate. In 1914, it was extended southwards to the Metropolitan Railway's Charing Cross station, on the bank of the Thames, to provide a loop that avoided the need to reverse trains.

Legislation in 1912 and 1913 permitted further extensions, and between 1923 and 1924, it was extended from Golders Green to Edgware, including a London County Council housing estate being built at Burnt Oak, and after this through trains were operated over the City & South London Railway south of Camden Town. To the south, the line was extended to Kennington to connect with the southern extension of the CSLR to Morden in 1926. The southward extension meant another tube link for Waterloo, with passengers for the West End having a choice of two lines, with the Northern Line, as it became, running to Tottenham Court Road at the eastern end of Oxford Street, and the Bakerloo to Oxford Circus, in the middle of Oxford Street. Both lines linked Waterloo with Charing Cross, but Waterloo also had a link along the Northern Line with Euston and, with just one change, King's Cross and St Pancras, and along the Bakerloo with Paddington. The latter was less important for, although the Great Western served the Midlands and South Wales, the London & South Western competed with the GWR on services to Exeter and Plymouth, while one could also travel from Waterloo to Reading, albeit somewhat more slowly than on the GWR.

The platforms at Hampstead remain the deepest on the London tube network at 192 ft below ground level, while the tunnel between East Finchley and Morden via the CLSR line at 17¼ miles was for many years the longest railway tunnel in the world.

Going overhead

By the outbreak of the First World War, London had the densest railway service in the world, both on the ground and under it. With the exception of the Metropolitan, the underground railways all provided single-class accommodation, but the 'Met' provided first-class and even had two Pullman carriages, until these were withdrawn during the Second World War, while first-class was also abolished on inner suburban and underground lines, never to return.

Despite many of the lines from the south approaching London on viaducts, there were no overhead railways as such. Liverpool had a railway that ran along the dock front, overhead so that it did not obstruct the dock entrances. There was nothing like this in London, but one reason for this was probably the fact that the London Docks were carved out of the land, while those in Liverpool were built out into the River Mersey, so that their landward end was straighter and more consistent than that of London, where there were docks on both sides of the river.

But, earlier, there had been two plans for central overhead lines.

One of the ideas put to the House of Commons Parliamentary Select Committee on Metropolitan Communications in 1855 was one from Joseph Paxton, the genius behind the Crystal Palace, and which reflected the by now unbounded confidence of the Victorians. Paxton's Crystal Palace had by this time been moved from Kensington to Sydenham, generating considerable volumes of off-peak suburban traffic for the London Brighton & South Coast Railway. For his next great achievement, Paxton favoured an inner circle railway, the Great Victorian Way, incorporating a shopping arcade no less than 72ft-wide, stretching all the way from Regent Street to the City, all of it under glass. Within this arcade, communication would be enhanced by a railway running 24ft above the pavement. The press did not like it, as the *Daily Telegraph* epigram at the beginning of this chapter shows. The newspaper went on to propose that instead of putting shopping arcades under railways, the railways themselves should be put underground. This was the same conclusion that the members of the Select Committee reached, also proposing that the main London termini should be connected with each other, with the River Thames, which still carried passengers at the time, with the docks and with the Post Office, at the time taken to mean the main establishment at St Martins-Le-Grand.

Later, in 1882, and then again in 1891, plans were laid to build an extension from Waterloo into the City, and which was dropped on grounds of cost and likely objections from the City and even the Port of London

TRAIN'S TRAMS:
George Francis Train, 1829-1904

Born in Boston, Massachusetts, in 1829, Train was orphaned when just four years old when yellow fever killed his family after they had moved to New Orleans. He returned to Boston to be raised by his strict Methodist grandparents, who hoped he would become a minister, but instead he went into business as a merchant, first in Boston and then in Australia.

Eventually, he arrived in England 1860, where he formed a horse tramway company in Birkenhead before moving to London where he soon met opposition. His trams were popular with passengers, but the rails stood above the road surface and were an obstacle to other traffic. Indeed, the following year he was arrested and tried for 'breaking and injuring' a London street. He left London for the United States, where he was involved in the formation of the Union Pacific Railroad, before returning to England in 1864.

He is sometimes considered as the inspiration for Phileas Fogg in Jules Verne's *Around the World in Eighty Days*, although Train managed to go round the world in just sixty-seven days in 1870, and followed this with two further trips. He called himself 'Citizen Train', and became a shipping magnate, a prolific writer, an unsuccessful presidential candidate, and associated with French and Australian revolutionaries, with the latter offering him the presidency of a proposed Australian republic, which he wisely declined. Indeed, he also associated with European royalty.

He seems to have learnt from the mistakes of his original tramway systems as he later promoted and built new tramways in Britain, overcoming opposition by offering to run the rails level with the street. Back in the USA, he became an eccentric, to the extent that in 1873 he was arrested and threatened with being sent to an asylum for the insane.

In 1903, he became ill with smallpox and died in New York, early in 1904.

Authority. The route such a line might have taken could also have caused problems. It would have had to go under or over the line from London Bridge to Charing Cross, and then there were the bridges for Blackfriars and Cannon Street to overcome. The extension of the London and South Western from Nine Elms to Waterloo had already caused problems, as at one stage a bridge over a road had to be built on the skew with the then unprecedented length for the time of 90 feet.

Another objection to an overhead railway was the infamous London fog, or even smog, which could be so thick that engine drivers on the lines between Charing Cross, Cannon Street and London Bridge had such difficulty in seeing signals that the service fell apart on such occasions. There was nothing romantic about 'a foggy day in London town'. Street urchins with flares used to guide carriage and omnibus drivers, but this was impractical for the railways as it was the need to see signals that was so important.

Nevertheless, by this time London's growth had meant that the way the city was run had to change. As early as 1855, the Metropolitan Board of Works took control of and standardised many public services across London, which now meant not just the City or even the City and Westminster, but many other boroughs as well. In 1889, the London County Council was formed, replacing the MBW and with its members being directly elected rather than appointed. Although it initially used the MBW premises, it was not long before the LCC had built its own County Hall, and it was not in 'old' London but across the Thames in Lambeth, by this time part of London. The offices were almost equidistant from the Houses of Parliament and Waterloo. The LCC started to acquire the tramways that operated in its area, creating the LCC Tramways that, by 1933, was to be the largest in the country with 167 route miles (269 route kilometres) and 1,700 tramcars. The railways had taken a hand in creating the conditions for the new political entity, having created the inner suburbs and then pulled them together.

Yet, even at the zenith of Victorian railway achievement, with ever faster, longer and heavier trains on the main lines, on suburban routes, the railways were facing a threat to their very existence. Nowhere was this problem more serious than in London. As the century drew to a close, the railway suburban services were suffering from growing competition from the electric street tramways that had grown up out of the original horse-drawn tramways that had posed little threat to the railways.

Chapter 8

The Threat of the Tram

Rumbling under blackened girders, Midland, bound for Cricklewood,
Puffed its sulphur to the sunset where the Land of Laundries stood,
Rumble under, thunder over, train and tram alternate go.

John Betjeman

I t was like a stab in the back, by one form of railed transport to another. The first victims had been the horse omnibus operators, who suddenly found that they were facing competition from a new mode of transport that was smoother and quicker and could take more passengers, literally for the same horse power. Nevertheless, all the horse bus operators had to do was move to routes that could not justify the construction of a tramway further out in the growing metropolis. The railways, of course, had no such flexibility.

As every schoolboy used to know, the first tram was run by a Mr Train, George Train, in fact, but Train's horse-drawn trams were not a success. They were first introduced in Birkenhead in 1860, and the following year he laid three lines in London. It was immediately clear that running along a smooth iron rail was far superior to being bumped along the road in a bus, and one horse could handle a tramcar that was heavier than a bus, and for passengers Train ensured that the interior was much roomier than the bus. It should have been an immediate success, but it wasn't.

In an age that was more suspicious of change than today, and also more xenophobic, for Train was an American, a foreigner, people were immediately suspicious. Naturally, the vested interests of bus operators and hackney carriage proprietors were also against the new invention which threatened to have mass appeal. Other road users also objected to the trams, and with good reason, for the rails were laid, in railway-fashion, in the street, so pedestrians and animals, and other wheeled vehicles, had to cross over them. The accusation that the rails were a danger to animals and to the wheels of other vehicles was not without foundation. Added to which, Train had gone for the heart of London, which he saw as Westminster, then as now a prosperous area, and at the time that meant the residents had their own carriages and did not use public transport.

All in all, it was no surprise that Train's London trams were off the streets within a year.

However, help was at hand from the very Westminster that had neglected Train's trams. The Tramways Act of 1870 provided a basis on which tramway systems could be established, and insisted that a new type of rail, one that was grooved and did not protrude above the road surface, be used. That same year, London saw trams again, and they were to remain for more than eighty years.

The Tramways Act was not a licence for tram operators to do as they pleased, but it did provide an easy statutory route for those wishing to establish a tramway. Hitherto, they had either to use light railway legislation or go to the expense and delay, and uncertainty, of a parliamentary bill. They could lay tracks in urban streets, the cost of which was almost a guarantee of monopoly on a route in contrast to the unbridled free for all that existed between horse bus operators, who would crowd out a busy route and ignore others offering thin pickings, but in return for the disruption the laying of tracks caused, they had to keep the road between the lines in good repair. Indeed, they had to look after the road surface for eighteen inches on either side of their tracks, and this was sufficient to discourage many schemes.

In some towns and cities, part of the tramway was on reserved track, away from the constraints of the public highway, but apart from a short section underground, this did not happen in London.

The legislators doubtless thought that these conditions were fair and reasonable and intended to encourage responsible behaviour by the tram companies, but there was a sting in the tail. Nationalisation of railway companies was already a political topic and as early as 1843 a London solicitor, William Galt, had written a series of four books on *Railway Reform*. In the Railway Regulation Act 1844, Gladstone included a measure giving the Government the power to acquire, from 1865 onwards, any company sanctioned following the 1844 Act. The Tramways Act 1870 also provided a means for the compulsory purchase by local authorities, but not the state, of tram companies after a period of twenty-one years, and every seven years thereafter. The intention was that a local authority unhappy with the performance of a tram operator could take it over, but in the late Victorian and Edwardian heyday of municipal pride, many councils saw owning a tram network as a form of status symbol, along with an imposing town hall. The outcome was that few tramway systems remained in private ownership. Many councillors also saw the profits from a municipal tramway system as offsetting the local rates and, once electrification became a possibility, a municipal tramway was seen as providing a base load for often over-ambitious municipally-owned local power stations and electricity supplies.

Another unforeseen but inevitable result of this was that many operators failed to invest in modernisation of their trams or their infrastructure for fear that they would in effect be making a gift of their investment to the local authority.

Many of the tram companies found the exacting demands of the legislation onerous and there were undoubtedly those who were glad to be relieved of the burden of tram ownership. Cheap fares did attract the volume of traffic, but costly tram networks needed to be kept busy all day. Unlike the railways, there was no goods traffic to augment revenues, and unlike the railways, their responsibilities did not end with the track and the vehicles. Not every tram company saw matters in this way. When the Provincial concern was forced off Portsea Island after Portsmouth Corporation exercised its right to buy, the company immediately crossed to the other side of the harbour and set up an operation running between Gosport and Fareham, happily in not one but two adjoining council areas which made municipal ownership more difficult. It was also the case that not every council realised that its ambition to own its own trams was a blessing. In Poole, in Dorset, the council eventually decided to abandon trams, and a bus company, Hants & Dorset, took over the town's local passenger transport. Hastings handed over the trams to another bus operator, Maidstone & District, but this kept the Hastings Tramways as a local trading name and eventually replaced them with trolleybuses.

Horses and iron horses

The first trams were horse-drawn and influenced by the early buses, so that when in 1870 the London Street Tramways Company ran its first service between Brixton Station and Kennington Gate, the tramcars were double deck with passengers sitting back-to-back knifeboard fashion. Another feature of bus operation was also adapted as an early print showed a lady, complete with hood, crinoline dress and umbrella, signalling frantically for a tram to wait, while the conductor looked studiously in the opposite direction. *Plus sa change!*

There seems to have been almost a burst of tramway mania, the London Street Tramways being followed by the North Metropolitan Tramways Company, with a line between Whitechapel and Bow. Even the hills of North London did not deter the tram, as the vehicles mounted Highgate Hill using a cable tramway, and these also appeared later in Brixton. By

1880, there were 500 trams trundling around the streets of London requiring the efforts of 4,000 horses. Nevertheless, the trams did not enter Central London again other than running over Waterloo Bridge and then through a subway to Kingsway. No doubt the disruption caused by installing and maintaining track was regarded as too much for the congested centre, but many years later the trolleybus was also denied access to the West End and got no further into the City than the Minories.

If the trams borrowed their configuration from the omnibus, they borrowed some of their operating practices from the railways. Soon, cheap workmen's fares were being offered. The trams needed the extra business as they had a carrying capacity that the horse bus could not match, and they needed to be the transport of the masses to justify the cost of installing expensive track. At last, this was a mode of transport for the common man, and had the advantage over the railways of running closer to most people's homes and closer to their destination as well; doorstop to destination transport! A typical tram could carry forty-two passengers, of which twenty were inside, with the lower deck passengers enjoying seats upholstered with horsehair, which was no doubt in plentiful supply, and covered in velvet. Access to the upper deck was by stairs rather than exposed steps, and the stairways were at both ends of the tram. Compared to the horse bus, which had to be built as lightly as possible, trams were solid, and despite the low fares to attract the working classes, they were not spartan. However, they were still restricted by the energies of the horse.

The trials of the horse were alleviated in some areas, and on some routes, by some dramatic infrastructure improvements. While not a tram route, Holborn had entailed horse-drawn buses descending the sides of the Fleet Valley and then up the other side, with a third horse added to the team to help on the incline, but the construction of Holborn Viaduct, completed in 1869, marked the creation of a new level east-west route between the West End and the City, part of a road network that ran from Oxford Street to St Pauls and on to the Bank of England. Before long, little of the viaduct remained to be seen as buildings hemmed it in on both sides.

True relief for the horse was soon to come from the adoption of steam power to the tramway network. The steam tram was in fact an unpowered tramcar hauled by a small steam locomotive. Tight regulations were enforced to ensure that the emission of steam and smoke was limited and that noises were suppressed, all to avoid frightening the horses that were still the prime mover in Victorian streets. Instead of looking like a scaled down railway locomotive, the tram locomotive looked like a box on wheels. There were two advantages to the steam locomotive, with the first being that it could work all day, unlike the horses, and needed less attention, while the second was that it could pull even larger trams, and with these seating as many as sixty passengers, with some having a covered upper deck, so that the advantage of the tram over the bus became even more pronounced. The steam tram gained widespread acceptance during the 1880s and 1890s.

A rival means of locomotion to the steam locomotive was the cable tramway, or cable car. These required a duct to be laid between the tracks and an endless cable installed, to which the tram was attached by a grip, hence the drivers were sometimes referred to as 'gripmen'. The cable was worked from a power station, which could use steam or electric propulsion to turn the cable, and increasingly the latter became commonplace as it enable a single power station to power several different cables. Attaching a tram to the cable enabled it to move, while releasing the grip and applying the brakes brought it to a halt. The cable tramway operating up Highgate Hill was Europe's first.

As the century drew to a close, London had around 130 route miles of tramways with more than a thousand cars, described by Carl Baedeker in 1895: 'The cars are comfortable and the fares moderate.' Indeed, the fares varied between ½d and 4d, which was a smaller range than the ½d to 6d, and occasionally 9d, of the omnibus. Either way, the visitor was warned both to indicate his intended destination to the conductor on boarding, to avoid mistakes, and never to proffer a sovereign for their fare but to keep themselves supplied with a variety of small change. By contrast, there were around 150 different bus routes crossing the centre of London, which remained a closed area for the tramways.

A variety of different operators had their vehicles rumbling and clanking along the streets. The South London Tramways served Wandsworth, and the London Tramways served Greenwich, Peckham, Streatham and Tooting, and the London Southern to Norwood; while towards the north ran the London Street Tramways to Hampstead and Highgate; and the North Metropolitan to Clapton, Dalston, Finsbury Park, Hackney, Leytonstone and Wood Green. There was also the Harrow Road and Paddington Tramways to Willesden and to the east the London, Deptford & Greenwich Tramways, or the South East Metropolitan which linked Catford with Greenwich; while the Woolwich & Southeast London ran from Woolwich to Plumstead and the Lea Bridge, Leyton & Walthamstow Tramways to Epping Forest.

This was a substantial mileage, but it was hardly a network.

The sparks effect

Railwaymen today talk about the 'sparks effect', meaning the tremendous growth in traffic that occurs when a line is electrified. In fact, today the change is from diesel to electric and the boost to traffic is less than it was when the change was from steam to electric, with a much cleaner and more pleasant travelling environment as well as much improved journey times.

While the first electric railways in the British Isles were intended for tourists, it soon became clear that the new means of propulsion had more than novelty value.

The first successful British street tramway to use electricity was in Blackpool and opened in 1885. This used a conduit in which the live rail was carried in a channel and a shoe or, in some descriptions a 'plough', picked up the current. In Croydon, electrification was also by means of a live rail concealed in a conduit. Maintenance of this, and indeed the cable conduits, was always a problem. Dirt and all manner of foreign matter, including horse dung, tended to clog the conduits. Far more practical was the overhead wire and the trolley pole, and this first appeared in Leeds in 1891. Travel by tram was transformed. Acceleration was quicker and costs were reduced.

The horse tram was finished, but the horse omnibus also found itself driven off those roads where an electric tram service operated. Replacing horse buses with electric trams proved to be viable, but where there was already a tramway laid, the change took effect quickly and for the person returning after some time away, it was nothing less than a revelation.

Arnold Bennett seems to have captured the impact of the electric tram in the reactions experienced by one of his characters returning to the Five Towns after an absence of more than twenty years:

> In twenty minutes he was leaving Turnhill Station and entering the town. The first thing he saw was an electric tram, and the second thing he saw was another electric tram. In Toby's time there were no electric trams in Turnhill, and the then recently-introduced steam trams between Bursley and Longshaw, long since superseded, were regarded as the final marvel of science as applied to traction. And now there were electric trams at Turnhill! The railway renewed his youth, but this darting electricity showed him how old he was.

This was, of course, fiction, and in the Potteries, far away from London, but there is no doubt that the author effectively captured the impact of the tram. One couldn't ignore the fact that one's tram was no longer horse-drawn, or no longer steam-hauled, as it was so obvious, even to those who profess to notice nothing about transport.

Soon, there were nevertheless plans for cross-country trams and even one in Essex from Southend to Colchester that would have included a ferry crossing. There was even a proposal for a Thames tram tunnel, but only the one under Kingsway was ever built. There seemed to be no limit to people's ambitions for the tram.

'A rather novel innovation is to be introduced on the London United electric tramways between Shepherd's Bush and Hampton Court,' reported the London *Evening News* in 1903. 'As an additional attraction for parties of trippers it is proposed to equip the line with tea and luncheon cars, so that refreshments may be served on the way without loss of time.'

This was a step too far and what we may call the 'Pullman' tram never materialised. Even so, London United did put a 'Special Saloon Car' into service, which was a single-deck tram with curtain-windows and wickerwork armchairs, while there were vases of flowers on the tables. This never ran in regular service but was available for hire by parties of up to twenty people. A charge of £1 10s was quoted for a return trip between Twickenham and Hammersmith.

It should not be thought that the trams were universally loved and popular. Many disliked the noise, what they perceived as their speed, and what could often be a fairly rough ride. The gradients for trams were far steeper and the curves far tighter than those on the railways, while the much shorter wheelbase, especially before longer cars with bogies were introduced, meant that the trams jolted and bounced. One had to climb up into a tramcar, rather than step off a platform onto a railway carriage, and in most British systems, the tram lines hogged the middle of the road, so one had to step off the pavement and through whatever traffic there might be before boarding, and alight into a busy roadway at the end of one's journey. When asked whether bogie cars would offer a better ride for passengers as well as increasing the carrying capacity of each tram, one tramway manager retorted that the conductor couldn't collect all of the fares in time and he was not prepared to lose revenue. Even in municipal ownership, revenue came before comfort.

Some tram operators, such as the North Metropolitan, even tried to run hourly express services, such as that between the Nag's Head and Moorgate, but how successful these could have been is doubtful as they would not have travelled far before coming up behind a 'stopping' service.

Especially as memories of the old horse buses faded, the tram was not everybody's' delight.

Private, municipal or nationalised?

There were other problems with the trams. In London there were company trams and then, once Parliament granted the necessary powers, municipal trams, but there was little attempt to create a network. Parliament in its wisdom had eventually enforced standard railway gauges for main line railways, but never attempted any such thing for the trams, so through running over another operator's lines, which was commonplace on the railways from the earliest times, was less common on the tramways.

Even when gauges were the same, sometimes the tracks would be out of alignment at the municipal boundary. In London, the boundary between East Ham and Ilford was a few hundred yards from an important traffic point, but Ilford's council would not allow through running for many years, even though it would have benefitted both operators. At the Rising Sun public house, the networks of Leyton and Walthamstow met, but were left for many years eight inches out of alignment. Even when the London County Council was created and acquired the local tramways, there remained the opportunity for friction at the boundary, as the journal, *Modern Transport*, reported:

> Loud and heated argument developed over the Abbey Wood to Plumstead section, which the LCC [London County Council] was slow to build; several times Erith offered to build it on behalf of London. Erith wanted to build it in 1902, obtained powers to do so in 1903, had them confiscated in 1904, was told in 1905 that the LCC could not build it for the time being, decided in 1906 to work it itself with motor buses, was told in 1907 that the LCC was anxious to build it, but not to operate it, and it would have to be leased by Erith on terms that were, to Erith, financially impossible, and finally for the 1908 session, Erith promoted (but withdrew) another Bill asking for its 1903 powers to be restored and also for running powers into Woolwich. Eventually the LCC constructed the line and opened it on July 26th 1908, but terminated it 80 yards short of the county boundary, and the council refused to join up with Erith rails and permit through running. It is doubtful if the LCC would ever have applied for powers for this route if Erith had not obtained them first. Abbey Wood was not then very built-up, and it was natural that Erith should show a far greater desire to get to Woolwich than that the LCC should desire to go to or towards Erith. Erith always hoped for a through service to Woolwich or even to London, and in constructing its track it allowed sufficient clearance on all corners to take the large LCC bogie cars.

All the Woolwich, Erith, Bexley and Dartford tramways were compulsorily acquired by London Transport on 1 July 1933, and a few months later the junction was at last inserted at Abbey Wood. The through tram service did not materialise.

Perhaps we shouldn't be surprised at the outcome of this sorry tale. If municipal undertakings lacked the entrepreneurialism to see a commercial objective, doubtless what railwaymen today would call a 'traffic generator', a nationalised body was even less enthused with the need to meet the demands of the market.

And yet, the tram was far faster than any street transport so far. The impact on the railways can be judged by the statistics for the London Brighton & South Coast Railway's South London Line, running from Victoria to London Bridge. This was the archetypal inner suburban railway, providing the fastest means of travel between the two termini and through congested South London, that is, before the advent of the electric tram. In 1902, the line carried more than eight million passengers, but competition from the electric trams more than halved this to less than four million in 1909.

It was this that forced the railways to consider electrification, initially on the South London line, with trains using overhead electrification and the service inaugurated on 1 December 1909. It was an instant success, so that in 1910, more than 7.5 million passengers were carried, and the figures were still rising, so that a return of 10 per cent was earned on the capital invested. Such a result encouraged the railways south of the river to start a rolling programme of electrification, although the South East & Chatham plans were delayed by the First World War and not implemented until after Grouping, when they were changed considerably by the Southern Railway. The widespread electrification of first the inner suburban lines and then the outer suburban may well have been another reason why London south of the Thames has been so badly served by the underground network, with only the Northern and District Lines penetrating to any extent.

Enter the motor omnibus

Early attempts to harness steam power to road vehicles had been less than successful. The early attempts had centred around the stage coach, but the result was too little and too late on the one hand, but on the other the resultant vehicle was so heavy and unwieldy that it damaged the turnpikes and posed a threat to bridges as well as frightening the horses. For many years the sole application for steam power was with traction engines slowly pulling heavy loads. Tight legislative controls from 1865 onwards also underlined the objection felt by many to steam on the road, except for steam-hauled trams after 1879. The infamous Red Flag Act of 1865 imposed a 4 mph speed limit on mechanical road transport and required a man carrying a red flag to precede any mechanical road vehicle other than a tram, and if this imposition by Parliament was not enough, it also bestowed upon local authorities the right to specify the hours during which mechanical road vehicles might use their streets. Later, this was limited to the power to ban mechanical road vehicles for eight consecutive hours out of every twenty-four.

Even so, the development of lightweight steam engines suitable for road vehicles was a quest that many would not give up. As early as 1873, a bill was promoted in Parliament to ease the restrictions, but this met determined opposition and the measure was lost. It was only when it became apparent that in several European countries success was being experienced with the internal combustion engine that Parliament relented, and the Locomotives on Highways Act 1896 removed many of the restrictions on vehicles of no more than three tons unladen, or with a trailer, four tons unladen. The speed limit was increased to a breathless 14 mph, although local authorities were given the power to reduce this until the Local Government Board intervened and reduced the speed limit to 12 mph.

All of this was very fine indeed, but for one point, which is that as far as public transport was concerned, there was nothing available to take to the roads. A few enthusiasts had their own personal motorcars, and that was all. One and two cylinder vehicles put-putted along with frequent breakdowns and undertook short journeys, often requiring attention along the way, but it was impossible to scale up the crude mechanical devices to the size of a bus. To be fair to the early pioneers, they also had to contend with poor road services and primitive suspension systems, so that the chances of mechanical reliability were much reduced.

Just as the first railway carriages were based on the design of the stagecoach, the first attempts at bus design were based on what was essentially a horse-drawn bus body, modified to take the internal combustion engine, a lightweight steam engine, usually with the driving cylinders on the back axle, or a battery electric motor. The alternative was to develop the larger private cars to produce an open wagonette, although later some of the latter were offered as convertibles or even had enclosed bodywork, but the number of passengers seated longitudinally behind the driver in these was usually no more than about eight.

The wrangling between not just the transport industry and government, but even between what Parliament would allow and the Local Government Board would permit, continued. But, in 1903, the Motor Car

Act raised the speed limit to 20 mph, although local authorities could reduce this to 10 mph in 'dangerous areas'. The Act introduced the registration of vehicles from the beginning of 1904 and provided for drivers to be licensed, but not tested. At the end of 1904, the maximum vehicle weight was raised to 5 tons, or 6½ tons with a trailer, with a maximum speed of 12 mph on condition that all wheels had rubber tyres, which at this time meant solid rubber.

This legislation was just in time to allow development of the motor omnibus. The first attempt at an urban motor bus appeared in September 1904, an open-top double-deck bus with sixteen seats inside on the lower deck, and eighteen upstairs, or 'outside'.

Nevertheless, as early as 1889, a battery electric bus was built by Radcliffe Ward, who founded the Ward Electrical Car Company, and was granted a licence from the Metropolitan Police before making the first of many trial runs.

'During the past weeks a vehicle without horses and without steam power has been at different times observed in the streets of London, travelling at the rate of 7 miles an hour, and threading its way through the maze of Metropolitan traffic,' reported the *Financial Times*. 'In character and form it resembles a large and rather cumbrous omnibus. The driver...occupies a platform which is equipped with steering gear...The new style of conveyance is the Electric Omnibus.'

Despite this report, plans for a service starting that July did not materialise. Others reports tell of trial runs of as much as seven or eight miles, which might seem little to us today, but horses pulling buses only worked a twelve mile day. Ward was sufficiently encouraged to form the London Electric Omnibus Company in May 1896, and after enjoying much publicity, in November felt able to announce the launch of an electric bus service. The Metropolitan Police licensed the vehicle, a ten-seat, single-deck bus, but its use was confined to demonstration runs.

The steam bus was the other promising arrival on the scene. In January 1899, the Motor Omnibus Syndicate Ltd was awarded a licence by the Metropolitan Police for a double-deck Gillett steam bus, which was a converted horse bus body, but only seating ten inside and fourteen outside, on a steam lorry chassis. A light canvas awning covered the upper deck, doubtless so that smuts from the chimney, which protruded through the awning, did not fall on passengers. This too failed to see regular service.

The internal combustion engine was not far behind. And indeed, it was ahead as it finally provided a regular service for Londoners. On 9 October 1899, two buses incorporating twenty-six-seat horse bus bodies and using four-cylinder twelve-hp German Daimler petrol engines, with steel tyres, opened a route from Victoria Station to Kennington across Westminster Bridge. Painted white, they belonged to the Motor Traction Company, which had been formed the previous year as the London Steam Omnibus Company, but never operated steam buses! The name was changed in September 1899. In spring 1900, the route was changed to run between Kennington and Oxford Circus, but by December, the buses were withdrawn.

It was left to Thomas Tilling's sons who put three Milnes-Daimler twenty-four horsepower motor buses into service in 1904. These were open top double-deckers, with sixteen inside seats and eighteen 'outside', on the upper deck.

Chapter 9

La Belle Epoche

Gaily into Ruislip Gardens
Runs the red electric train,
With a thousand Ta's and Pardon's
Daintily alights Elaine.
From *Middlesex*, John Betjeman

The Victorian era ended with the death of the great queen. The Edwardian era that followed was short, brought to an abrupt end by the First World War, but it was a period when the railway system in the United Kingdom was almost completed, and a period of peace and prosperity during which many people were able to enjoy the fruits of the progress made by the Victorians. Not for nothing have many historians described this period as 'La Belle Epoche'.

Queen Victoria had not enjoyed railway travel. She had made her first railway journey on 13 June 1842, travelling from Slough, then the nearest station to Windsor, behind the locomotive *Phlegethon*. Gooch drove the locomotive at an average speed of 44 mph, which alarmed Her Majesty, so that Prince Albert was moved to request that future journeys be conducted at lower speeds. The rule that her progress by rail was stately survived the Prince Consort's early death, but not her own. Impatiently, her son called for her funeral trains, the first from Stokes Bay, near Gosport, to Waterloo, for the lying in state and the state funeral, and afterwards, the second from Paddington to the Royal tombs at Frogmore, to be run at normal express speeds!

This also explodes another myth about railways and Queen Victoria, that her route to her beloved retreat on the Isle of Wight at Osborne House was the one used by most travellers to and from the island, the Portsmouth Direct, which is the line from Waterloo to Portsmouth via Woking and Guildford, and the crossing from Portsmouth to Ryde. It wasn't. The line suffers from many gradients and, at first, once opened through to Portsmouth in 1859, didn't run through to the harbour because for some years the Admiralty wouldn't allow it. Queen Victoria used to travel down the London & South Western main line to Eastleigh and then to Fareham, continuing on the short branch to Gosport, which her train would leave at the small station of Brockhurst (*not* to be confused with Brockenhurst, in the New Forest) and take the even shorter branch to Stokes Bay, where a short pier was built so that the Royal family could board a small steamer for the crossing to Osborne House, whose beautiful grounds stretched down to the Solent.

Edwardian confidence was if anything much greater than that of the Victorians: after all most of them were the same people! In London, this was the period of the first railway electrification and the first motorbuses. A Great Western steam locomotive, the *City of Truro*, set an unofficial steam record in 1904, of 100 mph, faster than any aeroplane for some years still to come. While the record was unofficial and over the following decades often doubted, more recent investigation has verified the claim. The Wright brothers, who had made their first tentative aeroplane flights in December 1903, made their first public demonstrations in 1908, initially in the United States, and then in France. The following year, the Frenchman, Louis Bleriot, flew a monoplane to make the first aeroplane crossing of the English Channel, and on the Medway, the Short brothers became the first licensees for the Wright series of aeroplanes.

Aviation might seem to have little to do with urban transport, but, as we will see later, when they developed, airports were to become significant traffic generators for the railways in particular.

Many portray the early years of the twentieth century as a time of peace and optimism. But apart from growing fears over the power and ambitions of Germany, and unrest in the Balkans, there were other signs that all was not well. In 1909, two Latvian anarchists stole £80 from a clerk in Tottenham. This was a time when the public as a whole rose up against a criminal, and several of them chased the two men across Tottenham Marsh. A policeman and a ten year-old boy were both shot dead and another fourteen people were wounded, before the anarchists tried to make good their escape by hi-jacking a tram. This was the most unlikely and unsuitable vehicle in which to make an escape, and no doubt to avoid being caught, the two men shot themselves. This was rare burst of excitement in what had become a well-ordered city.

In 1900, most trams were horse-drawn, but by 1914, the horse-drawn tram had gone from London. The expansion of the network continued, but started to slow after 1910 as the most obvious routes had been built. Even so, the total tramway route mileage grew from 1,040 in 1900 to 2,530 by 1914. Yet, at the peak of its success, the tram, which so threatened the suburban railways, was also challenged by the internal combustion engine which transformed the omnibus. After 1910, buses were increasingly powered by the internal combustion engine, which at the time was fuelled by petrol. The railways also saw electrification as the way forward for their suburban services, forced to consider change because of the threat to their traffic posed by the electric tram. Nevertheless, the first railway electrification was not in London, as we have already seen. The Inner Circle was London's first, in 1905. Growing competition from buses and trams had forced the District Railway to cut its fares from 1d a mile in 1901, and a further cut followed, increasing traffic but not the overall revenue.

The Great Western Railway took what might be considered as an outer-suburban branch for the first experiment the internal combustion engine on Britain's railways. In 1911, the company took delivery of a British Thompson Houston petrol-engined railcar, albeit a very small one, just 33¼ ft long, about half the length of a main line carriage, although longer than the then permitted maximum length for a bus. With a maximum speed of just 32 mph, the new railcar was hardly likely to compete with the best steam locomotives, but it was seen as being used purely on a feeder service and on local services with short distances between stations, acceleration mattered more than maximum speed. The new railcar was probably none too comfortable, with just two axles rather than bogies and a short wheelbase that would have left it pitching as it passed over track joints and points, while to accommodate a worthwhile forty-four seats, these were arranged in a three and two aside layout. Nevertheless, in February 1912, it entered service between Slough and Windsor, a branch of just 2.7 miles in length, taking eight minutes for the journey.

The small railcar, like many others that were to follow a half-century later when British Railways rediscovered the concept, albeit with diesel engines, soon proved to be too small for peak period traffic, when it often had to be replaced by a push–pull steam train. The media adopted an enthusiastic and encouraging tone when covering the new vehicle, but the GWR seems to have been disappointed, possibly because the new arrival was undersized. Either way, the new service did not last long, so steam once again reigned supreme between Windsor and Slough. It was to be another twenty years before the GWR once again experimented with the internal combustion engine.

The age of the electric tram and the start of the age of the internal combustion engine was still the age of the horse, especially for the collection and delivery of goods of all kinds, even if it had been displaced from public transport. There are no straight lines or abrupt endings in propulsion, and the edges are always blurred, but one thing was clear, and that was to hang on to their suburban traffic against competition from the tram, the railways would have to electrify.

The dawn of the commuter age

The sheer size of London meant that commuting pre-dated the railways, but the railway age gave a new dimension to commuting, and it was no longer a case of travelling from, say, Richmond or Kingston, to town, but of travelling from places much further afield. During the era of the stagecoach, regular travellers would catch the 'short stages' from dormitory towns such as Esher into London.

The term 'commuting' was not used at the time and indeed did not enter popular usage until well after the Second World War, being of American origin. In the USA, the term 'commute' was used to recognise the change between being a resident and a worker, or the payment for journeys in advance, 'commuting' the fares into a single advance payment. Before the term became widely accepted in the UK, the term was 'season-ticket holder', although in the north the term 'contract' was more widely used. A season ticket came to provide unlimited travel between two points, often including the use of intermediate stations, for a period of a week, a month, a quarter or a year, and regular travellers came to expect substantial discounts, even in excess of 60 per cent of the standard single or return fares on longer distances, despite putting railways, and other public transport operators, to considerable extra expense in providing extra rolling stock and personnel just for the daily peak periods.

This tradition of heavy discounts for peak period travel arose as the railways needed to fill seats on their trains at a period when early morning traffic was still light and the heavy commuter flows of more recent years had still to appear. The custom has become so ingrained that it is now impossible to change it.

The first recorded example of season tickets on Britain's railways was in 1834 on the Canterbury & Whitstable Railway, but these were not intended for workers, but for pleasure-seekers. As early as 1836, the London & Greenwich offered 'Free Tickets' for a quarter's travel, at £5 first-class, £4 second-class and £3 third-class. The London & Brighton introduced first-class season tickets between the two towns for the not inconsiderable sum of £100 in 1843, but by 1914, its successor, the London Brighton & South Coast, was offering this facility for just £43. The all-Pullman express, the 'Southern Belle', did the journey is just an hour.

It was not until 1851 that the Great Western introduced season tickets, and then only as far from London as Windsor and Maidenhead. Others, such as the London & North Western provided heavily discounted tickets at outer suburban stations to encourage new housing development. On the other hand, the pressures on housing in central London meant that the Metropolitan in particular found that there was a movement away from the centre to the cheaper housing of the outer suburbs, for which the term 'Metroland' was coined. The trend towards longer journeys to work really became significant with the dawn of the twentieth century, helped by a combination of electric trams and the electric trains that were the railways' response, but the lack of electrification in itself was no deterrent to the Diaspora of urban dwellers, and both Liverpool Street and Fenchuch Street soon became busy commuter stations. Initially, only first and second-class season tickets were offered, but soon all classes were available.

The First World War saw a dramatic increase in the sale of season tickets as, to cut unnecessary travel, ordinary fares were increased, but not season ticket rates. Between the wars, the Southern Railway in particular sought to encourage season ticket holders to its newly electrified lines, as we will see later. Working hours were longer at the time and Saturday morning working was normal, so the morning and especially the evening peaks were longer than became the case post-war.

A day 'up in town'

Living in Maidenhead, already home for many who worked in London, was Ruth Belville, whom we have met earlier taking the correct Greenwich Mean Time from the Royal Observatory to her clients across London. She had started her business, which she inherited from her father, living close to the Royal Observatory, but by the Edwardian era, she had moved to the other side of town.

'On average I make about thirty calls each Monday after visiting Greenwich, and it is a hard day's work,' she told a reporter from the *Maidenhead Advertiser*, which reported that she was 'carried all over London in tram, bus and electric train. In fact, she would be hard put to do the same journey today, make all of the calls and return home, especially since she also took the opportunity to do her shopping as she made her way back to Paddington.

Like many commuters her weekly visit to London started with a twenty minute walk from her house to the railway station at Maidenhead in time to buy a ticket and catch the 8.59 am to Paddington, which would have arrived at 9.37 am. Here her travel options had broadened considerably

THE MAN BEHIND THE COMBINE:
Charles Tyson Yerkes, 1837-1905

Born in Philadelphia in 1837, Charles Yerkes was initially involved in tramcar operation in Chicago before crossing the Atlantic and becoming involved in the development of the London underground system. He sought parliamentary authorisation for the Charing Cross & Hampstead tube line in 1900, and the following year he established the Metropolitan District Electric Traction Company, putting these ventures into a new company, the Underground Electric Railways Company of London in 1902. He moved quickly to electrify the District and build and equipped three tube lines, the Hampstead, Bakerloo and Piccadilly. His methods of financing his enterprises were new to British financiers and treated with suspicion, with most of his funds being raised in the United States. Nevertheless, he succeeded in raising £16 million (about £1,100 million today). Possibly his somewhat racy personal life and lavish personal expenditure was not to the taste of Edwardian London, and certainly his private art collection had to be auctioned after his death to pay his debts, but there seems to be no record of any fraudulent dealings.

Yerkes transformed transport in London, providing relief from the congested streets and connecting the main railway termini while standardising operating systems on the lines under his control, aided by a strong team of American railwaymen brought to London to ensure operating efficiency and overcome resistance to new ideas. His lines continued to develop after his death and his company expanded into trams, buses (known as the 'Overground'), and trolleybuses, eventually in 1912 acquiring the London General Omnibus Company, attracting much jealousy and with his transport interests becoming known as the 'Combine' to his competitors. However, any monopoly positions were strictly local. The entire transport empire passed into the control of the London Passenger Transport Board in 1933.

It is clear that the expansion of his business made the formation of the LPTB, the first transport nationalisation, much easier. The question is whether the continued existence of his empire and its natural expansion would have created a more efficient and commercially acute organisation than London Transport.

over the years. She was heading for Greenwich, so one option was to take the Circle Line to Charing Cross, but that was not the most direct route, although after electrification was completed in November 1905, it was no longer dirty, smelly and dusty with steam locomotives working hard as they accelerated between the frequent stops a into the cut and cover tunnels and then, all too briefly, into a stretch in cutting. The more direct route was the Baker Street & Waterloo Railway which had been extended to Edgware Road in 1907, and in 1913 this was connected to Paddington Station. The 'Bakerloo' would have carried her across the centre of London to Charing Cross to catch a train to Greenwich.

Another walk awaited her at Greenwich, but this time it was a steep twenty minute climb from the station to the observatory. There she would be grateful for the chair and the cup of tea offered her by the porter while her chronometer was checked for accuracy.

Her weekly round visiting clients then began. She would have most probably walked down the hill through Greenwich Park to Greenwich Pier, taking about fifteen minutes, before catching the steam ferry to the Isle of Dogs and then walking again to North Greenwich railway station, which was above today's Island Gardens Station on the Docklands Light Railway. An alternative would have been to use the tunnel for pedestrians and cyclists built in 1902, and although this would have taken longer, it may have been an attractive option in fog when the ferry services were unreliable and, in the days before radar, dangerous. She would then have taken the Millwall Extension Railway, part of the London & Blackwall Railway, to visit clients in the Millwall, West India and East India Docks, after which she would resume her journey alighting at Shadwell for the London Docks.

Ruth never discussed her clients and named but one or two, so it is possible that she may have left the observatory and caught a tram from Greenwich to New Cross to catch a train on the East London Railway to Shadwell for the London Docks. Here the alternative routes met and after conducting her business in the London Docks she could have caught the London Tilbury & Southend Railway train to Fenchurch Street.

We do know that Ruth next visited the Minories, the City and Clerkenwell, possibly walking briskly although she was by this time in her fifties and no doubt pressed for time, took the underground from Aldgate to Farrington, convenient for Clerkenwell, important for her because of the number of watchmakers and jewellers. She would then return by train to Moorgate and continue on foot to visit her clients in the City. Fortunately, her clients seem to have been clustered together in well-defined districts.

Leaving the City for the Borough, she could have caught the City & South London tube, but let's say that instead she caught the dark green No 90 bus that ran every five minutes, possibly one of the new motor omnibuses that were rapidly displacing the horse-drawn omnibuses that had served London so well for more than half-a-century. She would have called on her client, and then caught one running in the opposite direction for Fleet Street. From here, she called on more clients, before heading for the Strand, catching another bus, this time a white 'Waltham Green' No 5 bus that operated every six minutes through the centre via Liverpool Street and the Strand, and costing just tuppence. Like many of the bus services of the day, it did not start until 8 am, although it did run until midnight.

Her next cluster of customers were located in Kensington and Chelsea, so the District Railway was the most likely mode of travel, boarding at Temple Station and travelling first to Kensington and then perhaps she would walk to Chelsea. Afterwards, she would return to Dover Street, now known as Green Park, on the new Piccadilly & Brompton Railway, today's Piccadilly Line, to visit her clients in Bond Street and Regent Street. Perhaps she would have started her shopping at this point as, hardy though she undoubtedly was, she wouldn't have wanted to carry it with her all day. She would have caught the Bakerloo back from Piccadilly to Baker Street, where we know that she had a customer, before continuing to Paddington, possibly on foot. She then had to catch her train back to Maidenhead, almost certainly at the height of what would today be the rush hour, but the morning and evening 'peaks' were much less pronounced at this time as working hours were longer for the mass of clerks, typists, secretaries and shopworkers.

The Underground Group

Nevertheless, this is to race ahead a little, as another development was to take place that was as significant in its way as the formation of the London General Omnibus Company in 1855.

Victorian London seems to have attracted not just the best and most ambitious of British talent, but that from abroad as well, and especially from the United States, but the financier Charles Tyson Yerkes was to prove far more successful and his legacy far more enduring than that of the unfortunate Train with his trams.

Even before Yerkes arrived in London, the deep level tubes, of necessity using electric traction, was not only being approved by Parliament, but were being built and three had already opened, the short-lived City of London & Southwark, the Waterloo & City, of which more later, and the predecessor of today's Central Line, the Central London Railway.

The arrival of the Bakerloo line immediately transformed the position of London's Waterloo, for too long the most isolated terminus even though it served territory that was already favoured by affluent commuters and this had not only seen the launch of a horse bus service linking the terminus with the City, but also led to building of what was almost the shortest of all London tube lines and the only one to be operated by a main line railway company, the Waterloo & City Line. This opened in 1898 to give direct access to the City of London, and although nominally independent at first, from the outset it was worked by the London & South Western Railway which took it over in 1907. Using specially-built four-car trains, the line ran for 1½ miles under the Thames, without intermediate stations from Waterloo to the Bank, where in later years passengers could interchange with the Central London Railway. An electric hoist at Waterloo enabled vehicles to be removed for overhaul. The line passed into the control of the Southern Railway in 1923. It was to be the only tube railway not to pass into the control of the London Passenger Transport Board in 1933.

The Bakerloo line ran across the centre of the West End, serving such important points as Piccadilly Circus and Oxford Circus. It was acquired by the Underground Electric Railways, which had originally been formed by Yerkes to acquire the Metropolitan District Railway in 1902, and had already converted the MDR to electric traction, providing power from its Lots Road, Chelsea, power station and before acquiring the Bakerloo as well as the Hampstead and Piccadilly railways, both of which were still under construction.

Although regarded by suspicion as profiteers at first, not least because statutory undertakings (i.e. railways, authorised by Parliament) were being controlled by a non-statutory company, the company bought in a strong American management team that ensured efficiency and standardisation on its lines, with its third and fourth rail dc current supply becoming the standard for London that continues to this day. It also introduced multiple unit trains, lifts and escalators, and automatic signalling. The term 'Underground' became synonymous with the London network, especially after the other companies outside the UER group agreed to adopt the term for station signs and network maps. It also introduced a logo, a roundel with a horizontal bar, which has persisted to this day as the symbol for London Transport. No doubt this was due to its adaptability, as it could be used for an individual underground line or a station, and then later was used for buses and bus stops.

The UER on its own did much to transform travel and make the congested centre of London more accessible. While the Bakerloo ran across the centre from the south-east to the north-west, two of the other lines provided complementary links and connections. These were the Piccadilly, running from the north-east to the south-west and the Hampstead, which ran north-south and which also helped to ease the isolation of Waterloo.

When the Piccadilly Line opened as the Great Northern Piccadilly & Brompton Railway in 1906, it had what was then the longest deep level tube line in London, running 8½ miles from Finsbury Park to Hammersmith, with no less than 7¾ miles below ground. Its origins lay in a deep level scheme planned by the Metropolitan District, the Brompton & Piccadilly Circus and the Great Northern & Strand Railways, which were merged in 1902.

The line was extended during 1932–33, running over tracks abandoned by the District to Hounslow and South Harrow, and over the Metropolitan Line to Upminster using a new stretch of tube, while surface sections took it to Southgate and Cockfosters, giving an Uxbridge to Cockfosters run of thirty-two miles. A short branch was provided from Holborn to Aldwych, which was closed in 1994, although earlier it had its services suspended during the Second World War.

The third of this trio of essential deep level tube railways across the centre of London was what is known today as the Northern Line. For many years it was known more usually as the 'Hampstead Line' or the 'Hampstead & Highgate'. Originally authorised in 1893 as the Charing Cross Euston & Hampstead Railway, and there were very many variations to the original plans before it opened in 1907 as part of the Underground Electric Railway tube lines. At the time, it was known as 'The Last Link', running from Charing Cross to Hampstead via Euston, and brought to an end plans for a railway linking the South Eastern at Charing Cross with the London & North Western at Euston. While the CCEHR undoubtedly filled the need at the time, one can only speculate over the advantages of having a mainline link across the centre of London, which could have filled a similar role to the regional expresses running through Paris and in this case could have reduced the need to change trains as well as providing additional capacity on an overcrowded underground system. The problem, of course, was that at the time the CCEHR served more people and provided better links, and it was a case of one railway project or another, definitely not both. The CCEHR was completed with a branch to the Midland Railway's suburban station at Kentish Town, but before opening it was extended to Golders Green, in 1906 nothing more than a muddy country cross roads, and Highgate. In 1914, it was extended southwards to the District Railway's Charing Cross station on the bank of the Thames to provide a loop that avoided the need to reverse trains.

The platforms at Hampstead remain the deepest on the London tube network, at 192ft below ground level, while the tunnel between East

Finchley and Morden via the CSLR line at 17¼ miles was for many years the longest railway tunnel in the world.

In 1910, the Underground Electric Railways passed to the recently formed London Electric Railway. Steady extension then followed, with the Bakerloo Line reaching Paddington in 1913, and in 1915 it reached Queen's Park where it connected to the London & North Western Railway, and in 1917 used the LNWR tracks to reach Watford. A plan to extend the line south to Camberwell was authorised in 1931, reconsidered in 1949, but then abandoned.

Whatever his detractors thought of him, Yerkes transformed transport in London, providing relief from the congested streets and connecting the main railway termini while standardising operating systems on the lines under his control. His lines continued to develop after his death in 1905, with his company acquiring the London General Omnibus Company in 1912, attracting much jealousy and becoming known as the 'Combine' to his competitors. This was one advantage of working through a major holding company, for at the time the railways were allowed to operate feeder bus services connecting with their trains, but it was to be another seventeen years before they could invest directly in bus companies. Nevertheless, any monopoly positions were strictly local, and even the mighty 'Combine' faced considerable competition in many areas, especially south of the River Thames. Many of the tramway systems were under the control of local councils. It is interesting to wonder what might have become of the London tram network had it enjoyed a strong coordinating and guiding hand, such as that provided by Yerkes and his successors, rather than having been left as a series of isolated and often unconnected municipal fiefdoms. Given a free rein, the 'Combine' might even have produced many of the benefits of coordination that resulted from the creation of the London Passenger Transport Board, but with fewer restrictions and less bureaucracy.

'The twopenny lodging-house' and others

While the trams were the highlight of the Edwardian era in urban transport, another significant development was taking place on the roads, the motor omnibus. In fact, such was the poor reliability of the first motor buses as they appeared in the early years of the century, that manufacturers of steam buses and battery electric buses were also able to find a market for their wares. The steam bus had in fact advanced considerably since the early days of the steam engine and was no longer the heavy and unwieldy beast that stage coach operators had tried, and almost immediately abandoned. Coal was abandoned in favour of oil so there was no need for a fireman. One major operator, the National Steam Car Company, was even formed around the new generation of steam omnibuses, and its constituent companies eventually became the Eastern, Western and Southern National bus companies on being purchased by the railway companies after 1929.

The first steam, battery electric and motor buses were adaptations of the horse bus, albeit usually with solid rubber tyres on their wheels. The driver sat much lower down behind the engine, although on some vehicles, including those produced by Renault and on the steam buses, he still had a high driving position.

A few enthusiastic individuals operated wagonettes in London from May 1899, but the first attempt to establish a regular service in the capital was not until 1 April 1901 by the South Western Motor Car Company, which ran between Streatham and Clapham Junction via Balham. The entrepreneur behind this venture was Walter Flexman French, who was, following the First World War, to be involved with such famous bus companies as East Kent, Maidstone & District and Southdown. SWMCC used two Daimler wagonettes with a fixed awning and room for eight persons on longitudinal seats inside, while another two sat beside the driver. Nevertheless, even without the horses and no conductor, costs were high and passenger volumes low, so the service lasted just a few months. Perhaps the starting date was inauspicious.

On 18 September 1901, another wagonette service was started in London running between Piccadilly Circus and Putney. The promoter was one Francis Joseph Bell, whose publicity proclaimed that he had for 'two years carried on a successful service of ten motor omnibuses at Bournemouth'. Bell used seven vehicles on MMC chassis with solid rubber tyres and 10 hp Panhard-Daimler engines. Just eight passengers could be carried, of whom two sat beside the driver. Although normally open, the red wagonettes could be fitted with a roof and sides for wet weather.

The wagonette period was short-lived, but, as we will see later, slightly larger single deck vehicles also enjoyed a period of operation, perhaps similar to that of the single horse single-deck buses noted earlier.

Although the law demanded rubber tyres, many of the early mechanically-powered buses had steel tyres, and it was not until 1903 that a large bus appeared using rubber tyres, still solid, of course. Meanwhile, Thorneycroft, a builder of haulage vehicles, built a coke-fired steam bus for the London Road Car Company with the unusual feature that the horse-bus style body had the upper deck extended over the driver, who effectively sat just above the lower deck rather than on or just below the upper deck. This meant that while twelve passengers sat inside, no less than twenty-four could sit outside. As with the earlier steam bus mentioned in the previous chapter, this also had the chimney sticking up through the front end of a canvas awning, again doubtless to shield passengers from smuts, although it was also equipped with side curtains for inclement weather. A hint of railway practice was that the bus included sandboxes for starting on slippery road surfaces, possibly also another drawback of steel tyres. This was the first experiment with mechanical propulsion by an established horse-bus operator and it entered service between Hammersmith and Oxford Circus running via Shepherds Bush on 17 March 1902, charging a fare of 2d. The street urchins called it 'the twopenny lodging-house', clearly a reference to the chimney. The service lasted until May, when it was withdrawn, again because it was uneconomic.

The first large bus to be fitted with rubber tyres appeared on 3 October 1902 working Charles Claude Dennis's route from Lewisham to Eltham Green via Lee Green. This bus was built by Canstatt-Daimler to a design by Henry Lawson, who had been a prominent member of the motoring lobby and had organised the first 1896 'emancipation' run from London to Brighton. Completely open-topped with a high driving position, it had twelve seats on the lower deck and fifteen outside on the upper deck. This vehicle only remained in service until early 1904.

No doubt the LGOC felt that it was in danger of falling behind while other horse-bus operators experimented with new forms of propulsion. In June 1902, the company had ordered a petrol-electric chassis from Fischer, an American vehicle manufacturer, and which the LGOC claimed would be the first of nine such vehicles, each costing £450. In a petrol electric vehicle, the petrol engine drove a dynamo which charged batteries, from which the current then powered an electric motor. On arrival, in April 1903, the LGOC fitted a double-deck body, but the following month, the Metropolitan Police refused to grant a licence on the grounds that the vehicle was too wide. Nevertheless, it eventually entered service after gaining a special exemption, but it proved to be so heavy and fuel consumption so high that after some experimental running, in October the manufacturer was asked to take it back and refund the cost.

One problem was that it was still difficult to find a prime mover that was light enough and powerful enough to be suitable for a double-deck bus, even of horse-drawn proportions. Just as the horse-drawn double-deck bus was preceded by single-deck vehicles, something similar occurred in London.

The first of these, as opposed to a wagonette, was the Stirling twelve-seat single-deck bus introduced by the London Motor Omnibus Syndicate on a service between Oxford Circus and Cricklewood via Marble Arch on 26 November 1902. The completely enclosed body had a rear entrance with platform and nearside steps. Just four vehicles launched the service, and these were all withdrawn in autumn 1903. The business reorganised itself and emerged as the London Power Omnibus Company, and with two of the original vehicles and five new vehicles, launched a service between Marble Arch and Kilburn on 18 February 1904. This must at last have been successful as by the end of the year the fleet had grown to twelve vehicles, with the latest ones having fourteen and sixteen seats. A further sign of success was that in February 1906, the single-deck buses were all withdrawn and replaced by double-deck vehicles.

Despite this activity, the number of 'horseless' buses running in London was very small. In 1899, for example, there were just five, of which three were double-deck. In 1901, there were ten, all single-deck, but there was a surge the following year, with twenty-eight single-deck and two double-deck vehicles, but by 1903, there was just one solitary double-deck bus while the number of single-deck vehicles had dropped to eleven. Yet, by 1904, there were five double-deck and twenty-six single-deck buses in service. Despite this, at the start of 1905, there were only twenty motor buses in London: five of these were Milnes-Daimler double-deck vehicles, with three being operated by Thomas Tilling and another two by Birch Brothers. The Thomas Tilling vehicles set the pattern of urban double-deck buses for the next fifteen years, with sixteen seats inside and eighteen outside, with the driver sitting behind the engine in what has become known as the 'normal control' position. Unlike some of the steam buses, there was no attempt to cover the upper deck, which remained open, but rubberised sheets were placed behind the seat backs and these could be used to cover the passengers when it rained or snowed. It became the custom for the sheets, when folded behind the back of the seat in front, to carry advertising. Travel outside was not for the weak and even with spiral staircases and a platform, getting on and off required some agility. By this time, the same fare was being paid regardless of which deck one chose for the journey.

It was around this time that both the LGOC and the London Road Car Company started mechanised bus operation in earnest. They did not use the internal combustion engine, however, but instead both opted for steam buses and single-deck at that. On 8 October 1904, the LRCC introduced two Chelmsford buses with fourteen-seat bodies, and the same type of vehicle was introduced by the LGOC on 10 October, but only remained in service until 7 June 1905, having lost its owners £319 18s 5d in the meantime. The LRCC buses soldiered on until August before also being withdrawn. The Chelmsford name was later to change to Clarkson, but before this, the LRCC introduced a double-deck Chelmsford steam bus on 5 September 1905, running between Hammersmith and Oxford Circus. A much larger twenty-seat Darracq-Serpollet steam bus was introduced as an experiment in March 1909 by the Metropolitan Steam Omnibus Company.

Far ahead of their time were the single-deck Pullman buses introduced on 4 May 1908, which ran for a period providing a luxury service with armchairs and pneumatic tyres, but the latter innovation was still in its infancy and unable to bear the weight of a double-deck bus.

By 1908, it was also becoming clear that, except where low bridges or other obstacles made double-deck operation impossible, it was the double-deck bus that was the most efficient and economical means of transport in cities. The volume of traffic was there, but the better use of road space and personnel also meant that everything pointed in favour of the double-deck bus and, for that matter, double-deck tram. Contrary to popular belief, the double-deck bus was by no means unique to the British Isles at the time, but in widespread service in the cities of the northern hemisphere.

The reluctance to obey the letter of the law and use rubber tyres was a question of cost. It has been estimated that a set of solid rubber tyres on a one ton vehicle, a small wagonette, cost 10d per mile in 1902. The Great Western Railway sought to minimise these costs by negotiating what is believed to be the first tyre-mileage contract for its 22-seat Milnes-Daimler vehicles, which amounted to 3.0576d per mile, but even so, these vehicles remained in service from 30 January 1904 before being withdrawn at the end of the year due to the high cost and poor reliability of the tyres. One operator claimed that tyres would not last 200 miles before coming off the rims, when it was not unknown for a police officer to maintain that the vehicle then had to operate as a traction engine with a maximum speed of 4 mph!

Fortunately, by 1905, in an attempt to encourage the use of their products, the main tyre manufacturers started to offer contracts of 2d per mile for a set of tyres, so that the standard motor (or steam or electric) bus had wooden carriage wheels encased in solid rubber tyres. This started to transform the economics of horseless bus operation. Nevertheless, it does not compare with today when a bus operator will pay £19 per thousand miles and tyres can, with a little bit of luck, last for up 40,000 miles, 200 times the mileage in 1905.

New companies continued to appear, of which the most prominent was the London Motor Omnibus Company. Its traffic manager was a certain George Samuel Hicks, an experienced busman, who introduced some new ideas which have become commonplace ever since. It was Hicks who introduced the large fleet name, in effect a trading name, and all of the buses introduced by the LMOC carried the name 'Vanguard' in prominent letters. Vanguard commenced operations on 27 March 1905. Hicks next introduced route numbers, the first of which was used a little over a year later, on 30 April 1906, but surprisingly did not provide any indication of which direction the buses were travelling; this was left to Tilling who introduced front destination boards in September 1904. Hicks also ensured a high degree of standardisation in the Vanguard fleet, and stole a march on his competitors, by taking priority for deliveries of Milnes-Daimler vehicles, and so while the LGOC had obtained its first Milnes-Daimler on 29 May 1905, it was the first of few. As they sought to catch up, the established horse-bus operators were forced to look elsewhere.

The importance of route numbers should not be underestimated and it was a far more flexible method of advising waiting passengers of the route than the alternative, which had found favour with the North Metropolitan Tramways, of painting the cars in one of five different colours according to the route worked. It also enabled passengers to distinguish between vehicles that made a detour and those that were more direct.

The LGOC turned to the French concern, De Dion, the first of whose vehicles entered service on 19 October 1905 and until 1910, these became the most numerous type in the LGOC fleet. The rival London Road Car Company favoured Straker-Squire vehicles which were built under licence from Bussing of Germany, as well as Clarkson (formerly Chelmsford) steam buses. The pace of change accelerated rapidly, so that while there were just twenty motor buses operating in London at the beginning of 1905, by August there were a hundred, and by the end of the year this had more than doubled to 230, while by March 1908, there were no less than a thousand. The petrol-engined bus established itself as the mainstay of the fleet, but there were also 'gearless' petrol-electric buses and the London Electrobus Company had a small fleet of battery-powered vehicles that lasted from 15 July 1907 until March 1910. Nor should we forget the Metropolitan Steam Omnibus Company, which ran Darracq-Serpollet steam buses from 5 October 1907 to 16 October 1912.

Such rapid change does not come without cost. The new arrivals were at the end of their resources and the old-established horse-bus companies found the conversion to the internal combustion engine costly. It was the case that while horses were still in demand, the rapid conversion meant that there were too many of them and the market collapsed. On top of this, bus operators were free to compete with one another with little regulation by the standards of later years. As happened with the shipping lines, when regulation is not imposed, transport businesses have means of regulating themselves. This is important, for there is nothing more perishable than a seat on a bus or train, or berth on a ship, which makes the life of the butcher, baker and candlestick-maker relatively relaxed by comparison. The shipping lines sought salvation in the 'conference system' of coordinated sailings and charges, while the bus companies sought 'fusion' or 'amalgamation'.

The end result was that on 1 July 1908, the LGOC, the London Road Car and Vanguard fleets combined, leading many to refer to the LGOC as the 'Combine', although the fleet name in large letters on the sides of the buses now became 'GENERAL'. The new and enlarged LGOC had no less than 885 out of the 1,066 horseless-buses in London at then time. Of these, 1,015 were petrol-engined, one was petrol-electric, thirty-five were steam and fifteen battery-electric. The most popular make was Straker-Squire with 356, followed by Milnes-Daimler with 312 and De Dion with 165, while just seventy-five were built by Wolseley.

There was little standardisation, and there were still many horse-buses to be replaced. The Combine's chief engineer, Frank Searle, suggested that the company should design and manufacture a bus to its own requirements, using the former Vanguard engineering works at Walthamstow. The LGOC board accepted his recommendation and the first, known as the X, was completed on 12 August 1909. After some delay in licensing the vehicle because of objections by the Metropolitan Police to the noise it made, the first of sixty-one to be built entered service on 16 December 1909. The wits amongst the trade press described it as the 'Daimler-Wolseley-Straker type'. This was not unfair as Searle would have been foolish not to borrow the best feature from each.

'In the manufacture of the X type cribbed shamelessly,' he wrote many years later. 'Any parts of the 28 types which had stood up to the gruelling of the London streets were embodied in it.'

The 'X' provided valuable experience and was to lead to a still greater vehicle, the B type. The design of the B type began in March 1910 and the first bus was ready at Walthamstow on 7 October, entering service on 18 October. Despite the gloomy prediction of the Chief Officer of the London County Council Tramways, Llewellyn Fell, that 'twenty years hence motor buses will be exhibited as curios in museums', around 2,900 B types were built and did not disappear from service in London until 12 October 1926. The bus was also produced in single-deck form for services through the Blackwall Tunnel. Amongst the early routes to use the bus was the 16, running from Kilburn to Grosvenor Place, and not only had the LGOC adopted route numbers, but from 1908, it had also standardised its destination boards. Surprisingly, uniforms for drivers and conductors were not introduced until December 1910.

Meanwhile, on 31 October 1910, the tipping point was passed, when there were exactly 1,142 horse-buses and 1,142 horseless-buses licensed in London.

The 'B' was the first product of the Associated Equipment Company, established by the LGOC to provide its vehicles and the predecessor of AEC, which for many years was the supplier of most London buses even after the creation of London Transport in 1933. Sadly, AEC is no longer with us, having been merged with its arch rival Leyland in the 1960s.

It seemed that steam had lost the battle as the mode of transport for London's streets, but Thomas Clarkson, the manufacturer, retaliated by moving into bus operation, forming the National Steam Car Company. The NSCC started operations in London on 2 November 1909 with just four buses, but by the outbreak of war it had 184. The buses used paraffin as a fuel for its vehicles, but post-war, it was decided that National would also operate petrol-engined buses, and the last steamer went on 18 November 1919. Clarkson left the company in disgust. The company then started to develop services in the provinces, (as mentioned on page 118).

There was also a rear-guard battle fought for the petrol-electric. This held more promise. The Tilling concern had been interested in this type of propulsion since 1907, when it experimented with a bus known as the SB & S type, which proved capable of withstanding severe testing in London service. The chassis for the bus was completely redesigned and it had a much lower weight than earlier petrol-electric buses. The successor was the TTA1, which entered service in London on 11 June 1911, and afterwards was produced not only for service in London but also with Tilling's growing empire of provincial bus companies.

As war approached, further changes took place. The Metropolitan Police insisted that all new buses had to have provision for destination displays front and rear, while boards on the sides of buses stated the main route points. In April 1912, service numbers were encased in a glass box, illuminated from behind. Attention to public safety saw the provision of 'lifeguards' along the sides of buses, wooden slats under the chassis to make it more difficult for pedestrians to fall under the bus. Chassis, and thus floor, heights were much higher at the time with rigid axles and it was to be more than ten years before a rear axle with a lowered centre became available and vehicles became lower.

On the other hand, despite upholstered seats 'inside' in the lower saloon, protection for the outside passengers was still lacking. Apart from the steam buses with their light canvas awnings to protect passengers from smuts, the Metropolitan Police refused to sanction any form of covering on the upper deck.

Electrification

As mentioned in the previous chapter, the impact of the electric tram on the suburban railway services was considerable, being far faster than any street transport so far. While with hindsight, electrification was the obvious answer to both competing with the trams and improving productivity on the railway network, the railways were slow to adopt this and many of the first British electric railways were tourist attractions rather than workaday railways. Despite its connections, both personal and operational, at first with the Metropolitan Railway, when it thrust towards London, the Great Central was completely oblivious to electrification. This was not just because the Metropolitan was, and remained for many years outside the centre of London, steam-hauled, but also because the Great Central could not afford the costs of electrification. There were other reasons as well, apart from the innate conservatism of railway management. One was that electric trains at the time showed considerable improvement in journey times on stopping services, where the superior acceleration of the electric train put the steam locomotive at a disadvantage, but on fast and express trains, the electric trains failed to match the best that steam could offer.

It was not until more serious consideration of electric and diesel propulsion took place between the two world wars that other advantages began to be discussed. One of these was that less manpower was needed as even a single steam railcar still needed a driver, fireman and guard, while the fireman was dispensed with on electric and diesel trains, at least on the private enterprise railway for, as we will see later, having just one man on the footplate was a battle that British Railways shirked time and time again. Another point was made too between the wars, which was that electric and diesel trains only consumed fuel whilst on the move, unlike the steam locomotive, which had to be kept in steam, and indeed took hours to reach a working temperature. This argument, expressed in the journals of the day, sits strangely with the sight today at many stations and goods yards of a diesel engine sitting idly with its engine throbbing.

While a full-sized battery-powered railway engine, *Galvani*, was demonstrated in London by Robert Davidson from Aberdeen as early 1837, electrification in railway terms means trains powered by current picked up from either special rails or from overhead wires. A step forward came in 1879, when Werner von Siemens demonstrated a locomotive drawing power from a third rail at the Berlin Exhibition of that year, and then brought his invention to London to demonstrate at the Crystal Palace in 1881-82. This was followed by no than three electric railways being built in the United Kingdom between 1883 and 1885, two of them in what is now Northern Ireland, and the Volk's Railway at Brighton, the only one to survive.

Between 1890 and 1900, there were four more electric railways opened in Great Britain: the City & South London; Central London Railway; Waterloo & City; and the Liverpool Overhead Railway. Initially, these all used third rail electrification at 550-550 V dc. A significant advance was the invention in the United States by Frank Sprague of a system for controlling locomotives or self-propelled units, 'multiple units' in railway terms, operating in tandem or 'multiple', in 1898. This meant that two or more units could be coupled together and still need just one driver. The first trials of this system in Britain was on the Central London Railway in 1901, while the first to order electric multiple unit trains was the Great Northern & City Railway that same year, although by 1903, the CLR was first to actually put such trains into service. It was soon followed by the Metropolitan District and by the Metropolitan Railway, although the latter electrified only its underground or sub-surface sections, with trains steam hauled once in the open and electric engines used instead of multiple units. It was from this time that the London Underground Railways began using a central insulated negative rail for return current to avoid leakage from the return rails that could cause electrolytic corrosion of tunnel linings. It became the practice for the 'live' rail to be positioned outside the running rails.

As we have seen, competition from electric street tramways was beginning to make inroads into the traffic for suburban steam railways, and electrification was seen as an effective counter-measure.

The next stage was to consider using higher voltages, necessary if main line electrification was to be contemplated. The Midland Railway in Lancashire in 1908, and from 1909 the London Brighton & South Coast Railway, both favoured 6,600/6,700 V ac overhead electrification, but the latter's suburban plans were not completed until after the First World War.

There were distinct advantages and disadvantages to the different systems. Third rail direct current required less infrastructure work as bridges and tunnels could remain unchanged, but needed many more additional sub-stations. Overhead alternating current required fewer sub-stations, but overbridges and tunnels needed higher headroom while the trains themselves lost space to transformers. Some third rail systems used overhead wires in sidings and marshalling yards to ensure the safety of railwaymen, especially shunters, working on the ground.

The greatest enthusiasm for electrification in the London area by the surface railways was amongst the companies in the south. As already mentioned, the first electric services were introduced on the London Brighton & South Coast Railway's South London Line London Bridge to Victoria in 1909 using a 6,700 volts ac overhead system, described very confusingly by today's terminology as the 'elevated electric', and after this proved successful, the lines to Crystal Palace and Selhurst were electrified in 1912. This was completed during the same year, with services from London Bridge to Crystal Palace Low Level via Tulse Hill on 1 March, and to Streatham and Victoria via Tulse Hill on 1 June. What today would be described as the 'sparks effect' showed a tremendous increase in activity, with the pre-electrification services into the Brighton station running at 663 trains a day, but rising to 901 in 1912. At the other end of the South London Line, Victoria, the line to Streatham Hill and Crystal Palace Low Level was electrified from 12 May 1911, followed on 1 June 1912 by those to Norwood and the line Victoria to London Bridge via Streatham Hill.

On the other hand, it was not until Herbert Walker was poached from the London & North Western to become the London & South Western Railway's last general manager in 1912, that the company's suburban electrification started, including the rebuilding of Waterloo, until that time a collection of four stations built at different times to cope piecemeal with expansion, so that this had the distinction of becoming the first major railway terminus in the world built for an electric railway. The rebuilding of Waterloo took from 1910 to 1920, and so it is no surprise that the LSWR's first suburban electrifications were not completed until during the war years. Walker's eye for value meant that this was done on the 600-volt DC system using a third rail. Waterloo to Wimbledon via East Putney was completed on 25 October 1915, and on 30 January of the following year it was joined by the Kingston Roundabout and its Shepperton branch. On 12 March 1916, the Hounslow Loop was electrified, followed by the Hampton Court branch on 18 June. The so-called 'new' Guildford line, running via Cobham, was electrified as far as Claygate on 20 November 1916, and initially there was a steam push-pull service beyond for stations to Guildford, but the line had to return to steam working in July 1919, as demand on the other routes meant that the rolling stock could be used more effectively elsewhere.

Plans to electrify the South Eastern & Chatham's suburban services were overtaken by the grouping, having been delayed by the poverty of the two partners even though the powers had been obtained as early as 1903.

Not all of the other railways were so far behind. Between 1914 and 1922, the London & North Western Railway electrified its suburban services from Euston and Broad Street to Watford, using the third and fourth rail system favoured by the Underground Group of Companies. Post-war, and after grouping, these were extended to Rickmansworth. The Broad Street services were actually those of the North London Railway, whose operations were taken over by the LNWR in 1909, although the LNR remained as a separate company. The essentially suburban nature of the NLR meant that it was one of the first to suffer the impact of electric tramways, and this forced it to consider electrification. Electrification was approved in 1911 as part of the LNWR's scheme for its London suburban services, with electrification completed between Broad Street and Richmond in 1916, and then between Broad Street and Watford in 1922, using the third and fourth rail system.

On the Great Eastern at Liverpool Street, competition from the expanding London Underground and the electric trams meant that electrification was considered as early as 1903. Nevertheless, the Underground seemed to have stopped expanding and while Parliamentary approval was obtained, nothing was done, even though daily passenger numbers rose from around 200,000 in 1912 to 229,073 in 1921, but just fourteen trains had been added to the timetable. The cost of electrification was enormous, estimated in 1919 at £3.5 million (equivalent to more than £70 million today), with little prospect of achieving a worthwhile return. The alternative, a stop-gap measure, costing £80,000, was to change the layout of the approaches, the station arrangements and signalling, so that steam trains could continue to operate, but at the maximum efficiency. Despite these disappointments, overall traffic continued to grow, so that by 1912, Liverpool Street was handling a thousand trains daily. These included Britain's first all-night service, half-hourly between the terminus and Walthamstow, introduced in 1897. Walthamstow's population had grown from 11,092 in 1871 to 95,131 in 1901. This was not unusual and other suburbs saw similar expansion.

A map of London showing the built up area would have shown it confined to the City and West End in 1801, with the West End stopping at

Marble Arch, but by 1914, it stretched from Purley, south of Croydon, and as far north as Enfield, although it was patchy and Barnet, little further north than Enfield, was still in open country, and Orpington, not as far south as Purley, was also in open country. Much of this reflected the development of the railway services, and to a certain extent, that of the trams. Good, frequent, direct services meant development and urban or, perhaps more correctly, suburban growth. In 1906, Golders Green was a muddy country crossroads with a few buildings, but development started once the Hampstead tube reached it the following year. By the early 1920s, it was a built-up but prosperous suburb with substantial villas in leafy roads within walking distance of the tube station, the first outside the tunnel northbound and on embankment, and with a substantial depot for trains with, in front of the station, a large bus terminus.

On edge of the growing built-up area lay Coulsdon North on the LB&SCR main line to Brighton. At the time the station was known as Stoat's Nest. On 29 January 1910, an up express from Brighton split in two as it crossed points at the station and the last three carriages, a Pullman car and two third-class vehicles, derailed and crashed into the platform at around 40 mph, with the loss of seven lives and another thirty injured. The station was renamed the following year.

Clearly, the rewards were there for the railways, but even so the initial capital cost of electrification was to be a recurring problem, and after the First World War, only the Southern railway was to pursue this with the necessary enthusiasm and commitment. As we shall see, there were sound reasons for this, as the Southern was the one of the 'Big Four' railway companies most heavily dependent on passenger traffic, while the next most heavily dependent, the Great Western, had the smallest suburban traffic of any main line railway.

Chapter 10

The Great War

When we got to the station it was already packed. We couldn't get down to the platform, so camped on a landing halfway down. The air was as foul as the Black Hole of Calcutta and those people certainly were scared...I hadn't realised before how successful the raids are...

US serviceman on his arrival at a London railway station in 1917

No one today remembers the bombing raids of the First World War. While these did not compare with the 'Blitz' or *Blitzkrieg* of the Second World War, to a population not expecting to be bombed, they were bad enough.

The railways were largely unprepared for wartime and its demands, let alone the bombing. The sole exception was the London & South Western Railway, which during the Boer War had been the principal railway handling British forces destined for South Africa. Many of the troops passed through London's Waterloo Station while the cavalry's horses used the goods station at Nine Elms, and virtually everyone used the LSWR's port at Southampton. Yet, this was a much shorter war than the First World War, or Great War as it was known until 1940, and did not impact on the economy, the workforce, industry or transport, let alone the mass of the population, in the way that the First World War did. Continental populations, and their transport systems, were used to wars; the population of the British Isles, and transport management, were not.

One lesson had been learnt from the Boer War, when the LSWR had remained under the control of its own management, which was that concentrating so much traffic on London was inefficient, and in the years leading up to the outbreak of the First World War in 1914, the railway links between the coast and the military training and rear concentration areas on Salisbury Plain were improved.

The railways

A mechanism for the state to take control of the railways in wartime had existed from as early as 1842, when legislation was passed that allowed the government emergency powers over the railways; but at first the reason was that of internal security. It was not until invasion fears arose again in 1859 that consideration was given to the use of the railways in wartime. In the UK, parliamentary scrutiny of legislation authorising new lines began to take defence requirements into account. The War Office accepted the London Tilbury & Southend Railway's extension to Shoeburyness in 1882. The War Office also joined those opposed to the Great Western Railway's broad gauge, seeing it as slowing the movement of men and equipment in an emergency.

The original emergency powers simply gave the government of the day the authority to direct how the railways should be run, leaving operational control in the hands of the companies. This remained true with the legislation of 1844 and 1867, and even with the Regulation of the Forces Act 1871. Other recognition of the importance of the railways to the military included the creation of the Engineer & Railway Staff Volunteer Corps in 1865, so that experienced railwaymen would be on hand when needed. Amongst those who helped plan for the use of the railways in wartime was Sir Myles Fenton of the South Eastern Railway. In 1896, an Army Railway Council was established, which later became the War Railway Council.

War in Europe was widely expected, certainly in the United Kingdom and France. The Liberal government had begun to consider nationalisation of the railways, but this was put aside as war loomed. Even so, the state took far more extensive powers over the railways than had ever been anticipated, with the President of the Board of Trade, whose department was responsible for the railways, as well as ports and shipping, taking control of the railways and acting as nominal chairman of the Railway Executive Committee, REC, formed as early as 1912, to run the railways on behalf of the government. Membership of the REC included the general managers of the ten most important railway companies, and one of them, Herbert Ashcombe Walker, general manager of the London & South Western Railway since 1912, was chosen as acting chairman, despite being one of the youngest general managers. It could have been the LSWR's experience of the demands of the military during the Boer War that had resulted in Walker becoming acting chairman, or it could have been the commonsense argument that since so much traffic would travel over the company's metals and it owned the port of Southampton, that it would be best placed to coordinate matters and liaise with both the Army and the Royal Navy. The military training area of Salisbury Plain, the British Army's headquarters at Aldershot, and two of the Royal Navy's three main ports, Portsmouth

THE GREATEST RAILWAYMAN?:
Sir Herbert Ashcombe Walker, 1868-1949

Voted by readers of *Modern Railways* in 2008 as the greatest railwayman of all time, Sir Herbert Ashcombe Walker was the last general manager of the London & South Western Railway, and was in that company's tradition of recruiting its general managers from outside, in his case from the London & North Western Railway, which he had joined at the age of seventeen. He joined the LSWR in 1912 when he was forty-three, at a time when it had already started on third rail electrification and on the massive and desperately needed reconstruction of Waterloo. Despite being one of the youngest general managers, during the First World War he became acting chairman of the Railway Executive Committee, the body that ran the railways on behalf of the government, and his valuable work was recognised by a knighthood in 1917.

Walker has become famous for his extensive system of third rail electrification, completing that of the suburban network and extending it to the coast so that, by 1939, the third rail covered the Sussex coastline as far east as Hastings and extended into Hampshire as far as Portsmouth and, well inland, Aldershot and Alton. He also took the credit for the extension of the docks at Southampton that enabled it to become Britain's premier passenger port at a time when overseas travel meant travel by sea and air travel was still in its infancy. Others credit him with even interval or 'clockface' scheduling, on which he insisted, but many of the early railways had operated on such a basis, including the London & Blackwall, where high frequency lent itself to even interval operations.

It is true that Walker deserves acknowledgement for all of these, and indeed for the strong leadership that he provided throughout his time at the Southern Railway. Yet, to confine any appraisal of him to these matters alone is to overlook his other qualities. He had a strong grasp of financial matters coupled with what can only be described as common sense. Typical of him was the decision not to rebuild the whole of Waterloo because the 'Windsor' station was at the time a new structure and could be incorporated into the design for the reconstruction without damaging the completeness of the new terminus. Equally, one suspects that his enthusiasm for third rail electrification was based on the economy of a system that did not require the wholesale reconstruction of tunnels and overbridges, the cost of which could well have changed the economics of the programme completely. In many cases, carriages originally built for steam haulage were rebuilt as suburban electric multiple units, again a worthwhile economy, especially as the newer rolling stock was selected that otherwise could have been wasted by premature retirement. Walker also had an eye for publicity and recruited the young journalist John Elliot to handle the Southern's publicity. The LSWR had no great history of named trains, but the Southern Railway soon established a range of named expresses, showing that Walker did not adhere blindly to every LSWR tradition.

Walker was no slave to new ideas. Hiring a press officer was one thing, but modern corporate image-makers would have found him more than a 'hard sell'. He resolved a debate over the correct colour for the Southern's rolling stock by buying a length of green cord for his spectacles, cutting it into segments and giving each senior officer a piece, retaining one for himself. He then instructed them that the cord represented the correct shade of colour for locomotives and carriages, and any questions could be resolved by reference to the piece that would be kept in his office at Waterloo!

That Walker also took the long view and was aware of developments in transport generally can be gathered from the Southern's keen interest in acquiring bus companies, and where the entire company could not be purchased, taking a substantial shareholding, and the company was the first to build stations at airports, notably at Gatwick but also changing the name of an existing halt to create Shoreham Airport Halt, near Brighton, and was one of the more active members of Railway Air Services, which did much to develop domestic air services. His enthusiasm for main line electrification has led many to believe that his ultimate ambition was that of complete electrification of the Southern, but this seems unlikely given the sparse service and poor business prospects of many of the lines in Devon and Cornwall.

As a man, Walker has been described as quiet but authoritative, a consummate professional with a strong grasp of all aspects of railway operation, and a leader who always got the best from his management team. He had a strong sense of duty towards his shareholders and the travelling public. A weakness was the failure not to look for greater integration of the old companies that could have rendered economies in management. Integration was carried through efficiently in such places as the Isle of Wight, where three small island companies rapidly became one. It also has to be accepted that communications and automation were less sophisticated than today, so that keeping distinct divisions would have been seen as a practical approach rather than allowing over-centralisation. Undoubtedly, the network could have taken more line closures than was in fact the case, with short branches proving a drain on the finances of the Southern Railway at a time when market conditions were far from buoyant, while those closures that did take place could have been accelerated. There was a curious contradiction in that the man who managed a railway and shipping concerns, and several ports of which the most significant by far was Southampton, believed that airports should be provided by the state, rather like roads.

Walker retired in 1937 and became a non-executive director of the Southern until nationalisation. He died in 1949.

and Devonport, were served by the company. Everything suggests that Walker was a great success in this post, for which he received a knighthood in 1917. His career post-war was to show that he was indeed a visionary, and perhaps it was no surprise that, in a 2008 poll by the magazine, *Modern Railways*, to find the most significant railwayman of all time, Walker came top.

The REC's remit initially only covered railways in Great Britain, and it was not until 1917 that the Irish railway companies also came under its control.

Of course, the LSWR had no monopoly of cross-Channel traffic, which was also shared with four other railway companies, the Great Eastern, with its port at Harwich and London terminus at Liverpool Street; the South Eastern & Chatham, with its ports at Dover and Folkestone, and termini at Charing Cross, Cannon Street, Holborn Viaduct, Blackfriars and London Bridge; and the London, Brighton & South Coast Railway, with its port at Newhaven and termini at London Bridge and Victoria. The LSWR operated cross-Channel and Channel Islands services from Southampton, while the Great Western operated to the Channel Islands from Weymouth. Other shipping services were bringing men and horses across the Irish Sea, with Ireland an important source for both, while the entire railway network was pressed into service to meet the needs of industry as well as the armed forces.

Few had any real idea how modern warfare would affect the railways. Only a few considered attack from the air to be a serious threat, but as early as October 1914, the SECR had a lookout posted on Hungerford Bridge, carrying the line from London Bridge and what is now Waterloo East (then known as Waterloo Junction) into Charing Cross. The lookout was expecting not bombers but Zeppelin airships, and was there to stop trains running across the bridge.

While longer distance commuting was in its infancy at the time, the war years saw a number of cut backs and reductions in service. Unlike the Second World War, first-class travel was not abolished, but many trains that had been exclusively first class or even exclusively Pullman, such as the London Brighton & South Coast Railway's *City Limited* and *Southern Belle*, running between London and Brighton, were forced under wartime pressures to allow third-class travel. The number of services to the coast was substantially reduced, not least because the railways lost the ports of Dover and Folkestone to the military's exclusive use. Services to East Anglia were also affected, with Harwich becoming a naval base.

Suburban services were also affected, with reductions in services to save coal, as even electric trains used coal-fired power stations, and release men and rolling stock for war use. The South Eastern & Chatham Railway withdrew its service over the Metropolitan Extension from Victoria on 3 April 1916, so the South London Line had to deal with all of the traffic from stations between Victoria and Brixton. At the start of 1917, South Bermondsey and Old Kent Road stations were closed entirely, while other stations such as East Brixton and North Dulwich were closed on Sundays. Some stations, such as Old Kent Road, never re-opened. On other routes, Sunday train services were cut dramatically or disappeared altogether.

To discourage unnecessary travel, off-peak fares were increased and cheap day returns withdrawn.

There was relatively little damage to the railways from bombing during the First World War. Aircraft were in their infancy, and even a Zeppelin could only carry a limited bomb load. Most of the action affected Liverpool Street. On the night of 8/9 September 1915, several bombs fell on Liverpool Street, damaging the suburban and through lines, and fracturing a water main that flooded the suburban tracks. Nevertheless, partly because of the small size of the bombs, repairs were put in hand and a full service restored by 11 am on 9 September. The bombs also demolished a wall and shattered glass at Broad Street next door, where some horses were injured. A more significant incident followed during the air raid of 13 June 1917. Again the City was the target, and again three bombs landed on the GER's terminus at Liverpool Street: one of the bombs was a dud and failed to explode, another exploded on a platform and a third hit the dining car of the noon express to King's Lynn and Hunstanton, setting it alight. Two carriages between platforms 8 and 9 were being used for medical examinations, and these were smashed. All in all, sixteen people were killed and another thirty-six wounded, making it one of the worst bombing casualty rates in England during the First World War.

During the war the Great Northern Railway at King's Cross used Gas Works Tunnel as a shelter for main line trains whenever enemy aircraft approached, but the station was untroubled by German bombing during the war, even though a massive volume of freight traffic passed through the station on its way to the SECR, including train loads of explosives for the British forces fighting in France.

It was not at King's Cross but across the road from it at St Pancras that the worst loss of life on the railways occurred. On 17 February 1918, a stick of bombs was dropped across the station, but it was the one that fell just outside the booking office in the cab court that did the most harm, killing twenty people as they queued for a taxi. Railway traffic was not affected.

State control of the railways was intended to ensure that the system operated as one: an excessive measure as the pre-war railways had coordinated themselves very well indeed, partly through the workings of the Railway Clearing House,* which did more than simply balance inter-company tickets and freight receipts, and several companies did, collaborate, especially to ensure the smooth through running of the Anglo-Scottish expresses. Yet, state control did enable resources to be directed to wherever they might be most needed rather than some companies keeping their equipment to themselves while another part of the system suffered under wartime pressures. Many railwaymen had volunteered to join the armed forces while others were mobilised because of their reserve obligations, so that no less than 184,475 – 45 per cent of railwaymen of military age – enlisted. The military also helped itself to locomotives and rolling stock for service as far away as Mesopotamia: more than 600 locomotives were pressed into military service overseas and the ½ inch or so difference between the British and French track gauges mattered little.

There were increased pressures on the system over and above the obvious need for troop trains. Unforeseen by the planners on the outbreak of war was that the role of coastal shipping, in peacetime so important for the movement of bulk commodities such as coal, was severely restricted by enemy activity in the North Sea and the English Channel. Routine operations were severely affected as railway workshops were converted to help with the war effort, including the manufacture of armaments, while rolling stock was converted to provide ambulance trains. In the provinces, some minor railway lines were closed in wartime never to reopen.

Economy in manpower, fuel and materials all meant that services had to be reduced. There were fewer trains, and many were lengthened or combined, while overall speeds were reduced, although none of these measures was as restrictive as those imposed during the Second World War. First-class travel survived the war years, even on inner suburban lines and on the Metropolitan Railway, by this time the only part of the London Underground offering this facility.

New, rebuilt or reconditioned steam locomotives appeared in a drab grey colour scheme.

Despite it being a truly global war, the main centre of activity was in

---

*Although formed originally to settle accounts between railway companies, including through tickets, freight receipts and tolls for running over another company's lines, the Railway Clearing House did much to standardise systems, including such items as locomotive headcodes and signals, but in peacetime could only progress as far as individual companies would allow.

Europe, and the greatest pressure fell on the Channel Ports, with first Dover and then Folkestone closed to civilian traffic. The SECR became Britain's frontline railway, with the heaviest responsibility for the movement of men and materials to the coast. In London, Charing Cross also had the role of being Westminster's local station, and a special train, code-named *Imperial A* was held ready at all times for VIP journeys to the coast, being used for 283 journeys during the war years. Charing Cross was also the arrival point for many of the casualties of war: On 7 June 1917, after the start of the Battle of Messines at dawn, the first wounded arrived at Charing Cross at 2.15 pm that same day.

The state was to prove to be a short-sighted and improvident proprietor, so that financially, the war years were a disaster for the railway companies, despite compensation being based on pre-war earnings, ones of prosperity for the railways. Post-war, one general manager noted that the combined profits for the railway companies in 1913 had totalled £45m, but that by 1920, these had dropped to less than £7m, owing to improved rates of pay during the war when the railways were under direct government control. By 1921, immediately prior to government control ceasing, the railways were running at a loss overall of around £9 million. Part of the reason was almost certainly the cost of manpower. Railway wages in 1913 had totalled £47m, but by 1920 had risen to £160m.

On the roads

One of the great stories of the Great War was the use of London omnibuses to take troops to the front, and, of course, these were the famous 'B' class, but painted in drab British Army green. French troops, by contrast, were sent to the front in commandeered Parisian taxi cabs. In fact, no less than a thousand of the B type buses of the LGOC were requisitioned for war service, while another 233 were used on defence work around London and another fifty-two were used on a special air-raid service.

One vehicle that could not be whisked away from the streets of the capital to foreign parts, even those parts as close as France and Belgium, was the London tram. By the outbreak of war, in August 1914, the rapid expansion of the tramway network had virtually stopped and in Great Britain as a whole the total route mileage was 2,530, leaving just a few schemes to be completed between the wars.

The war brought an abrupt end to horse-bus operations in London for there were several short routes still in service in 1914 and the last ten horse buses for the LGOC had been completed as recently as 1905. The last route to be operated was that by Thomas Tilling between Peckham Rye and Honor Oak, but the British Army needed the horses, as well as the motor buses. As the war progressed, some horse buses were reinstated to compensate for the absence of so many B-type buses on war service.

For the traveller, the most noticeable effect of wartime was the appearance of women on buses and trams as conductresses, soon to be commonly known as 'clippies'. To ensure that modesty was maintained, especially when climbing the open, and often breezy, stairs to the upper decks, trousers were worn. No doubt many women found this a liberating experience and it was certainly far better than working in a munitions factory where the hazard of handling explosives was in fact nothing compared to the effect of the chemicals on their health. The first women to work as bus conductors in London were on the Tilling service 37, where they started to appear in spring 1915.

Chapter 11

Grouping and Recession

Omnibuses are everybody's vehicle, and the days have long gone
by when people of distinction were almost ashamed to be seen
riding in one, and ladies blushed at the thought.
The Wonder Book of Motors, 1927

The end of the Great War came complete with uncertainties for transport operators. The railways were still under the control of the Railway Executive Committee, but pre-war there had been a re-awakening of calls for nationalisation and a thorough investigation had only been prevented by the outbreak of war.

What no one could have foreseen was that competition from road transport was to become more serious for the railways, and indeed for the established bus operators, as men were discharged from the armed forces who had acquired mechanical knowledge or driving skills, and were joined by a flood of war surplus vehicles sold often at prices barely above their scrap value. Away from the towns, most transport was virtually unregulated. Not all of this activity was bad, as the more enterprising of the newcomers were to establish some of the country's major provincial bus operators.

Post-war saw one political innovation, the formation of a Ministry of Transport, which removed responsibility for road and railway transport, and canals as well, from the Board of Trade. The first minister was Sir Eric Geddes, a former general manager of the North Eastern Railway, who had become a civil servant during the war years before entering politics.

It is said that neither the new Ministry of Transport, nor its minister, foresaw the extent to which the railways would be affected by road competition, and indeed it was to be eleven years before any measure to control this reached the statute book, but given Geddes' experience of the railways and his subsequent career moves, one cannot help but question this. The ministry might not have foreseen the future, but Geddes surely must have done, driving through the Railways Act 1921 to the Statute Book.

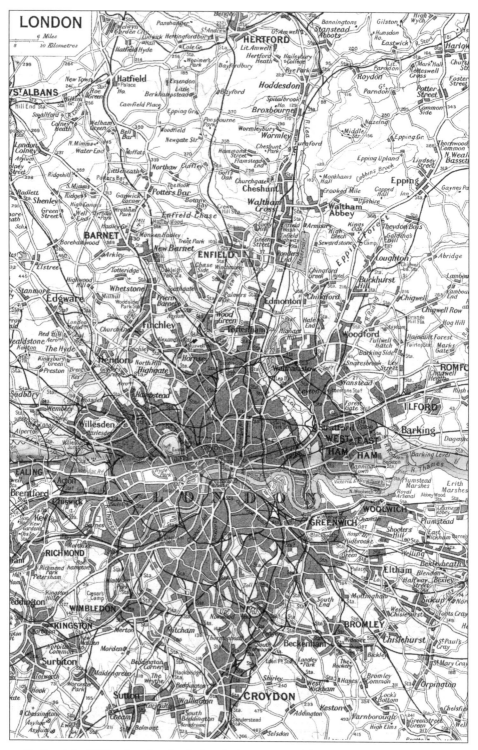

By the late 1920s, London had already been spread in all directions and was far removed from days when it just consisted of the City and Westminster.

The Act was concerned with one measure above all others, the grouping of the railways as an alternative to nationalisation. Wartime coordination of the railways had been viewed by many as a success, and the mood of the time was in favour of coordination rather than competition. Despite the growing losses of the railways at the end of government control, it still seems that memories of the high rates of return earned at one time by many railway companies remained strong amongst politicians. The feeling was that the railways needed firm regulation to avoid making excessive profits, and the mood of the time did not trust competition to do this. Inevitably, grouping was to extend the size and depth of the monopolies and reduce the opportunities for competition at the fringes. Originally, Britain's railways were to be grouped into seven companies, but in the end, this was reduced to just four.

First, there was the need to ensure that the nation's transport got back to operating on a peacetime basis as quickly as possible. The military's use of so many B-class buses had left the capital chronically short of road transport apart from the trams, and more than a hundred B-type lorries, still in Army markings, were pressed into service after being fitted with seats and a ladder at the back, operating routes such as that between Barnes and Charing Cross. It was to be another year or two before new buses started to appear in sufficient numbers, and while the first of these from the Associated Equipment Company, AEC, was the K-class and still open top, the driver was moved forward to the appropriately-known forward control position, and sat beside the engine over the front offside wheel. A stretched version followed, but a big step forward in 1923 was the NS, which had a much lower chassis, so getting on and off was much easier. The lower height meant that canvas top covers were used in wet weather from 1925, and the vehicles were later fitted with pneumatic tyres and windscreens for the driver.

In wartime, the state had failed to keep its promise of maintaining revenues at 1913 levels and protecting the equity of the railway companies, who were no longer seen as desirable stocks by many investors. A sum of £60 million (£1,164 million today) was eventually offered to the railway companies in compensation for the impact of wartime and state control on their finances. The problem was that Parliament would neither set the post-war railways free nor nationalise them. Not content with enforcing the grouping, it was also considered necessary to apply other controls as well.

The grouping was intended to ensure that the railway shareholders would receive what was described as the 'standard' revenue of £51.4

ARCHITECT OF RAILWAY GROUPING:
Sir Eric Campbell Geddes, 1875-1937

Indian-born Eric Geddes joined the North Eastern Railway in 1904, specialising in management techniques and by 1914 was general manager. He became a civil servant during the First World War, holding a succession of posts including munitions production, transport organisation and naval supply, eventually entering politics to become the first post-war Minister of Transport. The concept of grouping was his idea, and he had similar plans for the electricity supply industry. As Minister, he pushed the Railways Act 1921 through Parliament, but before it could take effect, he left politics and joined Dunlop, the tyre and rubber manufacturer, becoming chairman.

His final task in politics was to push through dramatic cuts in national expenditure, known to this day as the 'Geddes Axe'. In 1924, he was made part-time chairman of the new state-sponsored airline, Imperial Airways, whilst retaining his position at Dunlop. His final service to the state was to organise the delivery of essential supplies during the 1926 General Strike.

Geddes could be described as a meddler, seldom staying in any one position long enough to see new initiatives to their conclusion. Perhaps he complied with the cynical description of a whizz kid as being 'someone who moves on before the consequences of his actions come home to roost'.

million (£997.2 million today) annually spread across all four companies and based on the 1913 figure, which, fortunately, had been a remarkably good year for the railways. Despite the efforts of a Railway Rates Tribunal, this figure was never realised in practice because of the changes that occurred post-war and in particular the depressed state of the economy for most of the time. It seems limiting enough given the economic conditions prevailing between the wars, although deflation meant that costs actually fell, but it would have been impossible given the often high levels of inflation encountered in the four decades following the end of the Second World War.

Grouping

The Railways Act 1921 forced 120 companies, listed in Appendix I, of varying size into four large mainline groups. Not every railway was included, and a number of independent railways did survive, including a number of narrow gauge and light railways. Ireland was left alone, as Home Rule had occurred the year before the grouping.

For almost all of London's termini, the grouping meant a change of railway company with one notable exception, Paddington, where the Great Western Railway continued to hold sway, as not only by far the largest of the companies in what the legislation had termed the 'Western group of companies', but the only one of the group to operate to London. At Marylebone, ownership passed from the Great Central to the London & North Eastern, which also gained King's Cross from the Great Northern and Liverpool Street from the Great Eastern. At Euston, the London Midland & Scottish Railway took over from the London & North Western, while the LMS also replaced the Midland Railway at St Pancras and the London Tilbury & Southend at Fenchurch Street, as well as taking over the North London Railway at Broad Street. The Southern Railway came out of grouping with the largest number of termini, with the London & South Western Railway's Waterloo, Victoria shared by the London, Brighton & South Coast and the South Eastern & Chatham Railway group, as was London Bridge, while the SECR also had Blackfriars, Holborn, Charing Cross and Cannon Street.

Viewed with hindsight and the post-nationalisation structures of British Railways, the grouping did seem slightly illogical. If competition was to be removed, why leave such great opportunities for competition on many routes? Within the London commuter area, defying logic and most unexpected was the decision to leave the London Tilbury & Southend line with the London Midland Scottish as successor to the Midland Railway rather than transfer it along with the services from Liverpool Street to the London & North Eastern Railway, leaving two companies operating between Southend and the City of London.

Certainly, the grouping was not without its defects. The most obvious one was the failure to separate out the LNER services from London's Liverpool Street and Marylebone termini from those from King's Cross. Its boat trains to Harwich and its services through sparsely-populated East Anglia to King's Lynn and Norwich notwithstanding, there is no doubt that Liverpool Street was primarily a commuter railway with a secondary continental traffic and agricultural traffic, while King's Cross was at the end of a number of longer distance main line services in addition to serving the large industrial and mining areas of South Yorkshire and the North East of England, as well as the east of Scotland. This mattered for another reason. The LNER soon became a railway very much along the lines of the SNCF in France in that it cared very much for its prestigious main line traffic and produced fine expresses with motive power and carriages to be proud of, but it didn't care so much for its suburban and branch line services, which were often slow, drab and dirty. Despite promises, it never introduced electrification on its suburban network, confining itself to some electrification of its freight lines in the North East. No doubt, confined to King's Cross, the LNER, which was extremely short of money and had to struggle to finance modernisation from revenue since an approach to the shareholders would have been a miserable failure, could have been a more affluent railway, although severely affected by the miners' strike and by the downturn in the coal trade that followed it. There is the sneaking suspicion that the London suburban network would have been accorded a much higher priority had the Great Eastern remained independent. On the other hand, we should not forget that while the old GER had been amongst the first to suffer from electric tramway competition as early as 1901, it had failed to electrify, although railway historians accord it great praise for its successful and very efficient operation of a completely steam-hauled high density suburban service. Compared to this, leaving the London Tilbury & Southend line in different hands was a small matter indeed.

It is not just the combining of such disparate operations into one company that suggests that the grouping was a merger or two too far. The evidence suggests that managements struggled to make the grouping work. The Great Western fared best of all, as the only company to emerge intact from the grouping by simply bolting on the smaller companies to its own well-established structures, so that it was able to boast in 1937 of being the first and only British railway company to celebrate its centenary. Perhaps as a sign of the GWR's confidence, it abandoned the then current lake or all-over brown and reverted to chocolate and cream, usually with white roofs for passenger carriages. The London Midland Scottish was almost rent asunder by factional infighting between the old Midland Railway and the old London & North Western, with Euston versus St Pancras, to which the answer was seen as introducing a highly centralised structure. The London & North Eastern decentralised, which may have done much for local community relations, but one feels that opportunities were missed. As for the Southern, it almost immediately perpetuated the old pre-grouping set up by having Eastern, Central and Western sections almost equating to the former South Eastern & Chatham, London Brighton & South Coast and London & South Western railways. There was a fourth section, the London Section, but this was less prominent.

It seems that many opportunities to rationalise the network and operations were missed. It took the Southern some time to open up passageways between the Brighton and South Eastern sides of Victoria Station, which did not occur until 1924, while it took until 1928 for similar improvements to take place at London Bridge. There was delay too in appointing a single stationmaster for Victoria. There was some rationalisation of lines in the Thanet area to improve operations, but these should have been carried out by the SECR when it had been formed in 1899. Many stations were renamed to avoid confusion throughout Britain, but even so, old definitions were allowed to continue, such as Bedford Midland.

The grouping pushed the question of nationalisation into the background between the wars, largely because most of the inter-war governments were Conservative and opposed in principle. The Labour government of 1924 lasted but briefly while that of 1929 came at a time of financial crisis, and in 1931 was eventually forced to seek a coalition of national unity. Many Labour Party supporters saw this as a betrayal, but it simply underlined the fact that the governments of the day had so much more to worry about, and with large scale unemployment, the demands on the exchequer were huge at a time when tax revenues were adversely affected by recession. It was soon clear that the railways were themselves not an inviting prospect for any government, as the revenues predicted on grouping were not being realised. The idea of taking the railways into public ownership so that the country could enjoy the profits was a non-starter: there weren't any.

Electrifying the suburban lines

As we have already seen, the period before the First World War, while the railways were still fragmented, saw the start of electrification. Not all of this was in the London area. London was, as now, Britain's largest, busiest and most prosperous city, but one value of the old railway companies was that they were mainly not centred on London, and the local traffic of, say, Liverpool, was important to them. In fact, the London & North Western Railway electrified both on Merseyside and that part of its London suburban network acquired when it took over the North London Railway in 1909, approving NLR electrification in 1911. Between 1914 and 1922, the NLR lines were electrified, first between Broad Street and Richmond, completed in 1916, using the third and fourth rail system favoured by the Underground Group of Companies, and then between Broad Street and Watford in 1922, using the same rail system, with these extended to Rickmansworth after grouping. What is interesting about the North London electrification was that the railway was small in route mileage, but an important link for other railways wishing to reach the different dock systems along the north banks of the River Thames, and so much of its revenue was from freight, yet attention was still paid to passenger traffic.

That electrification was important and worthwhile can be demonstrated by the fact that, between 1913 and 1923, the number of suburban passengers carried by the London & South Western and the London Brighton & South Coast had grown by 26 per cent. In addition, after the war, working hours were shortened, so that the morning and evening peaks became more concentrated than had been the case pre-war or during the war years. This made steam working extremely difficult over the congested approaches to the London termini, and left electrification of suburban services as the only viable solution since widening the lines would have been hopelessly uneconomic given the dense residential and commercial development that had taken place alongside the tracks.

One problem with the LSWR system of direct current, dc, electrification was that it required a substantial number of sub-stations, and at first these had to be manned, and the cost of this was a marked disadvantage. However, railway grouping more or less coincided with the advent of the automatic substation, remotely controlled and requiring no manning. Electric trains needed a crew of two, a motorman and a guard, compared with the two enginemen and the guard of a steam train, did not have to have fires lit hours before being ready for service, required less maintenance and dispensed with stops for coaling and taking on water, and on stop-start suburban working were considerably faster than steam trains, all of which marked a considerable improvement in productivity. In addition, there was the inestimable benefit of dispensing with the shunting run to and from the sidings and turntables, with the almost constant demand for paths for light engines over already congested tracks.

The Southern Railway must have been sorely tempted to press ahead with the LSWR system of third-rail electrification, especially since the LBSC overhead system differed from that planned by the SECR, but delayed by the war. Nevertheless, in 1923, a consultant engineer was asked to consider all three systems and report on the best one, and meanwhile, work went ahead so that even after grouping, a new overhead, or in LBSC terms, 'elevated', electric scheme was introduced.

In 1924, the Southern announced that the Western Section electrification would be extended from Surbiton to Effingham Junction and Guildford, Raynes Park to Leatherhead, and from Effingham Junction and Leatherhead to Dorking North. This electrification scheme was the largest ever on a suburban system. Plans to open the 'elevated' extension to Coulsdon North and Sutton on 1 March 1925 were delayed by a month because of electricity supply problems. However, the other extensions to Guildford and Dorking North followed in July, while the Eastern Section was being electrified within a fifteen mile radius of London. At the same time several suburban stations were being re-arranged or having their platforms extended and new stations were built at Motspur Park and Carshalton Beeches, while those at Wimbledon and Sutton were being rebuilt.

The first electric services on the Eastern Section, the old South Eastern & Chatham territory, also started on 12 July 1925. Little incidental work had been needed for the extensions to Guildford and Dorking, but the same could not be said for the initial Eastern Section electrification, where the poor state of the SECR and its constituent companies had meant that there were disused stations to be removed and platform lengthening sometimes involved extra work on bridges as well as the approaches at St Pauls (today's Blackfriars) and Holborn Viaduct. The lines covered by the initial scheme included Victoria-Orpington via Herne Hill and Shortlands as well as Holborn Viaduct to Herne Hill, the Catford Loop between Loughborough Junction and Shortlands, and Nunhead to Crystal Palace High Level. The shortage of running roads also dictated some less than satisfactory timings, with the section of double track between Herne Hill and Shortlands dictating that services from Victoria and Holborn Viaduct ran just five minutes apart, leaving a gap of fifteen minutes to accommodate the many steam trains, including continental boat trains, using the same route. The new services started on a Sunday and worked well on the first day, but a number of breakdowns on the second day, some of which may well have been due to staff inexperience, led to serious disruption and it was to be well into the first week before everything was working smoothly. Problems with major timetable changes were to occur time and time again with electrification, largely because operating staff had to constantly refer to new timetables rather than simply working by experience and memory. This has been a problem that has persisted over the years, and even when the entire timetable for the South Western Division of what had become British Rail Southern Region changed in 1967 to coincide with the Bournemouth electrification, weeks, not days, of chaos followed.

The initial electrification was followed by a much needed re-arrangement and simplification during the second half of 1925 of the approaches to Cannon Street, which had been originally designed to allow all trains to and from Charing Cross to work in and out of the station. There was also extensive work at Charing Cross, where the platform numbering sequence was reversed.

Plans to introduce a second group of electric services on the Eastern

RAILWAYS OR ROADS?

The idea arose during the early years of the twentieth century that the Hungerford Bridge, carrying what were then the South Eastern & Chatham lines into Charing Cross, should be converted into a road bridge. There were objections to the SECR's plans to improve the bridge, and widen the station, but it was not until 1925 that serious problems with subsidence were discovered on one of the piers for Waterloo Bridge that the question of converting the Hungerford Bridge and transferring Charing Cross station to the south side of the river became a major issue. By this time, the debate had extended to converting the bridges running to Blackfriars, then known as St Paul's, and to Holborn Viaduct, to road bridges as well, with the London County Council's planners proving to be no friend of the railways.

The isolation of Waterloo and, before the Cannon Street and Charing Cross extensions, of London Bridge, has been mentioned earlier, so it seems strange that a return to this situation should have been seriously considered. True, tube lines had eased the isolation, and trams had made inroads into the suburban traffic, but adding the cross-river traffic of three stations, even though admittedly not large, to the existing tube network would have called for the costly construction of new lines as well as inconveniencing many travellers, especially commuters.

Nevertheless, a Royal Commission on Cross-River Traffic in London was set up in the summer of 1926, chaired by Lord Lee of Fareham. It reported in just four months, which must have been something of a record. The report called for a compromise. After rejecting the transfer of Charing Cross to the south side of the Thames as an unwanted disturbance to the railways 'which now serve many thousands of passengers daily', they recommended a new double-deck bridge to be built downstream of the Hungerford Bridge. The bridge would have a roadway on the upper level, with six railway tracks on the lower, and would be 60 feet wide. At the northern end, land would be acquired, although much of it was already in railway ownership as the SECR had long hoped to enlarge Charing Cross, for a new and larger site for the station, and once the bridge and new station were completed the railways would switch, leaving the disused Charing Cross station to be demolished and the land used for other purposes, with a hotel being suggested.

The LCC sought government support in the form of a 75 per cent grant, and also turned its attention to building a new bridge to replace those carrying the railway into Blackfriars and Holborn Viaduct. At this point, Sir Herbert Walker, general manager of the Southern railway, had to intervene. He pointed out that while to the 'ordinary man in the street it may appear that the Southern Railway has a superabundance of terminal stations on both sides of the river in London, but....under present conditions each one of these stations is essential to our traffic requirements...In fact, during the rush hours...we have at the present time very great difficulty at these various termini in dealing with the very large number of trains which have to run.'

Initially, this logic was to no avail, as the massive cost of relocating stations and building double-deck bridges caused the LCC engineers to call again for the station to be moved to the south side of the river. The Ministry of Transport supported this proposal, despite the Southern showing that more than 90 per cent of the 16,000-18,000 passengers arriving at Charing Cross between 7am and 10am each day needing to be on the north side, and hence likely to be faced with delay and inconvenience. Since those who did not need to be on the north side could have alighted at London Bridge or Waterloo, one wonders why the figure was not 100 per cent.

Both Westminster City Council and Lambeth Borough Council supported the Southern Railway's case. The question was decided when, during the financial crisis of 1931, the government warned the LCC that it could not continue its offer to meet 75 per cent of the cost. But the question cropped up again in 1935, by which time the SR's arguments were that the new bridges over the Thames at Lambeth and the replacement for Waterloo Bridge should be adequate for road traffic growth for many years to come.

Section, from 1 December 1925, had to be postponed until 28 February 1926, again because of power supply problems. These were the services from Cannon Street and Charing Cross to Bromley North, Orpington, Beckenham Junction, Hayes and Addiscombe, although trains on the Hayes to Elmers End branch switched to electric operation on 21 September 1925 to allow for staff training. Sufficient electric rolling stock and track mileage was available during the General Strike of 1926 for a service of electric trains to operate between Charing Cross and Dartford from 10 May until 16 May, but steam returned to the route afterwards. Electric trains returned to this route, but again on a temporary basis, from 6 June during the closure of Cannon Street for reconstruction to cope with traffic diverted to London Bridge and Charing Cross. The work at the two old SER termini also saw further colour light signalling installed.

The General Strike and the much longer lasting miners' lock-out associated with it, resulted in the temporary closure of the South London Line between 18 May and 20 September 1926. Closure, plus the extension of the City and South London tube line meant that traffic on the route was found to have fallen away considerably when the line re-opened. A major re-organisation of services associated with further electrification that came into effect in 1928 saw the South London Line service cut back, probably the only time in the history of Southern electrification that this action was taken. This instance of defeat simply reflected the fact that the line really was the wrong type of route to be operated by a main line railway, and could only have prospered in the longer term as a link in an urban railway, an above ground section of an underground line, otherwise it was extremely vulnerable to competition from the modern tramway. The route ran through a less prosperous neighbourhood, where the impact of recession was more heavily felt.

Once again a major launch of electric services had to be postponed, but only from 11 July to 18 July 1926, when electric services were introduced from Charing Cross and Cannon Street to Plumstead, and Dartford, permanently at last, via Blackheath and Woolwich, Bexleyheath and Sidcup.

The massive investment in electrification at this time was accompanied, as far as the Southern's management was concerned, by the distraction of the London County Council wanting to relocate Charing Cross to the south side of the Thames so that the Hungerford Bridge could be replaced by a road bridge. Similar plans existed for the bridges carrying the lines to Blackfriars and Holborn Viaduct, with a proposed Ludgate road bridge.

In addition to the conversion of the overhead electrics to third rail, the needs of the Central Section were not being ignored. The announcement of the conversion in August 1926, following the recommendation that third rail was the best and most economical way forward, also mentioned that third-rail electrification would cover the sections between London Bridge and Norwood Junction, Crystal Palace Low Level to both Beckenham Junction and Sydenham, from Purley to Caterham and Tattenham Corner, from Streatham North Junction to Sutton and Epsom, and from Sutton to Epsom Downs, as well as Wimbledon to Herne Hill, Tulse Hill and Haydons Road. A little more than a year later, further colour light signalling was announced, with another nine manual boxes replaced by power-worked cabins at Borough Market Junction and London Bridge. The speed at which these improvements were implemented was astonishing enough, although it no doubt also vindicated the decision to stick with third rail, but what was even more impressive was that a number of services were ready to be operated by electric trains using the steam train timings by 25 March 1928, when the services between Cannon Street, Charing Cross and London Bridge to Caterham and Tadworth changed, as did London Bridge to Crystal Palace Low Level through Sydenham. The new services, with accelerated timings and improved frequencies, were introduced on Sunday, 17 June 1928. Once again, the initial service went smoothly, but on Tuesday, 19 June, a points failure disrupted services during the evening peak, and while delays were not too long, mainly less than fifteen minutes, it took until 4 July for a full train service to be reinstated.

The next stage in the Central Section electrification followed on 3 March 1929, with Dorking North and Effingham Junction having electric trains to London Bridge as well as to Waterloo, with the former operating via Tulse Hill and Mitcham Junction. On the same day, electric services were introduced on Victoria to Epsom via Mitcham Junction and from Holborn Viaduct to Wimbledon via Tulse Hill and Haydons Road, while the Victoria to Crystal Palace Low Level service was converted from ac to dc operation and extended to West Croydon and Beckenham Junction, with the latter requiring considerable work as the line between Bromley Junction and Beckenham Junction had not been used by passenger trains for fourteen years, and peak period services were introduced between Streatham Hill and Victoria.

As a general rule, the pattern of services was three trains an hour at peak periods and half-hourly at other times. It was usual for frequencies to be higher than with the previous steam working, but this was most marked on the services from Holborn Viaduct to Wimbledon, which had enjoyed a rush hour service only previously, but the electric trains attracted passengers from the trams. The improvements were not without some rationalisation of services and stations, with Ludgate Hill and, on the southern loop from Tooting Junction to Wimbledon, the stations at Merton Abbey and Merton Park all closed on 3 March 1929. A new station was built at Epsom, replacing separate LSWR and LBSCR stations, while goods trains were concentrated on the former LBSCR sidings. Colour light signalling was also extended, with considerable rationalisation of signal boxes, providing a welcome economy in staff to offset the heavy capital costs being incurred.

By this time, all that was needed to complete suburban electrification was a degree of tidying up and infilling, and this was achieved on 6 July 1930 when electric services commenced to Windsor, from Wimbledon to West Croydon, and to Gravesend Central from Dartford. The Gravesend services were simply an extension of trains that would otherwise have terminated at Dartford. That same day, Cannon Street re-opened on Sundays. Earlier, on 4 May, trains from Victoria to Sutton were extended to Epsom Downs. By this time, the Southern Railway had almost 800 track miles electrified, which equated to just under 300 route miles.

End of the levy

There were four major political moves between the wars that were of significance to the railways. The first of these was the abolition of the tax on passenger travel, and followed soon afterwards by the first steps in the regulation of road transport; and then by the creation of the London Passenger Transport Board as the first transport nationalisation, while the Guarantees and Loans Act 1934 was a further stimulus to modernisation.

In his budget in 1929, the Chancellor of the Exchequer in Baldwin's Conservative administration, the then Mr Winston Churchill, announced the abolition of the Railway Passenger Duty that had first been introduced in 1832 and by the late 1920s was levied on all passenger fares above 1d per mile, on condition that the sums realised were capitalised and used for railway modernisation. While this was one of the few occasions when political interference with the railways proved beneficial, it is only fair to add that Churchill had not the interests of the long-suffering passenger in mind, but instead was concerned to reduce unemployment by encouraging investment through this form of 'pump-priming'. The measure didn't work politically as in the ensuing general election, a Labour government was elected.

On the Southern Railway it was easy to draw a direct connection between ending the duty and further expansion of electrification. The Southern's share of the capitalised duty was £2 million (around £100-120 million today), and it was estimated that extending electrification to Brighton and West Worthing would cost £2.7 million, including the provision of a much enhanced frequency with the number of departures more than doubled. To achieve a satisfactory return, an increase in revenue of 6 per cent would be needed. The company was not to be disappointed. The other companies spread the money around between passenger services and freight.

Accidents in commuter land

The Southern Railway inherited not only rolling stock from its predecessor companies, but also the infrastructure. The former South Eastern & Chatham Railway lines were often ballasted with shingle from the beach at Dungeness, which were round and smooth and did not offer stability, especially when wet; and when combined with the use of a K-class 2-6-4 tank locomotive, a type known to roll dangerously, the scene was set for a serious accident. This took place at Sevenoaks on 24 August 1927, when the locomotive of an express from Cannon Street to Dover started to roll and then derailed on the curve between Dunton Green and Sevenoaks. A

Pullman car struck the central pier of a bridge and jammed itself across the track, so that the rest of the carriages piled up against it, with thirteen killed and another sixty-one injured.

By 1935, Welwyn Garden City was a new suburb and already had some of its population commuting daily to London. The major accident on the London & North Eastern Railway, on 15 June 1935, did not involve a commuter train, but would have seriously affected commuter services for some days afterwards. The signal box controlled no less than six tracks, four of them for the mainline but with branch lines on either side. Three expresses left King's Cross heading north at 10.45 pm for Newcastle, 10.53 pm also for Newcastle, followed by a 10.58 for Leeds. The 10.45 passed through without any problem, but the inexperienced signalman did not clear the signals promptly, so the driver of the following train, the 10.53, seeing the distant signal at caution began to reduce speed so that he could stop at the home signal, which he expected to find at stop. In fact, the home signal was cleared before he reached it and he started to accelerate, but as his train steamed ahead, it was rammed behind by the 10.58, which completely destroyed the end carriage of the 10.53, while two of its own carriages telescoped into one another. In all, thirteen passengers were killed and another eighty-one injured. The signalman had clearly forgotten about the 10.53 when he cleared the 10.58. Despite the line having a manual block system of signalling, the inspector recommended the provision of a new block instrument and signal interlocking system, which became known as the Welwyn control.

By this time such basic measures such as the lock and block system were in use, but on the busy Southern Railway suburban lines, the system was modified so that a signalman could override it to avoid delaying trains should there be a failure in the system. At Battersea Park on 2 April 1937, the signalman at Battersea found himself in difficulty, and in the confusion he cleared his instrument on the up local line, allowing a train to come forward into a section already occupied. In the resulting collision between two electric multiple unit trains, ten people were killed and another eighty injured.

Road competition

The post-war period also saw competition from road transport that had no precedent. Before the war, this renaissance in road transport had really resulted in competition from the electric tramways which had been confined to the urban areas and their suburbs, and to passenger traffic, but competition from the motor vehicle seemed to know no bounds. Rural branch lines faced competition from the country bus, able to handle comfortably and profitably passenger loads that would not have filled more than a couple of compartments on the local train, and without the massive overhead costs of the railway. The main lines faced competition from the motor coach. Both branch and main lines faced competition from the motor lorry. It was not just a case of the greater flexibility and economy of the motor vehicle, their routes could be more direct. It was also the case that while road haulage contractors could pick and choose their traffic, and even specialise on a particular business; the railways were saddled with the burden of the common carrier obligation, a throw-back to the days when their rule of inland transport was unchallenged.

The seeming reluctance of many of the managers in the big four grouped companies to address the questions of integration and rationalisation had its counterpart in the reluctance of many railwaymen to countenance shedding uneconomic lines and uneconomic traffic. Even post-war, one company envisaged electric traction for most of its lines, including through goods trains, with diesel for the less busy lines and for stopping goods trains.

Regulation of road transport

Faced with a serious challenge from road transport, the railway companies tried to assess just how much business they were losing to road and lobbied for the government to do something about it. They were being tightly regulated themselves, so why shouldn't road transport be tightly regulated seems to have been the attitude. There was no question of 'setting the railways free', instead the lobby was for a 'fair deal for the railways'. The result was the first of a succession of road traffic acts, the first being the Road Traffic Act 1930, which established a system of licensing road haulage. It was to be another three years before a further Act of 1933 regulated bus services.

It is debatable whether the restrictions on freight or passenger transport were the more burdensome. The passenger operator would be tied to certain routes with either a general 'stage' road service licence or an 'express' road service licence with a minimum adult single fare, or, in the case of excursions and tours, certain departure points. Initially, bus and coach operators had what might be termed 'grandfather rights', enabling them to register their existing services, but new routes had to face the traffic commissioners, where the railways had a right to object to the granting of a road service licence. Potential customers had to be dragged off to the commissioners to testify that existing services did not meet their

An artist's portrayal of horse buses at a terminus. The nearer vehicle is one of the unusual Metropolitan Saloon Omnibus Company examples. The conductors can clearly be seen attempting to give change, while the crossing sweeper is waiting for a tip. (British Transport Commission)

Severe congestion on London's streets is nothing new, as this view of St Paul's from Fleet Street shows, with the London, Chatham & Dover train on the viaduct running to the station at Ludgate Hill.
(Author's collection)

The construction of the Metropolitan Railway, now the Metropolitan Line, using the cut and cover method caused whole streets to be closed, with considerable congestion on side streets. Yet, building beneath the surface was the only way, and cut and cover was only viable if the streets were reasonably wide and straight. Even so, notice damage to the buildings on the left in lower image. (Author's collection)

There is no hint of the chaos or disruption in the set of illustrations showing the new stations for the Metropolitan Railway, and no hint of the smoke and soot that acompanied travellers in the sub-surface sections and which swelled out into the short stretches in cutting. (Author's collection)

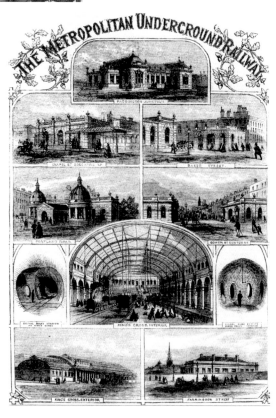

A handbill for a London &
North Western Railway
excursion to the Crystal
Palace, with a through train
rather than changing at
Euston, as would be the
case today. (Author's collection)

The early City & South London Railway carriages lacked windows and were known as
'padded cells'. (British Transport Commission)

The Bakerloo &
Waterloo Railway cut
right across London.
This shows a lady
passenger who has
paid 2d for her ticket
surrendering at the
barrier. (The Graphic)

The first railcar as such was introduced by the Great Western Railway between Slough and Windsor, but was not regarded as success by the company. The petrol engine is behind one of the driving cabs, further reducing the space for passengers. (Author's collection)

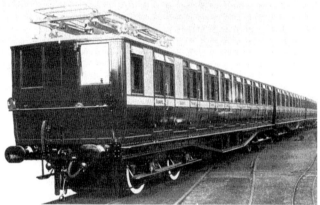

The London, Brighton & South Coast Railway favoured overhead electrification, as shown here, using the somewhat misleading term of 'elevated electric'. The overhead was replaced in the late 1920s by the Southern Railway's preferred third-rail. (Historic Model Railway Society)

The Metropolitan Railway used steam, even though much of its central London track was below street level. Here is an A-class locomotive. (Author's collection)

The famous B-type, the first mass-produced motor bus for London, is seen here at Victoria Station. There were also single-deck versions for routes through the Blackwall Tunnel. (British Transport Commission)

Even in 1926, before the mainline electrification started, the Southern Railway had all of the lines electrified, fast as well as slow, as can be seen here at Wimbledon. This provided flexibility in operations, and also reduced the cost of mainline electrification when this was taken to Alton and Portsmouth in 1937. (Historic Model Railway Society)

The man behind first
the London & South
Western electrification
and then the mainline
electrification of the
Southern Railway was
Sir Herbert Ashcombe
Walker, voted the most
outstanding
railwayman of all time.

Brighton was firmly in
the commuter belt by
the early twentieth
century, and
electrification made it
more attractive still,
helped by frequencies
that more than
doubled. (Author's
collection)

The image that so many people see of Waterloo if they arrive on foot is that of the grand entrance which accommodates war memorials to the fallen of the London & South Western Railway in the Great War, and of the Southern Railway in the Second World War. Were it not for the lines to Charing Cross on the viaduct, this splendid sight could be seen from the Thames and Waterloo Bridge. (Rupert Harding)

Initially, St Pancras did not have a massive commuter traffic, but this changed over the years, while today the station is ideal for the international commuter, with Eurostar trains direct to Paris and Brussels. (Rupert Harding)

Looking as if he was inspired by the great temple to steam that is St Pancras, the great poet Sir John Betjeman loved railways and old churches, so he doubtless saw a coming together of the two at the great London terminus. (Rupert Harding)

needs, although the bus operator could also seek support for its case from a local authority or a local employer who could also attend the hearing to support the bus or coach operator in his application.

To be fair, there was some need for legislation in the interests of the road transport industry and of its customers as much as anything else. Safety was one issue, with annual inspections of vehicles, and in the case of passenger vehicles the imposition of certain minimum standards through a certificate of fitness. Service reliability was another point, and bus and coach operators had to abide by the timetable attached to the road service licence for each route. Before the act, some operators had made a point of undercutting rival operators and forcing them out of business, after which fares were increased, so fares were also controlled, with operators having to seek permission to raise fares. All of this indicated some legislation was necessary to protect both the honest and reliable operator and the customer, but what emerged was little short of rationing. This was a period when the state started to assume more powers, and ironically it was in London, home of the 'City', the bastion of capitalism, where the process started.

Birth of London Transport

The main line railways retained their own lines within London when, on 1 July 1933, the London Passenger Transport Board came into existence under its own legislation promoted by the government earlier that year. Bus operators were not so fortunate, and many had to transfer depots, vehicles and routes to the new organisation, while those operating entirely within the 2,000 square mile area of the LTPB were taken over completely, including the municipal operators, of which the largest was the London County Council Tramways with 167 miles (269 kilometres) of route and 1,700 tramcars, by this time all electric. Despite an attempt to be left in private hands because of its largely rural routes, the Metropolitan was included in the new LPTB as it acquired most of the London underground network, including the District Line that used some of the Southern Railway's metals, while the Bakerloo and the District used those of the LMS to reach Watford and Barking respectively. The few exceptions to the take-over by London Transport were the Hammersmith & City Line operated jointly with the Great Western until it passed completely to London Transport in 1948, while the Southern Railway was able to hang on to the Waterloo & City Line, the 'Drain', until nationalisation, after which it remained with British Railways until 1994. It also seems strange that the lines of the North London Railway, at least those between Richmond and Broad Street, also remained in railway company hands, and only passed to London Transport's successor, Transport for London, in 2008.

Intended from the outset as an integrated road and rail transport organisation for London, the London Passenger Transport Area stretched out as far as Windsor, Guildford, Horsham, Gravesend, Tilbury, Hertford, Luton and Dunstable. The area did not tally with that of the London County Council or even the still wider area covered by the Metropolitan Police. Within this area, all suburban railway services were to be coordinated by a Standing Joint Committee consisting of four LPTB members and the four main line railway general managers, and all receipts from the area, less operating costs were to be apportioned between the LPTB and the railways. The apportioning was decided by the London Passenger Transport Arbitration Tribunal, which announced its findings on 11 June 1935. The Southern Railway's share of these receipts was fixed at 25½ per cent, a tribute to the traffic growth generated by its investment in suburban electrification, by this time completed. By contrast, the GWR's share, with the lowest suburban traffic of any of London's railways, was just 1.3 per cent. Naturally, the London Passenger Transport Board had the lion's share of the revenue pool, but even including its road transport operations, this amounted to 62 per cent, which seems low and puts the massive Southern contribution to London's transport into perspective. The London & North Eastern Railway, which its extensive network of suburban lines, mainly but not entirely from Liverpool Street, got 6 per cent, while the London Midland Scottish, with the North London Line and the London, Tilbury & Southern line, got 5.1 per cent.

Within the London Passenger Transport Area, no one could operate a bus service without the permission of the London Passenger Transport Board, or London Transport as it chose to call itself, so that a monopoly could perpetuate itself for all time. Even post-war when some local authorities attempted to operate services, London Transport simply asked them to pay for buses which it then operated. The LPTB also had the right to examine its own drivers, who were then not able to leave and work for another bus company without first taking a fresh driving test.

The influence of Yerkes and his successors on the London Underground ensured that there was a high degree of standardisation, with the main difference being between the sub-surface lines, known to London Transport for many years as 'surface' lines, and the deep level tubes. On the roads, however, there was little standardisation. The large fleets of the London General Omnibus Company and its subsidiaries, as such as East Surrey, were completely undermined by the host of different vehicles acquired from the municipalities and other companies, such as Thomas Tilling, taken over, and even more so by the large number of small independent operators, often with just a handful of vehicles, some very old, others very small. It was to take most of the period up to the outbreak of the Second World War for any real standardisation to be achieved, with the development of a substantial trolleybus fleet and the introduction of first the ST-class motor bus, based on the AEC Regent, then the STL, which was longer and had the staircase completely enclosed, and which was based on an improved AEC Regent.

London Transport did experiment, so there were unusual vehicles amongst its increasingly standardised buses. Between 1931 and 1937, AEC produced the 'Q', available as a single-deck bus or double-deck, with an engine mounted behind the front axle on the offside, so the door could be anywhere the operator specified and these vehicles were fully-fronted, that is they did not have the half-cab typical of buses of this period. Later, a rear-engined variant of the Leyland Cub single deck bus was produced, yet still with a half-cab and a streamlined bonnet where the engine should have been, and the larger Leyland TF-class, with an underfloor engine, and again a half cab.

Profitability

In addition to the ending of the levy on railway travel, the Guarantees and Loans Act 1934 was also intended to provide work, easing unemployment and lifting the country out of recession in what would today be regarded as an example of Keynesian economics and 'pump priming'. Here was yet another new incentive for the railways to modernise. In November 1935, the government agreed with the four main line railway companies to provide funds for major improvement schemes, at an interest rate of 2.5 per cent, lower than that generally available on the money markets at the time, through a Railway Finance Corporation, that would have its initial capital of £30m (£1,800 million today) guaranteed by the Treasury. Once again, the Southern, despite being by far the smallest of the railway companies, took an ambitious approach, with a loan of £6 million to fund further electrification and improvements at a number of stations, as well as construction of a new branch line to Chessington, mentioned later.

The failure of the railway companies to reach their standard revenues between the wars has already been mentioned. The reasons were varied, and included the recession that soon struck manufacturing industry within a few years of World War I ending, and although attention always focuses on the years of the great depression, British industry remained in recession for far longer. The country certainly was not helped by the General Strike of 1926 and the miner's lock-out that accompanied it and continued for long after the General Strike ended. The Great Western suffered a strike of its own at some depots in 1924. A consequence of the absence of mineworkers was that many markets for British coal, including export markets, were lost for good, resulting in lower traffic levels for the railways and for the ports, many of which were in railway ownership. The transport operators made much of the fact that volunteers from the population as a whole were quickly trained to take over jobs on the railways and the buses, but the General Strike itself did not last for long. It was violent at times, and in London a bus driven by a volunteer was stopped by protestors and set on fire.

A Railways Rates Tribunal existed to authorise any change in rates, although the railways, facing intense road competition, were free to charge 'exceptional rates' to retain traffic of as much as 40 per cent below the standard rate. They also tried to stimulate passenger traffic, or at least win some of this back from the coach operators, with the Southern, for example, introducing special 'summer fares' of a penny a mile. On London's buses, the fare of a penny per mile was also reintroduced, with the slogan, 'Mr Penny Mile is Back!'

Some idea of the discount afforded the purchasers of workmen's tickets can be gathered from that, even in 1947, the return workman's fare on the Waterloo & City Line, available to anyone travelling before 08.00 and which could be used on any return train, was just 3d, compared to a standard 3½ d single or 7d return.

Of course, there are those complete 'free market' supporters who would argue that transport shouldn't be regulated in this way. But the bus company or railway, or even the airline, is not like the butcher, baker or candlestick maker. As mentioned earlier, nothing is more perishable than the seat on any form of transport, for once it departs, if not sold it is lost forever.

If the railways couldn't defeat the road transport operators, then they could join them. They had for many years operated their own buses as feeders to their stations, but legislation in 1929 allowed them to operate other bus services or buy existing bus companies, but not within the London Passenger Transport Area once the LPTB came into existence. Later, they were to be allowed to buy road haulage companies and to operate air services as well.

Despite the effects of the Road Traffic Act 1930, the railways continued to suffer during the rest of the decade. In 1938, a 'Square Deal' campaign was launched to ease the restrictions under which they operated, but it received a poor press and aroused public hostility, the latter largely due to fears of increased fares and other charges. The road transport lobby that had done so well from the restrictions on the railways happily played on the fears of the public. Yet, a look at the results for the main railway companies in 1912 and for the big four during the mid to late 1930s tells its own story.

Taking the Southern Railway as an example, in 1912, the four companies that were to make up the Southern were mainly in profit, with the London & South Western paying a dividend of 5.62 per cent on its ordinary shares, while the London Brighton & South Coast paid 5 per cent, and of the two companies operated by the South Eastern & Chatham Managing Committee, the South Eastern paid 3.87 per cent leaving just the poor London Chatham & Dover to pay nothing. Yet, by 1935, after extensive investment in successful electrification schemes, the Southern Railway could only pay 4 per cent on its preference stock while the ordinary, or deferred, shares received nothing in 1935, while in 1936 the preference shares continued to attract 4 per cent and the ordinary stock received just 0.5 per cent. In 1937, the preference shares received 3 per cent and the ordinary 1.5 per cent, but this was a high point, because in 1938, although the preference shares received 4 per cent, once again the ordinary shares received nothing. Modernisation came at a high price if you were a holder of ordinary shares!

The Great Western Railway had also managed to pay 5.62 per cent in 1912, but the railway that gave the world what was for a short period the world's fastest scheduled daily service, *The Cheltenham Flyer*, could only pay 2.75 per cent by 1935, and this was maintained in 1936, and then actually rose to 3.5 per cent the following year before collapsing to 0.5 per cent in 1938. For the ordinary railway shareholder, a Post Office savings account must have seemed very attractive at times like this.

Of the companies that combined to form the London & North Eastern Railway, in 1912, the Great Eastern managed to pay 2.5 per cent and the Great Northern 4.37 per cent, with 6 per cent on the North Eastern, but the North British had struggled to pay 3 per cent on its preference stock and 1 per cent on its deferred stock, while the Great Central paid nothing. At least the latter's shareholders were prepared for what happened in the years 1935-38, when the LNER could not pay a dividend.

On the other side of the Pennines, of the companies that amalgamated to form the giant London Midland Scottish Railway, in 1912 the London & North Western paid a healthy 6.5 per cent, while the Midland, famous for the comfort of its trains, was not too well rewarded for its care with just 2.5 per cent on its preference stock and 3.87 per cent on its deferred stock. The LMS was renowned for its adoption of modern American management practices, and it also sorted out some of the sillier practices of its predecessor companies, amongst which the Midland, for example, had tended to build only smaller locomotives, so that double heading was frequently required, which, lacking the means of remote control usual on electric and diesel double or multiple-headed locomotives, also doubled labour costs and did not make the best use of coal. Despite this, the LMS failed to pay a dividend in 1935 and could only manage 1.25 per cent in 1936, and although this rose to 1.5 per cent in 1937, it disappeared once again in 1938!

It would be unfair to describe railway stock in 1938 as junk bonds, but it took an act of faith, even of blind optimism, for anyone to consider investing in the railways. The directors and managers of the grouped companies had maintained their railways to the best of their abilities, and had invested as heavily as they could, especially after the incentives of 1929 and later. This was most obvious on the Southern Railway, but the introduction of more powerful steam locomotives necessary for the longer distance services had taken second place to electrification. Even so, the Southern had tried its best to spread modernisation around its system. The Great Western as well had not simply been content to concentrate on its expresses, but had thought about the problems of rural branch lines with its diesel railcars. Given the picture of poor returns, one can have some sympathy for the other two companies, running a limited number of fine expresses but not doing much for the rural and suburban lines. The LMS did at least have a substantial number of fine mixed traffic locomotives, the handsome and rightly famous Stanier 4-6-0s, or 'Black Fives', that were to be largely copied by the post-war nationalised railway, and which were equally happy on the lighter expresses, suburban trains or on goods work.

The failure to rationalise

The railway companies had also been slow to rationalise, other than in their locomotive and carriage works, which many would suggest should have concentrated on overall and heavy maintenance and abandoned new construction in favour of using independent builders and competitive bidding. Only the Southern bought the products of independent builders to any great extent, although the GWR's diesel railcars were largely 'bought in'. There was also a very real reluctance to consider closing stations or branch lines.

Chapter 12

London's Transport

*See the 'world before your eyes' by the way which lies beneath
your feet – travel by Underground*

*'Take your partners for the next dance, please', but unlike Cinderella,
be sure to catch the Underground.*

Early LPTB advertisements for the Underground

Fond of advertising itself as 'London Transport at London's
Service', London Transport was a bi-modal road and rail monopoly
which also exercised control over the revenues of the mainline
railway companies. To its credit, for the first time, it gave London a highly
integrated public transport service, with a standardised fares structure,
albeit one based on railway costs rather than the much cheaper buses and
trams. The buses and underground trains it specified were for many years
if anything over-designed, but comfort, quality and durability was there
and London buses didn't rattle! On the downside, it was inflexible,
intolerant of anything that smacked of competition, bureaucratic and, of
course, the people it was meant to serve, the passengers, were at the mercy
of the trade unions representing its employees.

That London Transport was a complete monopoly and wielded
considerable authority far beyond the area of the London County Council
or that of the Metropolitan Police can be judged by the way it was treated
by legislation. In 1933, regulation of passenger transport extended to bus
and coach services. Each bus or coach route had to have a road service
licence, and after a period during which 'grandfather rights' enabled
existing operators to retain their services, new routes had to face scrutiny
by the traffic commissioners, and other interested parties could object,
including other bus operators or even the railways. London Transport was
exempt from this procedure, and other operators could not operate bus
services in its area without its permission, and those whose services crossed
into the LPTB area had to have a 'backing' licence.

The new London Passenger Transport Board eventually settled on the

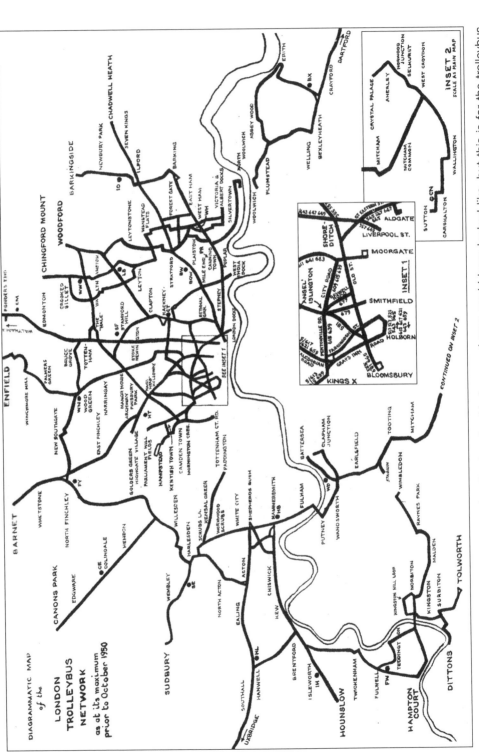

Without an electrician's inspiration, this is what the London Underground map could have looked like, but this is for the trolleybus

roundel with a bar through it as its logo, adopting a symbol used by the Underground companies from as early as 1909. Even so, some early advertisements show LPTB in a form of sloping figure of eight, with lines intended to demonstrate speed. Others show London Transport with a heraldic griffon placed between the two words.

In fact the roundel logo proved to be easily recognisable, memorable and flexible in use. It could be solid or open. A red roundel on a white background denoted a compulsory stop for buses, a green one a compulsory stop for Greenline coaches. A white roundel on a red background meant a request stop for buses, and a green background the same for coaches. On the underground, it could be used with the bar denoting the name of the line, or at stations the name of the station. Few trademarks have proved so durable, yet at the same time, adaptable to different circumstances. The name LONDON TRANSPORT was on the side of buses in gold letters, while on coaches the name was GREENLINE, but with London Transport in much smaller letters below.

Publicity

Despite the hardships of the Great Depression and the fact that, apart from the short-lived boom generated by the coronation of King George VI in 1937, traffic was down and remained so from 1919 to 1939, London Transport and the four grouped railway companies produced a steady flow of publicity material, much of it very high quality and fondly remembered. The LMS posters showing its workforce behind the scenes, getting locomotives ready in 'The Day Begins', or working on the line, were especially evocative, at least for railway enthusiasts. The Great Western actually thought of its passengers, and apart from posters, its promotion included a set of booklets and maps so that the traveller could learn more about the places through which the train passed.

For commuters, the Southern Railway had 'Live in Kent and be Content,' and 'Live in Surrey, Far from Worry,' to promote the ease of commuting on its newly-electrified lines. The alliteration of Kent/content and Surrey/worry had one drawback, there could be no such slogan for Sussex, for a long time commuter territory, but much more so once the Southern electrified the Brighton line. The Southern was never solely a commuter railway, and 'Sunny South Sam' was designed to draw holidaymakers to the south coast, but sadly the actor who posed as the railway guard in the campaign died shortly after it started and it never reached its full potential.

The railways did much of their own marketing and advertising

CREATOR OF THE FIRST INTEGRATED PUBLIC TRANSPORT SYSTEM:
Frank Pick, 1878-1941

After serving articles as a solicitor, Pick joined the North Eastern Railway in 1902, and became personal assistant to Sir George Gibb two years later. When Gibb moved to the Underground Electric Railways in 1906, Pick followed, and from 1909 was in charge of marketing. When the UER acquired the London General Omnibus Company in 1912, he became commercial manager for the entire group, often known as the 'Combine'. During the First World War, he was seconded to the Board of Trade, but returned to the UER in 1919 and was appointed managing director under Lord Ashfield in 1928. When the UER was absorbed into the new London Passenger Transport Board in 1933, he became vice-chairman, and took much of the credit for creating the world's largest integrated passenger transport system. He was also notable for his emphasis on good design, be it in marketing material, buildings or bus and trains.

During the Second World War, he became director-general of the Ministry of Information.

separately, but when offices were opened in Paris and New York to encourage visitors, they did so under the aegis of 'British Railways'. The term pre-dated nationalisation as it was also used from time to time on joint advertising for such services as luggage sent in advance, or to encourage dog owners to have their pet accompany them on journeys.

London Transport advertising was also good, and often event-based, which served the double purpose of alerting the race or theatre-going public to forthcoming attractions. Nevertheless, London Transport's biggest and most enduring contribution on the publicity front was the underground map, a schematic map which placed more attention on connections than on geographical accuracy, so that the stranger could get from A to C with a change at B with the minimum of confusion. Both these items survived the London Passenger Transport Board, the London Transport Executive and the London Transport Board, and are still used by Transport for London. The difficult task of creating a single entity out of the many bus and tram operators and of the underground fell to one man, Frank Pick, who also had a flare for publicity.

Rightly regarded as an outstanding example of twentieth century design, the London Underground map was designed by an unemployed electrical engineer, Harry Beck, in 1931. With a keen sense of humour, he once described the map as 'The Underground straight eight all-electric skit-set circuit diagram.' Apart from the River Thames, shown meandering through the map, and the position of the mainline stations on the underground network, the map showed no surface detail, and was regarded as being 'too revolutionary' by the Underground Group, but they soon changed their minds, and in 1933, a free pocket edition was issued for the first time. The map has withstood the test of time and the original eight lines have grown to fourteen. Harry Beck himself was in charge of the changes, until 1964. Today, the map is digitalised, which makes updating it easier. One cannot help but take the tube map as a quirk of fate. Who other than an electrical engineer would have thought of such a map, concentrating as it did on connections? That is not a criticism of the map; it is an appreciation as a modern-day commercial artist in one of the great design companies would be hard pressed to produce anything so clear, so easily understood, and so capable of standing changing times and changing fashions.

The new London Transport

The new London Transport soon set about extending its underground lines, eventually merging the City & South London and the Hampstead lines to make the new Northern Line, with a City branch and a West End branch, the only underground line to offer two routes through the centre in this way.

Not every underground railway passed in to its control. The Waterloo & City Line has already been mentioned, but another line that escaped the LPTB's clutches was the East London Railway, which did not pass into London Transport control until railway nationalisation in 1948, by which time the LTPB itself was no longer and London Transport had become the operating arm of the British Transport Commission's London Transport Executive. A compromise occurred on the Hammersmith & City Line, which the LPTB operated jointly with the Great Western Railway, while complete control passed to the London Transport Executive on mainline railway nationalisation in 1948.

In 1937, London Transport persuaded the Southern Railway to rename its terminus, St Paul's, to Blackfriars, so that the name could be used on the Central Line without causing confusion.

Even while the LPTB was in formation, the Piccadilly line was extended during 1932-33, running over line abandoned by the District to Hounslow and South Harrow, and over the Metropolitan Line to Upminster, using a new stretch of tube, while surface sections took it to

Southgate and Cockfosters, giving an Uxbridge to Cockfosters run of thirty-two miles. A short branch was provided from Holborn to Aldwych, which was closed in 1994. The Hounslow branch was extended in 1977 to London Heathrow Airport, the first deep level tube link to any airport in the world, and in 1986, a loop was added to serve Terminal 4.

In 1937, the Central London Railway was renamed the Central Line, having been completely modernised between 1935 and 1940 under the Treasury-sponsored New Works Programme. The original central third rail power supply was replaced by the LT standard third and fourth rail. Not all of the LPTB's ambitions could be completed in time. The extension of the Central Line to Loughton, Epping and Hainault opened between 1947 and 1949, when services from Liverpool Street to these towns ended, leaving the Central Line, so busy in the heart of London, the most rural of the deep level tube lines at its eastern end. Not all of the extension was on the surface, and it needed four miles of new tube tunnel before the former Great Eastern lines could be reached. A further extension to Ongar was electrified in 1957, but closed in 1994. To the west, what was by this time the Western Region of British Railways took the line to West Ruislip in 1948.

The Bakerloo had already extended itself to run over the London & North Western Railway's tracks to Watford as early as 1917. A plan to extend the line south to Camberwell was authorised in 1931, almost on the eve of the creation of the LPTB, reconsidered in 1949, but then abandoned. One extension that did take place was in 1939, when the line was used to reduce congestion on the inner section of the Metropolitan Line through a new tube link between Baker Street to Finchley Road so that Bakerloo trains could run to Stanmore.

The Metropolitan Railway, or Metropolitan Line as it became under LPTB control, had reached Uxbridge in 1904, Watford in 1925 and Stanmore in 1932. The extent of its rural lines, eventually reaching out to Chesham and Amersham, was used by the Metropolitan to argue against its incorporation into the LPTB, but without success. The New Works programme for the Metropolitan called for electrification to be extended to Amersham and the line between Harrow and Rickmansworth to be four-tracked, but while the plans were formulated in 1935, little happened before the Second World War, other than the extension of the Bakerloo trains to Stanmore over Metropolitan metals. Post-war, the national financial situation meant further delays. In some ways this was just as well. The line was becoming busier, and the original electrification plans involved using steam-hauled stock with slam door carriages and compartments converted to electric multiple units, using the same techniques that had served the Southern Railway and its predecessors so well. The implications of running such trains through the 'in town' section of the line, and the lack of emergency passage between the carriages when running underground meant that post-war such ideas had to be completely recast, and new rolling stock with sliding doors and 2+3 abreast seating was designed, known as the 'A' for Amersham stock.

The Bakerloo running over what had become London Midland Scottish Railway lines was as nothing to the status of the District Line, successor to the Metropolitan District Railway, which in 1933, had just 25 out of its 58¾ route miles over its own tracks.

Later renamed in 1937 as the Northern Line, the Edgware Highgate & Morden line, which had originated from the Hampstead Line and the City & South London Railway, benefited from a programme of works that eventually included new rolling stock in 1938, as well as extension of its network over London & North Eastern branches to High Barnet and East Finchley. Plans to extend the line beyond Edgware to Bushey Heath were dropped post-Second World War. When formed, the Northern included a Northern City section that was separate from the rest of its network, but transferred to British Railways in 1975. While less exotic than the Piccadilly, which served some of the most fashionable destinations, the Northern was no mean undertaking, and remains a vital link in the underground network. Until 1988 and the opening of the Channel Tunnel, the tunnel from East Finchley to Morden via Bank (the City branch of the Northern) was, at 17¼ miles, the longest continuous railway tunnel in the world, while the station platforms at Hampstead are the deepest on the London underground at 192 feet below ground level.

On the roads

As Appendix II shows, the LPTB absorbed a large number of road transport undertakings, of which many were operating trams and just one, the London United Tramways, was operating trolleybuses. There were many bus operators, including a number of small operators in the rural areas cast into the London Transport pot, but others were well established.

In contrast to the railways, most of which were in one large group, the 'Underground', and highly standardised within each railway or 'line', as they became under the LPTB, the bus and tram undertakings showed little standardisation. For the LPTB, the day of the tram was, if not over, then with a limited future. Much neglected and overlooked today, except in a

few countries such as Italy, the trolleybus offered most of the benefits of
the motor bus and many of those of the tram. Indeed, even in the early
1930s, the trolleybus was more reliable than the motor bus, while it was also
more flexible than the tram and installing a trolleybus route did not involve
digging up the roads. Oddly, the first LUT trolleybuses, which looked like
six-wheeled variants of the current motorbuses, even to having a half cab
whereas later versions were fully fronted, were slow, and the rapid
acceleration and good hill-climbing of later vehicles, which made them so
suitable for the hills of north London, was conspicuous by its absence. The
public nicknamed them 'diddlers', but whether this was a knock at the
acceleration, or lack of it, or the noise of the compressors, has been lost in
time.

In some cities, the trolleybus was seen as a cheap means of extending the
tram network, but in London, they were soon seen as replacements. The
new LPTB quickly decided to replace all trams in London with 'more
modern vehicles'. Conversion began in 1935 with trams in south-west,
west, north-west, north and east London being replaced by trolleybuses,
and rapid progress was made until 1940, when wartime shortages brought
the programme to an end, leaving the 'South London' trams and the
'Kingsway routes' 31, 33 and 35, as the only tram routes left operating to
survive the war.

Few seem to have mourned the passing of the trams. The often rough
ride and draughty interiors from having an open doorway at both ends,
meant that many found the trolleybus a big step forward in comfort, and it
was quiet.

The London bus scene was far from chaotic when the LPTB was
formed. There were indeed the 'pirate' bus operators who would move
onto another company's route and run one bus just before and another just
behind, known as a 'chaser', to catch the incumbent operator's passengers,
and offering lower fares. But for the most part, the LGOC and its
associates, of which Tilling had become one, saw cooperation as more
important than competition, giving the system stability. The LGOC route
numbering system was also used by its associates from before the First
World War, but an impetus to standardisation came with the London
Traffic Act of 1924, which imposed a route numbering scheme on all bus
operators in the central area, known as the Bassom Scheme, after the then
chief commissioner of the Metropolitan Police. The full length of a route
was allocated a number, whilst short workings used letter suffixes. There
was no great urgency on this matter and it was not until 1934 that the
LPTB overhauled the route numbering system, which had to take into

account country operations as well and the municipal tramways. The early system was:

Routes 1 to 199, London red double deck services;

200-290, London red single deck services;

290-299, central London night bus services;

300-399, London country or green bus services north of the River Thames;

400-499, London country or green bus services south of the River Thames;

500-699, trolley bus services.

Greenline coaches were given letters instead of numbers until after the Second World War when numbers in the 7XX series were allocated to these services, which continued to grow and later included a number of routes that did not cross the central area. Wartime staff shortages and the need to conserve fuel also saw many of the 2XX routes converted to double-deck whenever practical, so the 240 became double deck, but the 240A did not and essentially became a feeder into the 240, while the 210, with a low bridge, remained steadfastly single deck. Later, 'N' prefixes were introduced for night buses.

Chapter 13

Electrification and the Long Distance Commuter

*You... must learn what we are here for. It is not just to please the public
but to enable us to pay ordinary dividends each year and so be able to
raise capital for further electrification...I am happy to carry more people
for more money. I don't mind carrying fewer people for more money, but...
to carry more people for more money... that's the way to go bankrupt.*

Sir Herbert Walker, General Manager of the Southern Railway, 1923-1939,
to John Elliot, c.1930

Sometime, probably during the late 1920s, but certainly no later than
1930, Sir Herbert Walker opened a meeting with his officers with the
simple statement: 'Gentlemen, I have decided to electrify to Brighton.'
Many believe that Walker would have wanted an all-electric Southern
Railway, but, this seems unlikely given the infrequent nature of many of
the services in Devon and Cornwall as well as some of the lines on the Isle
of Wight, although a Solent tunnel from near Lymington to Yarmouth was
proposed. The LBSCR had ambitions to operate all of its passenger
services, and possibly goods as well, using its 'elevated electrics'.

There was also an incentive for further electrification. In his budget in
1929, the Chancellor of the Exchequer, the then Mr Winston Churchill,
announced the abolition of the Railway Passenger Duty that had first been
introduced in 1832, and by the late 1920s was levied on all passenger fares
above 1d (0.4p) per mile, on condition that the sum was capitalised and
used for railway modernisation. At the time, the Southern had enjoyed
some success in stimulating leisure traffic to the main resorts with its
special 'summer fares', offering third-class returns of 1d per mile. The
Southern Railway's share of the capitalised value of the duty was just over
£2 million, while the cost of electrifying the main line from Victoria and
London Bridge to Brighton and West Worthing was estimated to cost £2.7
million.

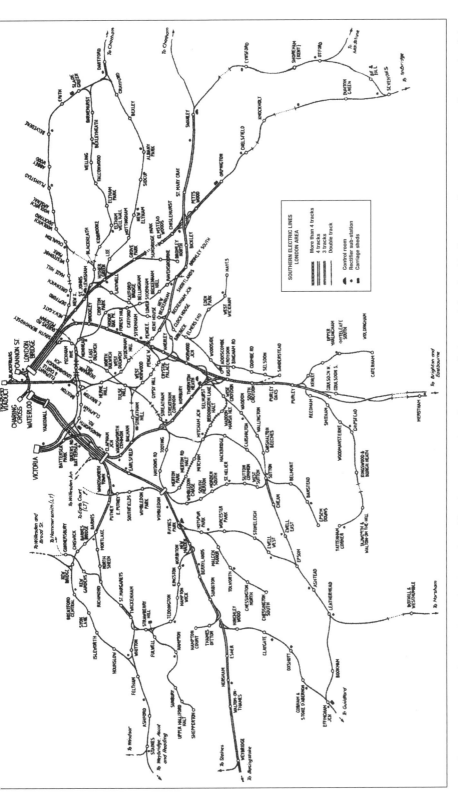

The Southern Railway's massive suburban electrification meant that there was little need for the Underground to penetrate too far south of the Thames. It continued to Portsmouth and all South Coast towns as far east as Hastings.

The plans were announced publicly at the Southern Railway AGM in 1930, when the shareholders were told that this first main line electrification scheme would use the same 660 volt dc system already in use, not least because it held the possibility of existing suburban stock being used on weekend excursion trains. Once again, the Southern planned a massive increase in frequency, more than doubling the existing service, and also promised to continue the practice of non-stop expresses between Brighton and London, including the use of Pullman carriages. Not only would electrification take place, but it would be accompanied by a further extension of colour light signalling, with the colour light signalling for the stretch of track between Coulsdon North and Brighton to be the longest in the country. As part of the scheme, at many stations, including Brighton, platforms would be lengthened, while Haywards Heath station would be rebuilt. A former railway rolling stock paint shop at Brighton would be converted to a twelve-road carriage cleaning and inspection shed, with a mechanical carriage washer in the sidings, and another carriage shed would be built at West Worthing. To justify the cost of electrification and the enhanced service, a 6 per cent increase in revenue would be required.

Work started in 1931 following on in true Southern fashion from the completion of the suburban network, and thirty-six out of the 162.5 track miles were completed by the end of the year. It was possible to operate an electric train service as far as Three Bridges and on the short piece of electrification between Redhill and Reigate, on the North Downs line to Guildford, on 17 July 1932, and although basically just hourly, this was a great help in training motormen and also provided experience for depot staff. Once again, the time taken to complete or commission work seems to have been incredibly short by modern standards. It took just fifteen minutes on a weekday morning, 6 October 1932, to commission the colour light signalling from Balcombe Tunnel Junction to Copyhold Junction. At Brighton, it took just five hours early on Sunday, 16 October, to commission a new signal cabin that replaced six manual boxes and this despite the work taking place during heavy rain.

Trial trains were running between London and Brighton from 2 November 1932, and the an official inauguration took place on 30 December 1932, when the Lord Mayor and sheriffs of London, the board of the Southern Railway and its senior officers, all travelled to West Worthing on one of the new standard sets that included a Pullman car, to meet the Mayor of Worthing, and then on back to Brighton to meet that town's Mayor, before the entire party moved off to luncheon at the Royal Pavilion.

Provision of rolling stock was very lavish, and all of it was new. Basically, the new electric multiple units included three five carriage Pullman sets, the first electric multiple-unit Pullmans in the world, six carriage corridor sets with one Pullman car amongst its ordinary carriages, and a variant of this with additional first-class accommodation for services to London Bridge, used on the fast and semi-fast services. There were also four carriage compartment sets in which one carriage had a side corridor and lavatories, and these were used on the stopping trains. Off-peak, six trains an hour were provided, four from Victoria, including one for West Worthing, and two from London Bridge. The non-stop service to Brighton, advertised as 'on the hour, in the hour, every hour', showed little improvement over steam timings, although the working timetable was for fifty-eight minutes to ensure a punctual arrival. The other trains, advertised as 'six trains per hour all day – comfort and frequency – you won't need a timetable', were an improvement, with 'semi-fasts' taking seventy-four minutes to Brighton and even stopping trains, just ninety-eight minutes, despite lingering at Redhill to detach a portion for Reigate. Contemporary advertisements show a man waiting for his girlfriend, saying that he would 'wait for just six more trains'. Brighton was already part of the London commuter belt, so peak services had to be considerably augmented, with five fast trains between 17.00 and 18.30, four of them running non-stop and one making just three stops. The only stock that was not new was for the Brighton-West Worthing local service, using three-car suburban stock from the Western Section. These ran every fifteen minutes, with alternate trains missing the halts. There was one closure, with the halt at Bungalow Town between Brighton and Worthing being closed on the day that electric services started – but it was not to be closed for long as it was also convenient for Shoreham Airport (now known as Brighton Airport) and when it re-opened it was as Shoreham Airport Halt.

A new system of headcodes was introduced for the Brighton electrification, with even numbers used for trains running between Brighton and Victoria, and odd numbers for trains to and from London Bridge.

The first month of operations showed an immediate jump in traffic, with revenue up 5 per cent, and at holiday periods, traffic grew even more, with 78 per cent more tickets sold over the Easter Holidays, while on Easter Monday, passenger numbers rose by 127 per cent, so that on that day, between 18.00 and 22.00, no less than twenty-eight trains left Brighton for London, most of them fast.

This was success on a grand scale. The interesting point was, however, that travel by express motor coach between London and Brighton also increased.

Anxious to make the best use of the investment in the Brighton line, it was decided to extend electrification to Eastbourne and Hastings via the coastal route, rather than taking the direct route to Hastings through Sevenoaks and Tonbridge. This was because the Southern was pressing ahead with electrification at a time when the British economy was still shaky, and in addition to feeding off the Brighton electrification, the chosen route to Hastings also enabled Lewes, Eastbourne and Bexhill to be served. The direct route to Hastings would have been electrified had not the Second World War and nationalisation intervened, something borne out by both a later Southern Railway announcement on electrification and by the extension of electrification from Orpington to Sevenoaks.

The short section of track between Bickley Junction and St Mary Cray was opened to electric trains on 1 May 1934, while electric services from Sevenoaks via both Swanley Junction and Orpington started on 6 January 1935. Again, the standard twenty-minute frequency in peak hours, half-hourly off-peak was adopted, with trains from Charing Cross, Cannon Street and Holborn Viaduct. On eight coach trains, the three leading carriages only ran beyond Orpington or Swanley Junction. This was an investment in the future, calculating that rapid growth in residential areas would soon fill the then empty rural spaces beyond Orpington. As before, the Southern's confidence was to prove to be justified, and the company helped with its advertising campaign with the slogan 'Live in Kent and be Content'.

The Eastbourne and Hastings electrification also included the line from Haywards Heath to Horsted Keynes, and from Lewes to Seaford, and some additional work in the London area, including extra sidings at New Cross Gate. While incidental works were not numerous, a tunnel at the London end of Lewes station had to have one of its curves eased to allow modern rolling stock to use it and an overbridge at the station rebuilt so that the platforms could be lengthened, while platforms were also lengthened at Eastbourne. Contrary to popular opinion, lengthening trains is not an easy or inexpensive option. There was also some station rebuilding, including elevating the halt at Cooden to station status as Cooden Beach, while no less than ten stations had electric lighting installed for the first time. A new carriage shed with four roads was built at Ore. One unusual aspect of the preliminary work was the replacement of track re-laid with steel sleepers with wooden sleepers, essential for safety with electrification.

The formal opening took place on 4 July 1935, once again with the Lord

Mayor and Sheriffs of London accompanied by the usual hosts travelling to meet the mayors of Eastbourne, Bexhill and Hastings. Services actually started on 7 July. While the new electric multiple units ordered for the Eastbourne and Hastings electrification lacked the Pullman car, which was replaced by a first-class coach with a pantry, Brighton sets with single Pullman cars operated as far as Eastbourne with many of the newer sets relieving them on the Brighton line, suggesting that the original provision of Pullman carriages was far too generous even for the Brighton line. The best trains took just eighty minutes to reach Eastbourne, and this was cut to seventy-nine minutes by 1939, but post-nationalisation it stretched to eighty-one minutes and then eighty-five.

As with the original Brighton and West Worthing electrification, a much improved coastal service was introduced, with trains running every half hour from Brighton to Seaford and every half hour to Eastbourne, with both these services serving passengers travelling between Brighton and Lewes. However, all was not well, for despite the frequency of services being more than doubled, passengers east of Eastbourne took exception to trains running into and out of that station instead of dividing at Polegate, as had been the practice during steam working.

Meanwhile, there had been another development on the Brighton Line. The opening of what was billed as the 'largest indoor swimming pool in the world', at Brighton, on 29 June 1934, was taken as an opportunity to rename the *Southern Belle* as the *Brighton Belle* by the Mayor of Brighton when the train arrived at noon.

The Southern's confidence in electrification was soon justified. At the AGM in February 1936, Mr R Holland-Martin, the chairman, was able to announce that revenue on the Sevenoaks electrification had risen by 41 per cent, almost 50 per cent more than that estimated to cover the costs of the work, while the Eastbourne and Hastings schemes had seen revenue rise by 16 per cent, more than twelve times the amount needed to cover the costs. It is clear from his statement that in addition to meeting interest on the capital costs, in many cases costs had also risen with electrification because of the enhanced train services provided, although electric trains needed a minimum crew of just two compared with the three of a steam train.

There was yet another new incentive for the railways to modernise. The previous November, the Government had agreed with the four main line railway companies to provide funds for major improvement schemes at an interest rate of 2.5 per cent, lower than that generally available on the money markets at the time, through a Railway Finance Corporation, that would have its initial capital of £30m guaranteed by the Treasury. The

Southern, despite its being the smallest of the railway companies, decided to take a loan of £6 million to fund further electrification and improvements at a number of stations, as well as a new line from Motspur Park to Chessington South. The new electrification schemes were to include both routes to Portsmouth, the direct line via Guildford and the old LBSCR line through Horsham and Arundel, as well as the Thames Valley line between Staines and Reading, and in Kent, there would be additional electrification between Swanley Junction to Gillingham and Gravesend to Maidstone, as well as Sevenoaks to Hastings, but the last-mentioned was delayed by the Second World War and nationalisation, and indeed, only barely managed to electrify a short time before the end of the twentieth century, and then on a cheapened basis with stretches of single track.

New lines

Another project that had been delayed, although one suspects not so much by the First World War as by uncertainty and the sometimes slow expansion of the underground system, was a line between Wimbledon and Sutton. This had been authorised in 1910 for the Metropolitan District Railway, with Wimbledon as the southernmost of the three branches of the District. As originally conceived, the line would have been a continuation of the District. The project was revived in 1923 because the Southern was anxious about further extensions of the City & South London tube beyond Morden, and it was agreed that the tube would not be extended and that the Southern would build the new line. Work started in 1927, with opening as far as South Merton on 6 July 1929 and at Sutton on 5 January 1930, providing a convenient link between the London Section and Central Section. Six new stations were provided on the line, including one at St Helier where the London County Council was building a vast new housing estate for 10,000 people, and this was the only station to have a goods yard, doubtless for household coal traffic. Electrified from the outset, the line cost £1 million and required a high embankment and twenty-four bridges to carry it over the many roads in the area. The double track ended on the opposite side of Wimbledon from the District platforms, and instead of connecting with the underground system linked with a line originally worked jointly by the LSWR and LBSCR to Streatham Junction, and services operated over the line between Holborn Viaduct and West Croydon.

   An ambitious scheme to create a new seaside resort and dormitory town at Alhallows on the North Kent coast, across the Thames Estuary from

Southend-on-Sea caused the Southern to build a single track 1¾ mile branch line off its Gravesend-Port Victoria line. After special excursions, on 14 May 1932, the line opened on 16 May. It was steam-worked from the outset, with a regular service to and from Gravesend, but with a few peak period trains to and from London. It was not electrified when the third rail was extended east from Gravesend in 1939.

The spread of the London suburbs between the wars, with three bedroom semi-detached houses being built by speculative builders for as little as £200, was a driving force in the extension of the Southern's network. One area enjoying such development was Chessington in Surrey, and the Southern decided to build a 4¼ mile branch off the line from Raynes Park to Epsom at Motspur Park. The new line was mainly either in cutting or on embankment as the countryside was undulating, while the heavy clay subsoil also required the extensive use of dry filling material, mainly taken from London slum clearance. The terminus, Chessington South, was in cutting and had a goods yard as well as a number of unusual features, such as having an island platform, possibly because the original plan was that the line should continue to Leatherhead. Electrified from the outset, the line opened as far as Tolworth on 29 May 1938, and to Chessington South on 28 May 1939. A major traffic generator for the line was Chessington Zoo, providing a useful two-way traffic flow on weekdays, and keeping the line busy on Sundays and holidays.

Some of the new lines reflected the way in which the railway had grown. At Ramsgate, the SER and LCDR had separate termini, and the SECR had other priorities when it took over management from its two cash-strapped predecessors in 1899. It was left to the Southern to rationalise the situation, building a new by-pass line 1½ miles long between St Lawrence on the former SER line and just south of Broadstairs on the former LCDR route, with two stations on the new line, one being a single new Ramsgate station and the other at Dumpton Park. The two termini were closed, as was the SER Ramsgate-Margate line, made redundant by the new line and the station at Margate Sands. The new line and its stations opened on 2 July 1926.

The SECR had achieved some connections between its former routes, and the Southern made further improvements with two short curves at Lewisham, opened on 7 July 1929. The first curve assisted the progress of goods trains for Hither Green marshalling yard from the LMS and LNER, while the second put Lewisham Junction station (later renamed Lewisham) on a loop off the main line between St Johns and Hither Green, allowing more suburban services to be routed through the station.

At the time of the Chessington branch being constructed, the Southern had already started work on the first of the two Portsmouth electrification schemes, the Portsmouth Direct via Guildford, and in this case known to the Southern as the 'Portsmouth No1 Electrification Scheme'. The Guildford New Line had already been electrified, but could not be used by the new scheme which had of necessity to use the main line, requiring electrification from a point just south-west of Surbiton to Portsmouth Harbour, the longest main line electrification scheme at that time, a distance of more than sixty route miles. As with the Brighton and Eastbourne schemes, the Portsmouth No 1 would include a number of other schemes, including electrification from Woking through Aldershot to Alton, in itself hardly a minor work, and from Weybridge to Staines. All in all, this required a track mileage of 242 miles and was estimated to cost £3 million.

The Portsmouth Direct required very extensive incidental works, including rebuilding the station at Woking and extending its four through platforms to 820 ft each, but while the stations at Guildford and Haslemere also received platform lengthening, sadly neither was rebuilt and for many years the former was left with very low platform faces so that passengers almost had to climb up into the train. Havant was also rebuilt, but with the down platform served by a loop off the running line, and with a bay for the short Hayling Island branch, which was not to be electrified, suggesting that even the optimistic Southern had some doubts over the long term future for this short branch with its highly seasonal traffic. There was also platform lengthening at the high level station at Portsmouth & Southsea, as the town station was now called. The opportunity was taken to extend colour light signalling. The goods yard at Portsmouth was moved, providing a relief line between Portsmouth & Southsea and the depot at Fratton, while new carriage sheds were built at Wimbledon, Fratton and Farnham, with carriage washers at the first two.

In late 1936, trial trains were operating north of Woking and between Weybridge and Virginia Water, and on 3 January 1937, electric services were introduced between Staines and Weybridge, while electric trains were also operated from Waterloo to Guildford and Farnham but using steam timings, again to help train operating staff. The trial trains were able to operate into Portsmouth Harbour from 11 April, and a limited number of weekend departures were operated by electric trains from 29 May. Finally, the new electric train service from Waterloo to Portsmouth Harbour and Alton was introduced on 4 July 1937, with the first train having the coat of arms of Portsmouth painted on its front corridor connection. This, of course, was the most obvious difference between the new Portsmouth rolling stock and that prepared for the Brighton and Eastbourne lines, the corridor connections through the driving cabs of the electric multiple units meant that complete access could be had throughout the train, and this may also have been a factor in using four car rather than the less flexible six-car multiple units.

The citizens of Portsmouth must have been regarded as being less well-heeled than their Sussex counterparts, because a restaurant car was provided rather than the Pullmans of the lines to the Sussex Coast towns, probably because Portsmouth was not a commuter city at the time, as the steam expresses between Portsmouth and Waterloo had taken two hours, and there had been just four daily. In fact, Pullman services are only viable on lines that have few stops, so that there is time for a full meal to be served, and yet are short enough to allow just one sitting, otherwise a restaurant car service with two sittings is more likely to be viable.

The fast trains on the Portsmouth routes normally ran into the Harbour station, but the inaugural train terminated at Portsmouth & Southsea Low Level for the necessary civic niceties to be observed.

The Alton line stock, also used for the Portsmouth stopping trains, consisted of two car units without corridor connections and with only one carriage having a corridor.

The new service consisted of an hourly fast train stopping at Guildford, Haslemere and Portsmouth & Southsea, although later many trains stopped at either Havant or Woking, as did many peak period extras, with a half-hourly stopping train that ran fast to Surbiton and divided into Portsmouth & Southsea and Alton portions at Woking.

The service was accelerated, with the fast trains taking ninety-five minutes compared to the two hours of the steam trains, the difference in performance compared to the Brighton fasts being partly accounted for by the number of stops and also by the steep gradients on the line which were of little consequence to the electric trains. The Portsmouth direct had not enjoyed a particularly good service before electrification, but electrification meant that on a summer Saturday there were four fast trains every hour.

In retrospect, it seems strange that such a major city as Portsmouth should have suffered such a poor service for so long, as the largest city on the South Coast with a resort at Southsea, the extensive Royal Dockyard and many other naval facilities in and around the town, while it was the quickest route for passengers travelling to Gosport and even Fareham, using the steam launches across the harbour. It was the main port for travellers taking a ferry to the Isle of Wight, with those from Portsmouth to Ryde having the advantage that it was also the shortest and quickest route to the island's main resorts at Ryde, Sandown, Shanklin and Ventnor. This history of neglect ended in July 1937, and was put to rest completely the following year with the 'Portsmouth No 2 Electrification Scheme' taking the old LBSCR line through Horsham, Arundel and Chichester.

The decision to electrify railways has not always been universally popular, despite the benefits which have led to the term 'sparks effect' being applied to the traffic growth generated by electrification, or even, in some cases, the mere announcement of plans to electrify a line. Landowners and farmers in West Sussex objected strongly to the Portsmouth No 2 Electrification Scheme, concerned about the dangers to persons and livestock. A deputation went to meet the Southern directors, and questions were even raised in the House of Commons. Suggestions were made that the third rail should be boxed in, which was quite impractical, or that the current should only be on when a train was about to pass, which was almost as bad, or that certain sections of line should have overhead conductor wires. The Southern's management pointed out that adequate fencing was always used, and that the only people at risk were those who trespassed on the line.

Work on this scheme required 165 track miles of electrification and was far advanced when the Portsmouth Direct electrification was inaugurated. Incidental works were again considerable, with additional sidings electrified at New Cross Gate and carriage sheds erected at Streatham Hill with a carriage washer, and the Slade green workshops were extended, while a new carriage shed was built at Littlehampton. Almost inevitably, platform lengthening was necessary at Sutton, Dorking North, where the down bay became a loop, Pulborough, Arundel, Littlehampton and Chichester, Barnham and Bognor Regis, as well as to a lesser extent at many of the small halts along the coastal stretch of this route. There was a further extension of colour light signalling. One of the most costly items was the rebuilding of the bridge over the River Arun at Ford in Sussex, which had originally been built with lifting spans to allow ships to pass under, although this had only been used rarely, yet which also needed Parliamentary approval. The line had to be closed for the weekend of 23-25 April 1938 to enable the new spans to be lifted into position. An electricity sub-station at South Stoke, near Arundel, had to be built on 50ft concrete piles sunk into the Arun Marshes, so that it could remain above flood level.

Trial trains started to run in May 1938, and in June there were a number of specials run between London Bridge and Bognor Regis. The new services started on 3 July 1938, using further examples of the rolling stock built for the original Portsmouth electrification, plus a variation on these with a buffet car manned initially by the Pullman Car Company, and painted in a new lighter shade of green. In addition, the service was diverted from London Bridge to Victoria, with London Bridge being used only for rush hour extras.

The service was less frequent than on the Brighton and Portsmouth lines, with an hourly departure from Victoria with the front section for Portsmouth Harbour and the rear for Bognor Regis with the buffet car. Trains were initially divided at Barnham, but over the years, this varied, and sometimes the trains were divided at Arundel. Journey time to Portsmouth Harbour was 2 hour 12 minutes, and to Bognor, 1 hour 42 minutes. A new coastal electric service was introduced at the same time with two trains an hour between Brighton and Portsmouth and one an hour from Brighton to Littlehampton and Bognor, and this was amalgamated with the existing West Worthing service so that there were now six trains an hour running west from Brighton, with three of them terminating at West Worthing. In addition, the Victoria-West Worthing service was extended to Littlehampton. The extra services were slightly less than on previous electrification schemes, at around 95 per cent, but revenue still rose by 13 per cent in the first six months of operation.

A far smaller scheme was involved with the electrification of the line to Reading, since much of the route had already been covered by earlier schemes, so that just eighty-eight track miles were involved. In a sense, while the actual electrification to Reading itself was new, those from Ascot to Ash Vale and Aldershot and Guildford were infilling between existing schemes. Although station platforms were lengthened at a number of stations, the new length was just 540ft rather than the 820ft favoured on the main lines. Trial trains were operated from 30 October 1938, with a formal opening on 30 December, with the new services introduced on 1 January 1939. The new service was not strictly suburban, but the pattern of services reflected suburban practice, possibly in order to find paths through such congested spots as Richmond, with a peak period service of every twenty minutes and half-hourly off-peak. Trains usually ran fast between Waterloo and Staines, and divided at Ascot with the front section continuing to Reading and the rear to Guildford via Camberley and Aldershot, where the unit had to reverse. The overall journey time to Reading was seventy-five minutes, somewhat slower than on the GWR, but here the justification for electrification was the number of intermediate commuter or dormitory towns along the Thames Valley. The increase in frequencies was around 85 per cent.

The final electrification scheme, again an extension of existing schemes, before the outbreak of the Second World War was to Gillingham and Maidstone. This was slightly more extensive than the Thames Valley route at 117 track miles. Incidental works were extremely heavy, with many clearances having to be eased to allow 9ft-wide carriages, with platform extensions at Holborn Viaduct and additional roads electrified at Cannon Street, while a new station was needed at Swanley where the Gillingham and Maidstone East lines divided. A carriage shed was erected at Gillingham with a carriage washer. In some senses, this extension made far less sense than pressing ahead with the Sevenoaks to Hastings scheme would have done, since the route was still to carry many steam-hauled trains and the role of the electric trains was seen mainly as to collect traffic from intermediate stations. The line also carried a considerable volume, at least by Southern Railway standards, of goods trains, which were still worked by steam.

An oddity was the construction of platforms for a station at Lullingstone, where a site for a proposed new airport for London had been identified, but this was never built, probably due to the outbreak of the Second World War, and the platforms were later removed.

Trial running commenced in May 1939, and there was an official opening on 30 June, when the directors and senior officers of the Southern Railway travelled from Charing Cross to meet the mayors of Maidstone, Chatham and Gillingham. The new service was introduced on 2 July 1939. There was an hourly service from Victoria, stopping only at Bromley South and at Swanley, where the trains would divide, with the front portion running fast to Otford and then all stations to Maidstone East, while the rear portion continued all stations to Gillingham. Timings were sixty-five minutes to Maidstone East, sixty-three minutes to Gillingham. There were additional trains during peak periods to and from Holborn Viaduct. Now that the electric network had become so extensive, new opportunities for electric trains were opened up, and it was possible to operate special summer excursion trains from Gillingham to Portsmouth via London Bridge, Epsom, Effingham Junction and Guildford.

This marked the end of one of the most ambitious electrification schemes ever, and amongst the most extensive at the time, giving the Southern the world's largest suburban electric railway network. The increase in frequencies that accompanied electrification is almost beyond belief. At Waterloo, for example, off-peak services had gone from just two main line departures an hour in the steam era to twenty-one, and during the peak from four to twenty-nine, while on Sundays they had gone from one to eighteen. On the busy Central Section at Victoria, off-peak departures had gone from one an hour hauled by steam to eighteen, and in the peak from two to twenty-eight.

The annual report and accounts for the Southern Railway for 1938 provided some interesting information on the running of a railway. During that year, 46.7 million miles had been worked by steam at a total cost of £3,079,000, while 37.47 million miles had been worked by electric at a total cost of £1,642,000. Wages for the steam mileage amounted to £1,668,000, but for the electric mileage were just £327,000. Electricity itself was expensive, costing £1,190,000 against £1,295,000 for coal and water, but obviously this was more than offset by greater labour productivity. The volume of stores used was also less for the electric trains, at £10,000 against £60,000 for steam, but this may have been affected by the fact that the electric trains were on average much newer. The high volume of shunting movements for steam trains has already been mentioned, but for the electric trains, only 123,000 miles out of more than 37 million were due to empty working or shunting.

The Southern had taken the few isolated electric services of the LSWR and LBSCR and created a network of 1,759 track miles, with 3,040 motor, trailer, restaurant and Pullman cars on its electric trains, with a total of 176,905 seats, against 3,618 steam passenger carriages with a total of 185,339 seats.

The 'Jazz Service'

Although competition from the expanding London Underground and the electric trams meant that electrification was considered as early as 1903 for services from Liverpool Street, which had passed from the Great Eastern Railway to the London & North Eastern Railway on grouping, and parliamentary approval obtained, nothing was done. Even without the 'sparks effect', daily passenger numbers rose from around 200,000 in 1912 to 229,073 in 1921, but just fourteen trains were added to the timetable. The cost of electrification for the Liverpool Street suburban services was enormous, however, estimated in 1919 at £3.5 million (equivalent to more than £70 million today), with little prospect of achieving a worthwhile return. The alternative, a stop-gap measure, costing £80,000, was to change the layout of the approaches, the station arrangements and signalling, so that steam trains could continue to operate, but at the maximum efficiency.

The new service was officially described as the 'Intensive Service', but was named the 'Jazz Service' by one evening newspaper, partly because jazz music was the rage at then time and also because to speed loading, second-class carriages had a yellow line painted above the windows, and first-class had blue lines, while third remained unmarked. Sixteen-carriage trains of four-wheeled carriages operated with twenty-four per hour at peak periods on just one line between Liverpool Street and Bethnal Green, still using manual signalling and 0-6-0 tank locomotives that had first appeared in 1886. Trains spent just four minutes in a platform, while platforms 1 to 4 had their own engine docks and layouts that enabled locomotives to be shunted without going beyond platform limits. At peak periods, trains started every two minutes in sequence from platforms 4 to 1, followed by a four minute gap for arrivals.

A miners' strike in 1921 meant that the intensive service had to be suspended to save coal, and again during the General Strike and prolonged miners' lock-out of 1926. Nevertheless, the pressure began to ease not just because of the additional trains but because commuters were moving further out into the country. The LNER's chief engineer, Sir Nigel Gresley, improved the standard of the elderly four-wheel rolling stock by producing five-car articulated units with a much improved ride. But, traffic continued to fall, with the daily number of passengers peaking at 244,000 in 1923, but dropping to 209,000 in 1938, and eventually to 171,000 in 1959. Despite much ribbon development along the line from Liverpool Street to Southend, the stimulus of electrification was not there and anyone who had decided to live in suburbia would have chosen a town on the Southern over the LNER. No doubt the fall in passenger numbers would have been even more dramatic had the extension eastwards of the Central Line been opened before the outbreak of the Second World War.

Chapter 14

The Second World War

We may need you to get the children away to safety.
Ernest Brown, Minister of Labour, to leaders of the Amalgamated Society of
Locomotive Engineers & Firemen, August 1939

For the passenger, used to steadily improving services on the main lines, and some of the branch lines as well, the outbreak of the Second World War came as a nasty shock. Together with the blackout, cuts in railway services were amongst the earliest indications that life had changed for the worse. In a period when car ownership was the exception rather than the rule, petrol rationing affected relatively few, and food rationing was some months away. The four days on the eve of war breaking out that saw the evacuation trains run and during which off-peak services were cut to the minimum were bad enough, but although normal services were restored afterwards, this was not for long.

Many differences arose in wartime railway operation when comparing the two world wars. The most obvious, especially when viewed in retrospect, were the almost complete lack of amenities such as sleeping cars and restaurant cars on Second World War trains, while these facilities were reduced but never abandoned completely during the First World War. First-class disappeared from London suburban journeys during the Second World War, but did not during the earlier conflict.

Perhaps more important, there was another difference between the two conflicts that did not appear in the timetables, but became apparent as the war dragged on. During the First World War, railway travel had been the safest mode of transport; during the Second World War, it became the most dangerous as the men, fuel and materials being moved by the railways made them prime targets. It was not necessary either for a railway line to be bombed, as an enterprising fighter pilot could be just as effective in putting a steam locomotive out of service as a bomber crew, with the difference that the former was in and out quickly, away before anti-aircraft gunners could get into their stride. It wasn't necessary to blow the wheels off a steam locomotive or put it into the middle of a large crater as a boiler riddled with machine gun bullets, or even better, blasted apart by cannon shell, was of no use and would take some considerable time to repair, requiring highly skilled manpower and scarce raw materials, including non-ferrous metals. In some cases, as with a branch line train near Guildford, the fighter pilot strafed the carriages, killing and wounding passengers.

Keeping the railway running was to be another problem, but one common to both wars. Men who were experienced and highly skilled could expect to be mobilised if they were reservists or called up, despite much railway work being a reserved occupation, or might already have volunteered. Once again there was the prospect of locomotives and other rolling stock being requisitioned by the military, often for use abroad. Worse still, the railway workshops were forced to devote much of their capacity to war production, including even guns, tanks and landing craft, rather than keeping the railway running. The result was that, increasingly, the railways began to assume a battered, war-weary and unappealing appearance. Yet, traffic continued to grow, much of it military. The civilian population also made increasing demands on the railways, with many more people in work and often working well away from home, even if everything was done to discourage unnecessary travel, and, understandably, people still tried to take holidays. The virtual loss of the North Sea for the movement of materials, and especially coal, meant that this traffic had to be transferred to the already overstretched railways.

Heavy use of the railways in wartime was understandable, neglect wasn't. The Germans realised, until everything began to fall apart in 1944, that good railway maintenance was a vital part of the war effort. When they realised that the Bielefeld viaduct was a high priority British war target, and only survived because of the difficulty of hitting it, they built a camouflaged double-track diversionary route which ran down and up into the valley from both sides. By the time a bomb had been developed that didn't need to hit the viaduct, but instead undermined it and brought it toppling down, the diversionary route was well established and railway traffic was able to continue as before.

Reductions and restrictions

Wartime meant that the railways had to economise in the provision of their services, saving fuel and making locomotive power and rolling stock available for the many specials required by the armed forces. The cuts went far beyond the railways and affected ferry services, which were very badly disrupted as ships were taken over by the Ministry of Transport, with many needed to help move the British Expeditionary Force (BEF) to

France and then to keep it supplied. Others took on roles such as hospital ships or even minesweeping.

There had been much rehearsal of wartime operating conditions on the railways over the previous year or so. Railwaymen had practised working in black out conditions, which meant that no lights could be shown externally, with all windows screened, while station platforms could only be lit by blue lights or, as there were still many lit by gas, specially shaded gas lamps, and drivers and motormen had to pull up their trains beside oil lamps placed on the platform as markers. Steam locomotives had canvas draped between the engine cab and tender to hide the light of their fires, while the side windows that had appeared on the more modern locomotives were blanked out.

Despite the prospect of war, the railway unions were threatening strike action in August 1939. Negotiations between the companies and the unions had broken down when the government intervened. 'We may need you to get the children away to safety', warned Ernest Brown, Minister of Labour, playing his only trump card.

For the traveller, amongst the changes was that the blackout acted as a spur to extending loudspeaker announcements to stations, and while initially station name signs were no longer lit, those under station canopies were allowed to be illuminated later provided that they were swung round at right angles to the platform. Those stations that had had their names painted on the canopies to help airmen with their navigation had them blanked out. A final safety measure at stations was the removal of glass from roofs and canopies, essential since even a small bomb could create so many shards of broken glass as to be an effective anti-personnel weapon.

Initially, excursion and cheap day tickets were withdrawn, but day tickets were reintroduced on 9 October 1939, although with tighter conditions that meant that they were not available before 10.00 and could not be used on trains departing from London between 16.00 and 19.00 Monday to Friday.

After the evacuation was over, services returned to normal only briefly, for on 11 September, government-inspired cuts were imposed, inflicting hardship on passengers as normal commuter traffic remained virtually at pre-war levels. Some large companies had dispersed, especially those with strategic importance such as the railways themselves and the shipping lines, which moved their head offices, but it was not possible for everyone to do so. The usual twenty minute suburban frequencies were cut to half-hourly, while off-peak and Sunday services became hourly. Some suburban services were cancelled completely. Not only did this lead to overcrowding with many passengers left behind, it also meant that station dwell times were extended as passengers struggled to alight from trains or climb aboard. Journey times were further extended with a national railway speed limit of 45 mph. After the uproar that followed, normal services were reinstated on weekdays from 18 September.

Nevertheless, this was simply a temporary reinstatement and indicated that the blanket reductions of 11 September had prepared too hastily. Wartime meant that services *had* to be reduced. Reductions in passenger services followed on 25 September for both the Great Western and London Midland Scottish, with the London & North Eastern following on 2 October, and the Southern Railway, with its extensive commuter network, on 16 October, but this time with better allowances for peak period travel. Off-peak, most main line services lost their hourly trains to be replaced by a service every two hours, often on extended timings as trains called at more stations. Off-peak suburban services were hourly. On some lines services were curtailed late in the evening, but others had special late services after midnight for the benefit of shift workers. The national maximum speed limit was increased to 60 mph during October.

Catering arrangements were reduced. Pullman and buffet cars were withdrawn and restaurant car service ceased on most routes. These cutbacks must have once again aroused some public reaction and been regarded as too severe, for on 1 January 1940, Pullman cars reappeared as did pantry cars and more buffet cars.

Some idea of the impact of the cuts and extended journey times can be gathered from a comparison between October 1938 and the same month a year later. On the LNER, the Norwich service was cut from eighteen trains daily to twelve, and the 115 miles were covered in 206 minutes compared with a pre-war best of 130 minutes and an average of 170 minutes. On the Southern, the service to Southampton was cut from twenty-eight to twenty trains daily and the timings for the seventy-nine miles was stretched from a pre-war best of eighty-five minutes and a 1938 average of 110 minutes to 123 minutes. Portsmouth, doubtless because of the Royal Navy, saw its services cut slightly from forty-five to forty daily, while the journey took an average of 118 minutes in 1939 compared to a 1938 best of ninety minutes and an average of ninety-eight minutes. The needs of the armed services were paramount and commuter traffic on its own wasn't enough to save a service, for the Brighton line suffered one of the heaviest reductions in the number of trains, more than halved from 100 trains daily to forty-six.

There were many reasons for the extended journey times, of which the maximum speed limits were just one. Wartime shortages of materials and the disruption of the normal renewals and maintenance programme would take its toll, with many 'temporary' speed limits, while war damage became extensive, especially in the London area and along the southern and eastern coasts. Trains had extra stops and extra carriages. Long distance trains from some London termini had to be divided in two to fit the platforms, with the first half pulled out of the station, and then backed on to the second half to be coupled, before the journey could start. At intermediate stations, such over-long trains had to make two stops so that passengers could board and alight.

The railways were also beginning to suffer from inroads made into their rolling stock with locomotives requisitioned by the military and carriages converted for use on ambulance trains, some of them for the military while others were converted for the evacuation of civilian casualties in anticipation of widespread disruption by heavy bombing, although the latter were never needed.

Other measures were also necessary. Locomotives were modified, with a number fitted with condensing gear to save water and pipes for obtaining water from streams, anticipating widespread disruption to water supplies following bombing.

Limiting a railway service has many disadvantages, especially during bad weather when the frequent passage of trains and movement of signals and points can help to stop icing. Late December 1939 and all of January 1940, saw exceptionally severe weather which froze the conductor rails on the electrified lines and, having started on a Sunday when only a limited service was operating, froze many trains in the sidings. This was to be a problem throughout the war years which coincided with a period of exceptionally severe winters.

Reduced facilities

In addition to trimming services, as the war progressed, other restrictions were applied. On 6 October 1941, under the directions of the Minister of War Transport, all London suburban trains became third-class only, with the definition being that this applied to any train starting and ending its journey within the London Passenger Transport Board's area. The reasons for the move were practical, the idea being not only to make the best use of all accommodation on the reduced number of trains, but also to recognise the difficulty in finding the right class of accommodation in a hurry during the blackout. To drive the point home, carpets were removed from first-class compartments and the first-class indications on the compartment doors painted out, while timetables and departure indicators described trains as 'Third Class Only'. Blackout or not, regular travellers seemed to be able to find their way to the most comfortable part of the train and gravitated towards the superior legroom and elbow room, and plusher upholstery, of the former first-class compartments, so that these soon became shabby with intensive use.

While mainline trains retained first-class accommodation, it was important to discourage unnecessary travel. The lack of sporting events and the fact that the coastal resorts had their beaches wrapped in barbed wire, meant that the normal leisure pursuits were not available. Again on the instructions of the Minister of War Transport, on 5 October 1942, off-peak cheap returns were scrapped, leaving seasons as the only 'cheap', or discounted, tickets.

A means of reducing fuel consumption was to reduce heating, so the pre-war system of switching on full heat on mainline trains between October and April when the temperature fell below 48 degrees F at any one of a number of monitoring points, and half-heat when the temperature fell below 55 degrees F, had been reduced to having full heat when the temperature fell below 45 degrees F and half-heat when it fell below 50 degrees between November and March.

The 'Blitz' created new wartime traffic. At Chiselhurst in Kent, the caves provided a natural air raid shelter, and many people would 'commute' by train to Chislehurst each evening to seek shelter in the caves. This was just one example, but Paddington was amongst those termini seeing 'reverse commuting' in wartime, first at the height of the Blitz and then during the period of V1 and V2 rocket attacks.

Shortages of skilled staff in the workshops and the conversion of many of these to war production, as well as shortages of materials, meant that the intervals between routine overhauls were extended. Economy measures on the Great Western were typical and included a new colour scheme for passenger carriages of reddish-brown with a bronze waistline and black roof, while locomotives were painted plain green without any lining out on being sent for overhaul or repair. The colour of the locomotives soon became immaterial as standards of cleanliness dropped.

While Britain's air raid warning system was excellent, it was always difficult to be precise about the intended target or about the number of aircraft. Inevitably, there would be areas close to a target that were included in the 'alert', and yet attracted little attention. In fact, a solitary aircraft could cause considerable inconvenience and loss of working time by prolonging an alert. There were those, of course, who became blasé about air raids, but railways were obviously high priority targets, so a relaxed attitude was asking for trouble.

Fortunately, it was soon found that many members of the ARP movement were in fact keen aircraft enthusiasts with equally keen eyesight, and who could be counted on to tell whether an aircraft was friendly or not. It was found that by placing such people in positions with a good field of vision, such as on top of a high roof, a good assessment of the threat could be made and the decision on whether or not to continue working or to seek shelter followed.

The railway in wartime

The changes in working or operational practices do not give a real impression of what it must have been like on the railways in the blackout, or of the problems of individual railwaymen, and women, having to report for work after a broken night's sleep in a crowded air raid shelter, or of coming off a night shift in the morning to find that their home no longer existed, and perhaps face the loss of family members and neighbours as well. In fact, the strain of losing his house in an air raid is believed to have been a factor in the serious accident on the GWR at Norton Fitzwarren when the driver mistakenly followed the signal for an adjoining line.

The efficient working of a railway required skill and experience, but under wartime conditions, most adults had to be available for either the armed forces or prepared to be directed to essential war work, and as skilled men volunteered or were conscripted into the armed forces, many of their places were taken by women. None of the war's belligerent nations mobilised the population as completely as the United Kingdom.

Despite many railway jobs being classified as 'reserved occupations', the railways saw a growing number of their personnel leaving to join the armed forces for the duration of the war. Before the war ended, the number of GWR personnel in the armed forces would rise to around 16,000. In the case of the Southern Railway, some 9,000 men were replaced by 8,000 women, who even undertook some of the heavier jobs, including those of porters. At first, the new recruits did not have uniforms, but this was quickly remedied. Uniforms were important on a railway not only because much of the work was dirty, but also for security and so that passengers knew who to turn to for advice and help.

Despite the cut in the number of trains, passenger traffic was 3 per cent higher in December 1939 than a year earlier.

Air raids often caught trains in exposed positions and it was decided that to keep moving was safer than stopping. At first, the instruction was given on all railways that on an air raid warning being given, passenger trains were to stop and passengers allowed to alight and seek shelter if they wished, after which the train would continue at a maximum speed of just 15 mph. As the full impact of the blitz took effect and air raids became so frequent, this slowed traffic down to an unacceptable extent, and the instruction was revised with trains allowed to proceed at 25 mph from early November 1940. The danger of a derailment to a train running onto bomb damaged track at high speed during an air raid was obvious, but away from the most heavily blitzed areas, many drivers took a chance and often ignored the speed limit, guessing that the risk of bomb damage was relatively light.

For the passengers, many journeys had an air of uncertainty. They would set out on their usual train or the one that had replaced it in the wartime timetable, but depending on the previous night's air raids, punctual arrival at their destination was something of a gamble. When Waterloo was closed, or the line between Waterloo and Clapham Junction was closed, passengers had to alight at Clapham Junction and queue for a bus. The replacement bus service was sparse and barely able to cope with shortages of fuel and vehicles, while busmen had also been called up. Nor could one assume that the roads were open, and in many cases diversions had to be made to avoid burning buildings or the journey was slowed by fire hoses in the road.

Even when all was well, the blackout meant that reading was difficult, although limited light was permitted after an initial period once all windows were blacked out, with just small gaps to allow passengers to see if they had arrived at their destination.

Shortages of skilled staff in the workshops and the conversion of many of these to war production, as well as shortages of materials, meant that the intervals between routine overhauls were extended. The railway companies were also severely restricted in the type of steam locomotive that they could build, but new building was allowed both to replace locomotives lost to enemy action and also to ensure that sufficient power was available for the many military specials. In theory, just two standard types were allowed, but before this happened, on the Southern Railway, where there was a dire shortage of large locomotives, the wily chief mechanical engineer, Oliver Bulleid, introduced his famous 'air-smoothed', as opposed to streamlined, Pacifics, or so-called 'spam cans', because of their shape, by convincing the authorities that these were really mixed traffic locomotives. He compensated by also introducing a utility 0-6-0 design of unsurpassed ugliness that lacked anything that could be eliminated to save on scarce materials.

State control

Shortly before the outbreak of war the Government moved to take control of the railways. One difference with the situation on the outbreak of the First World War was that instead of the President of the Board of Trade, the Railway Executive Committee came under the control of the Minister of Transport, later, in 1940, to become the Minister of War Transport. The then Minister, Captain Euan Wallace, actually seized control of the railways on 1 September 1939, two days before the outbreak of war, using powers granted under the Defence Regulations Act 1939, with the Emergency (Railway Control) Order.

Once again the minister operated through a Railway Executive Committee, which had been formed the previous September, which included the general managers of the four main line railways and of London Transport. The London termini were obvious targets, so the railways had already evacuated many of their administrative personnel to the outskirts and to the provinces. The Railway Executive Committee itself found safety in an abandoned underground station on the Piccadilly Line at Down Street, between Green Park and Hyde Park Corner stations, which provided office accommodation and dormitories.

The Railway Executive Committee was chaired by Sir Ralph Wedgwood who was chief general manager of the London & North Eastern Railway, and when he retired early in 1939, he was asked to remain as chairman of the REC. His deputy as chairman was Sir James Milne of the Great Western Railway, while Wedgwood's successor at the LNER also became a member of the REC. The other members were Sir William Wood of the London Midland & Scottish Railway and Gilbert Szlumper of the Southern Railway, with Frank Pick of the London Passenger Transport Board. The REC secretary was G. Cole Deacon from the Railway Companies Association. Later, when Szlumper was transferred to the War Office as Director-General of Transportation (sic), his place both as general manager at Waterloo and on the REC was taken by Eustace Missenden.

The REC worked through a series of section sub-committees which were, for the most part, based on the structure of the Railway Clearing House with its sub-divisions. There were a few additional sub-committees, however, including one set up to prepare for sabotage. In all, there were sixteen sub-committees, and pulling together their work must have been a challenge. As it happened, sabotage was not a major problem and was more likely to come from members of the Irish Republican Army than from any German agents.

Compensation and control

Meanwhile, the shareholders were still waiting to learn what compensation they would receive for what effectively amounted to the requisition of their property. The haste to grab control of the railways was in contrast to the tardiness in finalising the arrangements. In 1939, using the new Emergency Powers (Defence) Act 1939, the Government was dragging its feet. Encouraged by the delay in reaching agreement, the Labour MP for Bristol South asked the Minister for Transport, on 22 November, whether he would consider nationalising the railways. The Minister rejected this at the time, assuring the House that he was confident that agreement would be reached shortly, and also reminding them that unified control had already been achieved through the Railway Executive Committee. Another month passed, and the question of nationalisation was becoming more serious, as rumours that could only have been officially inspired that nationalisation was being considered began to circulate, obviously intended to apply pressure to the railway companies.

'It cannot be for the good of the community that such a monopoly as a main line should be controlled by any group of individuals, however public spirited', ran one statement on the matter, completely ignoring the fact that the railways were no longer controlled by the companies, but instead by the REC. Many railway journalists saw opportunism in these threats, arguing that those in favour of nationalisation would find their arguments less convincing in a period when policy could be considered at leisure. Even so, it was not until 7 February 1940 that the Minister was able to give the House of Commons the news that agreement had been reached.

State control made the railways contractors to the Government, with all revenue passing to the government which then allocated shares from a pool, initially set at a guaranteed £40 million (around £2,152 million today). The Southern share of the pool was fixed at 16 per cent, the same as for the GWR while the LPTB received 11 per cent, the LMS 34 per cent and the LNER 23 per cent. These percentages were based on the average net revenues for the companies and LPTB in the three years 1935-37, which the government took as each company's standard revenue. Once the guaranteed £40 million had been paid, any balance was allocated to the five train operators on the same percentage terms up to a maximum of £3.5 million. After this, if there was a further balance, the revenue over £43.5 million would be divided equally between the government and the pool until the pool total reached £56 million. At this stage, if the revenue share allocated to any of the companies then exceeded its standard revenue, the excess would be shared out proportionately among the other companies.

Costs of maintenance and renewals had to be standardised, while the cost of restoring war damage would be met up to a total of £10 million in a full year. Privately-owned wagons were also requisitioned by the Ministry of War Transport, and the individual companies had to meet the costs and revenue attributed to the wagon owners out of their share of the revenue pool.

This was a 'take it or leave it' type of agreement, with the government leaking threats of nationalisation if the companies failed to agree, although these were officially denied. While the years in question had been bad ones for the British economy, the final year 1938, had been even worse and the railways had had great difficulty in getting the government to understand this. The railway companies had never achieved the revenues anticipated by the Railways Act 1921. All that can be said for the deal was that the government was anxious to avoid inflationary pay claims from railway employees, but the inescapable fact was that the railways were having their revenues more or less fixed while costs were bound to rise as they struggled to meet the increased demands that wartime would place upon them. The upper limit on the costs of war damage was either political expediency to keep the unions quiet and retain the Labour Party in the wartime coalition government, or simple naivety since normal insurance measures were not available in wartime.

In addition to taking over the 'Big Four' and London Transport, the Railway Control Order also applied to joint committees of any two or more of these railways, and to other lines, including the East Kent and the Kent & East Sussex. The government had earlier warned the railways that as many as 800 locomotives might be required for service overseas, but as the war did not follow the pattern of 1914-18, not all were required.

While the railways were expected to give up manpower and equipment for the armed forces, the impact was less than during the First World War in which 184,475 men were conscripted. Some 110,000 men had to be given up for national service, with more than 100,000 actually conscripted into the armed forces, while 298 steam locomotives and forty-five of the still rare diesel locomotives, all of them shunting engines, were also taken for service overseas. These figures were in addition to the use of railway workshops for war work, which naturally moved a further substantial number of personnel away from railway work.

The financial basis of state control of the railways in wartime had been imposed. However, it was soon clear that the original scheme had many deficiencies, and as early as December 1940, a short Act of Parliament allowed those railways under the control of the Minister of Transport to make agreements with the Minister to cover financial matters arising from the period of control. The railway companies were given the freedom to enter into arrangements provided that the Minister laid an order.

Part of the problem was that the government never really understood, or perhaps even cared about, the problems encountered by the pre-war railways, let alone the difficulties facing them in this new conflict.

As usual, the Treasury was unsympathetic and unrealistic. The Chancellor of the Exchequer, Sir Kingsley Wood, decided that war damage would not be treated as an element within working expenses, which could be offset against the guaranteed sums paid by the government, but instead were to be charged to the capital account, transferring these uninsurable costs from the government to the railways. On 7 April 1941, in his budget speech, the Chancellor announced that its policy was to combat inflation and restrict price increases as far as possible, and that included railway fares and rates for goods traffic. This was important news but it took more than a week for the minister, Moore-Brabazon, to write to Lord Stamp of the LMS, as chairman of the Railway Companies Association, but Stamp was killed that night, 16 April, in an air raid.

Moore-Brabazon moved on, and so it was left to his successor, Lord Leathers, to explain to the railway companies the bad news about pricing and war damage, and even then, June 1941, the advice was oral, almost as if the government was ashamed to commit itself to paper! Instead of the original agreement of a £40 million guarantee and a share in net revenue in excess of that amount up to £56 million, there would be a fixed annual guarantee. The railway companies were in an impossible situation, with the nation still expecting German invasion and having come through the Blitz. To argue would be construed as being unpatriotic, and many would have had memories of how war profiteers had been vilified by the press and politicians in the First World War, although no one had ever suggested that such charges applied to the railways. The railway companies were negotiating under duress, and the government had clearly already settled on the fixed figure of £43 million, eventually referring to the changes in the light of the previous year's legislation permitting an amendment. The government promised to make good any deficiency in the fixed figure, but would also take any surplus.

Division of the £43 million and the relative shares were to be:

Great Western	£6,670,603	15.5%
Southern	£6,607,639	15.4%
London Midland Scottish	£14,749,698	34.3%
London & North Eastern	£10,136,355	23.6%
London Transport	£4,835,705	11.2%

Clearly, there were winners and losers, although the variation in percentage terms was marginal. The Southern and Great Western were both slightly worse off in percentage terms, the former the more so, while the LMS, LNER and LPTB all made marginal gains. Shareholder protests that the deal was mean in the extreme was countered by socialists claiming that the deal was far too generous.

'Certain sections of the community, always vocal in these matters, have not disguised their disappointment that the government has decided not to adopt the advice they have given so freely and with so little practical knowledge, to nationalise the transport system of the country,' thundered the *Railway Gazette*. 'The new agreement, which provides for renting the railways by the State, has also been criticised on the grounds that its terms are unduly generous to the transport system. How little substance there is in these protestations is easy to see if one is prepared to delve far enough into the facts of the case, to divest one's mind of prejudice, and to approach the problem from the basis of equity. On this basis, the original agreement can by no means be judged generous to the proprietors of the railways; nor can the second. At best it provides a very meagre return upon the capital which has been invested in the undertakings and without which, allied to the patience which, perforce, has been exercised by a long-suffering body of stockholders, the railways of this country could not have reached their present high standard of efficiency, which has contributed so greatly to the successful prosecution of the war.

Of recent years there has been all too prevalent an idea that the standard revenue which was fixed by the Railways Act, 1921, as fair and reasonable and in the public interest is beyond the possibility of attainment – that the £51,359,000 at which it now stands has become but a mythical figure. It should be remembered that Parliament considered the attainment of that standard revenue was so expedient in the public interest that it placed a duty on the Railway Rates Tribunal to fix charges so as to enable a company to earn its standard revenue. Although it is a fact that Parliament's object was not attained...this has been due very largely to acute and unregulated competition by road interests. There can be no doubt that in present circumstances the railway companies could earn their standard revenues...Moreover, the use now made of the capital provided by the railways is much greater than in the period before the war, and includes the use of assets that were then operated at a loss, but were continued in use to meet conditions which now exist. Taking into consideration…the London Passenger Transport Board, a total of £56,853,000 would be required as the total standard revenue of the whole of the undertakings, and it is this figure that should be borne in mind when comparisons are made with the fixed annual revenue of the five major parties in the revised arrangements which provide for a rental of £43,000,000 in addition to the net revenue from certain excluded items.

The excluded items were the railways revenue from associated businesses such as bus operations. The *Railway Gazette* continued to emphasise that the railways had made considerable sacrifices in accepting the deal, but were obviously influenced by two factors, the national interest, and that, while the earnings even for 1941 were far in excess of the sums provided by the deal, there could be developments that would reverse this situation, such as invasion. It went on to remind its readers that the railways would now have to pay for restoring their own war damage, and that there could be no grounds for suggesting that the £43 million annually was a subsidy to the railways, but instead it was clear that the railways were subsidising the government. Gross expenditure by the five railway undertakings controlled by the REC during 1940 had amounted to £203.5 million, of which more than £150 million was accounted for by labour costs, while the capital cost of the five undertakings amounted to £130 million. The £43 million included the revenue from ancillary businesses, and amounted to a return of less than 3.5 per cent on the capital.

Further adjustments were not made in the later stages of the war when it was clear that the invasion threat was long past, even though the net earnings of the railways were by this time well in excess of their fixed annual payments by upwards of 100 per cent for three years running. In fact, the surplus profits taken by the government for 1943, 1944 and 1945, reached a total of £155 million. By this time, the railways were not simply serving the British armed forces, but in addition they were playing their part in supporting the build-up of men and equipment for the invasion of Europe. There were also the leave specials, and not just for British servicemen, who wanted to get home to see their families, but for Americans whose idea of a good time off-duty meant heading for London.

While in theory, the railways could keep the money earned by their investment in road haulage and bus companies in the pre-war years, these were also constrained by the requisitioning of their property by the military, while buses, for example, could be directed from one company to another, as demand fluctuated. Companies in what had been, pre-war, holiday areas, suddenly found themselves with large military training camps and other bases to serve. They might be expected to provide vehicles without notice for troop movements, and this was especially the case for those in what would be regarded as 'invasion areas', such as the Isle of Wight, for example. Road transport was also constrained by its fuel supply, which on the outbreak of war was cut by 20 per cent, and later controlled thoroughly. Many bus operators experimented with low pressure gas, towing trailers behind the double deck buses and sometime putting gas bags on top of single-deck buses, but this was generally unsatisfactory. It was, in any case, easier to convert the petrol-engined vehicles than those with the increasingly common diesel engine, and when gas was used, it was given to the petrol-engined vehicles.

As noted earlier, the inclusion of the railway operations of the London Passenger Transport Board in the government's compensation scheme dismayed the main line companies, largely because they expected travel on the London Underground to fall during the war years. There was also the wider issue that the compensation scheme was inadequate for the demands being placed on the railways and inflexible, indeed the revised scheme was even worse than the original.

While the wartime London Underground system was smaller than that of today, most of the network was already completed while extensions to the Piccadilly and Central Lines were well advanced.

London at War

The London Underground faced two conflicting problems during wartime. The population of the London Passenger Transport area actually fell by 2.7 million to 7,147,000 between 1939 and 1944, largely due to evacuation, and the reduced travel caused by the blackout and German bombing, reduced traffic substantially at first. On the other hand, heavy movement of forces personnel brought heavy and sometimes unpredictable traffic peaks, while for service personnel from the British Empire and, later, the United States, even without the bright lights London continued to be the prime destination when on leave. This service leave traffic was encouraged with the offer of a ticket, costing a shilling, which gave visiting service personnel the use of most of London Transport's bus, tram, trolleybus and underground services for a day, starting at 10.30 am.

Because of the original mass evacuation of children, the war started busily enough for the underground network, with London Transport and the four mainline railway companies told to make arrangements to evacuate 1¼ million people, mainly children, although in the end only 600,000 were moved. While the main line companies handled the real evacuation, London Transport was responsible for getting them to the departure stations, which were usually not the mainline termini, and in addition to the underground system, more than 5,000 buses were also used.

This was at a time when fuel supplies to London Transport's bus services were cut by a quarter, although to a small extent this was offset by the cancellation of the cross-London Greenline limited stop bus network, with the Greenline 'coaches' converted to ambulances. The number of standing passengers on buses was increased from five to eight, the legal limit at the time, but the cuts in services meant that the Underground, contrary to expectations, became busier. Many commuters started to cycle for part of their daily journey, and at suburban stations London Transport introduced arrangements, wherever space allowed, for these to be left at the station during the day. At some of the interchange stations in central London, snack trolleys were introduced for service personnel.

In common with the surface railways, the London Underground was badly disrupted by the bad weather that started after Christmas 1939 and continued throughout January 1940. The surface sections suffered and despite de-icing trains being used and steel brushes fitted to trains in passenger service, conductor rails often re-froze between trains. In one case, a train was stalled at Osterley on the Piccadilly Line having left Hounslow West at 4.13 pm. The following train was coupled to it a quarter of an hour later, but despite scraping the rails, they froze again before the trains could move very far. Eventually, both trains arrived at Northfields at 11.45 pm. In normal conditions, this journey would have taken ten minutes.

Protecting the system

Preparing for war imposed some engineering and logistical feats on the London Transport railways. The deep level tubes may have seemed safe and secure from German bombing, but they had an Achille's heel in the fact that both the Northern and Bakerloo Lines ran under the River Thames, with both having their own lines between Charing Cross (now known as Embankment) and Waterloo, and the Northern also running between Monument and London Bridge. At the time of the Munich Crisis in 1938, when a sudden outbreak of war, possibly without prior declaration, was widely expected, the Bakerloo and Northern Line tunnels under the Thames were plugged with concrete, but this was a temporary measure.

Early in 1939, plans were drawn up for floodgates on either side of the Thames to protect the lines running under the river, needing eighteen floodgates each weighing almost ten tons, in all, and much of this work was completed before the outbreak of war, although the Northern Line between London Bridge and Monument did not re-open to traffic until May 1940, having been closed for the previous eight months. The practice was to be that on receipt of an air raid warning by a traffic office at Leicester Square, the gates would be closed as soon as the line they protected was free of trains, something that could be verified by track circuiting. Closure of the gates took just a minute, and procedures were put in hand to allow the severed sections of line to continue to work independently. In the case of a gate malfunctioning, steel diaphragms were placed nearby, but the gates could be worked manually if needed.

There were also additional floodgates, smaller and weighing just 4.5 tons each, at Charing Cross (now known as Embankment), to isolate the passages leading from the District and Circle Lines to the Northern Line. Further floodgates were installed at vulnerable sections of the District and Circle Lines as west as South Kensington, while on the East London section of the Metropolitan Line, vertical lift floodgates were installed at the southern end of the Thames tunnel.

Elsewhere on the system, precautions were taken to protect it from burst water mains and sewers.

A further line of defence was the positioning of detector devices on the bed of the Thames as a safeguard against acoustic bombs that could be set off by the noise and vibration of a train running through a tunnel. At times, services had to be suspended on the lines under the Thames while the Royal Navy swept the river for mines.

Electricity supply cables were duplicated to ensure continuation of supply in the event of bomb damage.

Disused deep level tube stations were used by the government, including the Railway Executive Committee which took over Down Street station on the Piccadilly Line, closed in 1932. The Aldwych branch was closed for the duration of the war and used to store equipment and other valuable items, including much of the collection from the British Museum, amongst which was the Elgin Marbles. The unopened Central Line tunnels for the extension eastwards into Essex between Leytonstone and Gants Hill were used as a factory for the defence equipment manufacturer, Plessey, and a narrow gauge railway line was laid so that supplies could be moved quickly and easily to the workbenches and completed work taken away. The tunnels provided 300,000 sq ft of floor space and were used by 2,000 people working day and night shifts.

The deep level tube tunnels soon became a popular spot for those seeking shelter from the air raids once these became heavy during 1940. This practice was discouraged at first, but Londoners started to break into tube stations after they had closed for the night, and finally the authorities gave in. Officially, the station platforms were allowed to be used from 7 September 1940 and sanitary and drainage arrangements were installed quickly at eighty-one stations, with sewage pumped to the surface. Most of the 'shelterers' slept on the platforms, but in due course bunks were provided for 22,800, although the peak population in the shelters, reached on 27 September 1940, was 177,000, with another 17,000 using the extensions to the system that still had to be brought into use. Admission to the tube stations was by ticket, provided free by the local authority on a permanent season ticket basis, or on a nightly basis by the ticket office at the tube station if space permitted. Arrangements were even made for feeding the shelterers, sometimes by the Salvation Army, but there was also a 'Tube Refreshments Special', converted tube train travelled the deep level lines carrying supplies to 124 canteens set up throughout the system. All in all, at the peak 120,000 people were fed each night by one means or another.

Many of the inner city tube stations became so overcrowded that special trains had to be operated to disperse 'shelterers' to less busy stations. There were also strict rules on how close to the platform edge the 'shelterers' could sleep while trains were still in operation, with them having to pull back four feet from the edge after 6.15 am in the morning.

Not that the shelters were always as safe as the public imagined.

Caught on the tube

No one expected the sub-surface lines, sometimes referred to by London Transport as the 'surface' lines, of the Circle, District, Metropolitan and Hammersmith & City Lines to be safe from heavy bombing. Indeed, having been built on the 'cut and cover' technique, these lines ran in and out of the open, with some of the stations even having glazed roofs, although this was removed on the outbreak of war.

An early casualty was Praed Street on the Circle Line, a convenient station for travellers to and from Paddington. On the night of 13 October 1940, just after 11 pm, three bombs landed in Praed Street itself, outside the Great Western Royal Hotel. The first two exploded in the street, causing considerable damage to the surrounding buildings, but the third exploded on the Circle Line underground station, which at the time was fairly busy with many passengers waiting for trains. Girders and large wooden beams went crashing down into the station, adding to the chaos and the casualties. Immediate rescue came from the air raid precaution

(ARP) personnel of the Great Western Railway at Paddington Station, so that all of the casualties were at hospital within an hour or so.

An early indication of what could happen even with the deep level underground of the tube lines came on 12 October 1940, at Trafalgar Square Station on the Bakerloo Line, when a bomb penetrated the pavement and killed seven people. The next day, another bomb struck Bounds Green on the Piccadilly Line, causing part of the station tunnel to cave in and killing nineteen people while another fifty-two were injured.

There was even worse to come. On 14 October 1940, a bomb pierced the station tunnel roof at Balham, fracturing water mains which flooded both tunnels and swept gravel and other debris into the station, killing four London Transport staff and sixty-eight shelterers. The Northern Line had to be closed for three months, compared with the ten days or so that was more usual in other cases of bomb damage. Earlier that evening, London Transport's headquarters at 55 Broadway, under which lay St James's Park Station on the Circle and District Lines, received a direct hit.

On 21 October, the line between Edgware Road and Addison Road was closed due to severe bomb damage, and never re-opened.

Given the concerns over the system's vulnerability to flooding, there was a near escape on 12 November 1940, when the station at Sloane Square on the District and Circle Lines, which had only re-opened after rebuilding some eight months earlier, was destroyed by bombs. A conduit carried the West Bourne stream over the station, and it was fortunate that this was not broken otherwise a substantial section of this busy line, along which lay six main line termini, could have been flooded.

Nevertheless, the worst accident on the London Underground system and the worst during the Second World War on the railways had nothing to do with the enemy or with trains. On 3 March 1943, the still unopened Central Line station at Bethnal Green was being used as an air raid shelter, and as the warning sounded, the local population headed for what they thought would be safety. A woman carrying a baby tripped as she went down a short staircase of just nineteen steps, with the press of those behind meaning that others fell. Within a few minutes 173 people, sixty-two of them children, were killed by suffocation and crush injuries.

Waterloo suffered badly during the Blitz, as we will see shortly. Later, while the Blitz was roughly halfway through, the sub-surface booking hall for the Bakerloo and Northern lines was badly damaged on 5 January 1941. Less than a week later, the worst incident of all came on the night of Saturday, 11 January, at 7.57 pm. During a long air raid that lasted from

6.25 pm to 9.30 pm, with 145 enemy bombers operating over London, a high explosive bomb was dropped by either a Junkers Ju88 or a Heinkel He111, and this crashed through the road into the circular subway under the surface of Bank Station, before exploding at the top of the Central Line escalators, destroying the ticket hall and three escalators, and blowing out the windows of two trains standing on the Central Line platforms. Yet again, a water main was fractured, and lighting failed as far away as Holborn Station, 1½ miles away. Three minutes later, in the blackout, a bus on route 21 crashed into the crater. Inevitably, there were heavy casualties, with four London Transport personnel and fifty-three other people killed, while three London Transport personnel, fourteen passengers and fifty-two others were injured – many would have been people who believed that they were safer underground than on the surface.

The damage at Bank had little impact on the Waterloo & City Line as the service was suspended due to the problems at Waterloo, but the Central Line service was stopped immediately, but resumed at 7.11 am the next morning, although for a period trains ran through Bank Station without stopping; later trains stopped so that passengers entered and exited the station by way of the Northern Line station at Monument, with which there were connecting pedestrian tunnels. It seems incredible that it only took two months to restore Bank Station to working order.

This time, the Royal Engineers had to take over repair work, creating a box girder bridge 164 feet long to carry road traffic across the large crater between Queen Victoria Street and Poultry to Cornhill and Threadneedle Street. The RE were able to do this using large prefabricated assemblies that had been built and put in stock before the war ready for just such an eventuality.

Yet another major interruption to services came after the exceptionally heavy air raid of 10 May 1941, with damage that resulted in a five-month suspension of services between King's Cross and Euston Square on the Circle and Metropolitan lines.

Despite the difficulties of using deep level tube stations, further deep level station platforms were built below some existing stations on the Northern and Central lines, with no less than eight of these at an average depth of 80 feet below ground level built at Belsize Park, Camden Town, Goodge Street, Stockwell, Clapham Common, Clapham North and Clapham South, as well as at Chancery Lane. In all, ten were originally proposed, with the hope that with the return of peace these could form part of a deep level express tube network – the progenitor of today's much delayed 'Cross Rail' scheme. These new extra deep level tunnels were built in pairs and were 1,400 feet long, far longer than that needed for even a surface train, were of 16 ft 6 in diameter with a floor built halfway up, and each location had 8,000 bunks fitted. These were ready from 1942 onwards, but first used in mid-1944. Each end of the section of tunnel had a double spiral staircase and a lift for five persons – completely inadequate had an express tube network ever been built.

The two deep shelters that were not built were to have been at the Oval on the Northern Line, where the water table was too close to the surface for work to proceed, and at St Paul's on the Central Line, where an Act of Parliament prohibited construction of such works so close to the Cathedral.

The threat from the air was taken very seriously indeed. Even the deep level tubes had some sections on the surface, such as between Golders Green and Edgware on the Northern Line which, except for a short length of tunnel north of Hendon Central, ran on the surface. Between Hendon and Golders Green, the Northern Line was very much an 'overground', running on embankment or viaduct.

As with the surface railways, colour light signals had to have extra long hoods fitted. Also with blackout in mind, on all lines, train windows were covered with cream netting, except for a small area in the centre. The cream netting gradually turned black. Many passengers found it tempting to peel off small areas, and advertisements featuring a character called Billy Brown then appeared in tube carriages with the message:

'I trust you'll pardon my correction
That stuff is there for your protection.'

There was further advice to passengers, warning them not to leave a train (clearly aimed at those on the surface lines) between stations during air raids or after an alert had been sounded unless requested to do so by a member of staff. Gas attacks were widely anticipated, and the advice was to close all windows and ventilation, not to smoke, and not to touch any exterior part of a carriage, and, of course, always to carry a gas mask.

London was the primary target for both the V-1 and V-2 flying bombs, and not surprisingly no less than 149 of these 'revenge' weapons fell on London Transport facilities. The first of these came in mid-June 1944, when the viaducts carrying the District and Piccadilly Line tracks between Hammersmith and Ravenscourt Park were badly damaged. While the engineers managed to restore train services, albeit at low speed, in just two days, another V-1 landed close to the point of impact of the first, and caused further damage so that it was six weeks before full services could be restored.

Overall, the war years saw the London Underground system suffer more than 2,000 incidents resulting in damage to the infrastructure, and there were 1,050 cases of damage to rolling stock, with nineteen railway carriages completely destroyed. As with the surface railways, massive arrears of maintenance accrued as the workshops went over to war work, including making parts for tanks and armoured fighting vehicles and the overhaul and modification of more than 500 armoured fighting vehicles. The main effort, however, was in aircraft manufacture, including more than 500 Handley Page Halifax heavy bombers, built by people of whom four-fifths had no previous engineering experience. Perhaps the oddest part of this effort took place in the subway running from Earl's Court station to the exhibition hall, where a part-time voluntary work factory was established in mid-June 1942 to produce aircraft components, and which continued its work for three years, not closing until after the war in Europe had ended. The unopened eastern extension of the Central Line was used to manufacture electronic components.

London and the Underground survived the blitz; despite there being only one night without an air raid from the night of 7/8 September for the next sixty-five nights, and that was because of bad weather. Yet, bad though it undoubtedly was, it could all have been much worse. Some years before the war, the Luftwaffe had decided to produce large numbers of dive-bombers and medium bombers rather than the heavy bombers favoured by the British and Americans. There might not have been a London Underground system had even a handful of heavy bombers been available to the Luftwaffe in 1940 or 1941. Even the deep level tube lines would have been gouged out and doubtless the resulting mess would have been flooded with water and sewage. Had just 4,000-lb bombs been used, incidents such as those at Balham and the Bank would have become commonplace. Even these would have been enough to bring the system to a complete halt.

The main line termini

The surface lines of the 'Big Four' fared little better. Waterloo was vulnerable with its approaches mainly on viaduct and the station itself built up high with cellars underneath. St Pancras, built on a deck, would also have suffered disproportionately. These were not the only vulnerable termini, London Bridge and Liverpool Street were others. The tunnels at Liverpool Street, King's Cross and Euston could all have been blocked, closing the stations for months.

Waterloo, with a spirits store under the station which soared above surrounding streets, suffered accordingly. On 7 September 1940, a bomb fell just outside the station and seriously damaged the viaduct over John Street. Railwaymen and the Royal Engineers worked to restore services, but the station was closed until 19 September, and services could not be fully restored until 1 October. The disruption affected more than just passengers, and at one stage there were 5,000 bags of unsorted mail. The overnight newspaper trains switched to Clapham Yard, and after further enemy action moved to Wimbledon, and then to Surbiton after bombing destroyed the roads around Wimbledon station. Waterloo was one of the worst affected of the Southern termini in London, as it was out of action due to incendiary bombs from the night of 29/30 December 1940, until 5 January 1941, which itself was not a quiet night as the old LSWR offices in York Road were destroyed that night and the underground lifts and booking hall badly damaged. A further closure came after the raid on the night of 10/11 May 1941, when around fifty high explosive and incendiary bombs and parachute mines set fires blazing and destroyed the Necropolis Station before penetrating to the basement arches setting alight large quantities of spirits stored there: the station could not function until a partial re-opening on 15 May. The disruption to services was severe, with many passengers delayed by several hours as the crowds overwhelmed the replacement bus service from Clapham Junction, with a queue of more than a mile in length at one point and the road towards Waterloo difficult to drive over as it was cluttered with many fire hoses. One unexploded bomb was to remain undetected until work started on an office building in York Road in 1959: at 2,000lbs, had it exploded during the intervening years, the destruction and loss of life at the height of the rush hour would have been terrible. The original LSWR terminus at Nine Elms also lost its roof on 10/11 May.

To the north of Waterloo and on the other side of the Thames, Charing Cross, so important during the First World War, was left on the sidelines as with the evacuation of the BEF from Dunkirk, there was no longer any need for senior officers to make hasty trips to France. During 8 October 1940, a daylight raid inflicted serious damage on a train standing in the station, but the worst raid of all was during the night of 16/17 April 1941, with the hotel and station both badly damaged by fire and other fires started on Hungerford Bridge. Three trains in the terminus were set alight along with a fourth on the bridge, while further disruption was caused when a landmine was discovered near the signal cabin with its parachute caught on the bridge girders. The mine was eventually defused and removed, but not before a fire under platform 4 had come within four yards of it. Charing Cross was closed throughout 17 April. Another closure followed a further raid on the night of 10/11 May. On 18 June 1944, a flying bomb blew out a span of the original bridge near the south bank, but trains managed to continue using the station by using the newer section of the bridge, although full service could not be resumed until 4 December.

At another Southern terminus clinging to the north bank of the Thames, Blackfriars saw services reduced as a wartime emergency measure from 16 October 1939, including the complete withdrawal of rush hour services to Dartford via Lewisham. The worst night of the blitz was that of 16/17 April 1941 when a bomb wrecked the old Blackfriars signal cabin on the south side of the river. Immediately, flagmen were put into position to signal trains through the section and work the points, but worse was to come when either a large bomb or landmine destroyed the bridge over Southwark Street and seven flagmen seeking refuge in a shelter were caught by the blast, with three being killed outright, another three dying in hospital from severe burns, and just one surviving to make a slow recovery in hospital. With military help, a temporary bridge with two running roads was ready in fifteen days, but a permanent replacement repair was not in place until 9 October 1942. The terminal roads at Blackfriars were locked out of use until the end of the war, while temporary signalling arrangements were provided.

It was not until 12 August 1946 that a full restoration of services could be made at Blackfriars, with wartime cuts in services reversed and a new signal cabin at Blackfriars opened on that day and the terminal roads re-opened. The station's platforms were re-numbered 1 to 5 from east to west at the same time.

The problems at Blackfriars also impacted on Holborn Viaduct, whose trains ran past the Thameside terminus. Services were badly affected following the collapse of the bridge over Southwark Street during the heavy raid on the night of 16/17 April 1941, and while services were reinstated when a temporary bridge was erected, more was to follow. Earlier, the old hotel building was hit on 26 October 1940, and on the night of 10/11 May, it was hit again, and completely gutted by fire, with the damage to the station itself so extensive that it could not be used by trains until 1 June, and a temporary booking office had to be provided.

East of Blackfriars and closer to the centre of the City, Cannon Street was closed between 10.00 and 16.00 and after 19.30 daily, and from 15.00 on Saturday until Monday morning with effect from 16 October 1939. Even rush hour services were severely curtailed in wartime, so that by 1944, there were just twenty-four peak hour departures, only one of which was for the Kent coast. Before this, on the night of 10/11 May 1941, the station was bombed and caught fire, with railwaymen braving molten glass dripping from the roof to rescue locomotives and carriages, but one of the former, *St Lawrence*, was caught by a bomb on the bridge.

Severe damage to London Bridge could have had the potential to close both Cannon Street and Charing Cross, and while this did not happen, the station also suffered during the war years. Its importance to the other two termini can be illustrated by the fact that, in 1939, London Bridge handled 250,000 passengers daily, with no less than 80,000 of these on the trains continuing through to the City and West End. The station handled 2,407 railway movements daily, and in the morning peak hour received ninety-four trains, of which forty-six terminated while twenty-nine continued to Cannon Street and another nineteen to Charing Cross. On 9 December 1940, the signal box had a parachute mine settle against its wall with its parachute caught on a signal, and displaying great heroism, the three signalmen continued working while a naval officer and a rating defused the mine. On the night of 29/30 December 1940, the station, while not in the City, shared in the massive raid using incendiary bombs, and at 00.27, the upper floors of the station buildings were gutted by fire, which also destroyed many station offices. In an attempt to get the station working again, a wooden temporary ticket office was sited on the main concourse.

Broad Street was put out of action on the night of 3/4 October 1940, and remained closed for several days. It also had to close on 13 October and 11 November following further enemy action. Services to the LNER were cancelled to make way for war traffic, but reinstated post-war. Heavy air raids on London's East End also meant the withdrawal of services east of Dalston Junction, which were not reinstated after the war.

Broad Street's neighbour, Liverpool Street, suffered even worse than during the earlier conflict. When bombs fell on Platforms 1 and 4 during the Blitz, a train was wrecked and this took some days to remove. The East Side booking office was also damaged as was platform 18, while a delayed action bomb exploded in the engine sidings beyond platform 10 and killed two men, despite being surrounded by four trucks of ballast. A bomb that fell on Broad Street threw a wagon onto the roof of Liverpool Street. The station buildings also suffered heavy damage, with the clock tower burnt out, and it took British Railways until 1961 to replace the clock.

Marylebone itself escaped unscathed during the Second World War, with a few incendiary bombs soon extinguished, but the tunnel approach through St John's Wood was badly damaged, forcing Marylebone to close between 5 October and 26 November 1940, with single line working until August 1942. The goods depot was destroyed by fire on 16 April 1941. Finally, towards the end of the war, the signal box was hit by a flying bomb, killing two men.

One of the more fortunate of the London termini during the war years was Euston, left comparatively unscathed. In 1940, at the height of the Blitz, a bomb damaged the roof of the Great Hall, while another bomb landed between platforms 2 and 3 and wrecked offices and damaged part of the hotel. In fact, only Fenchurch Street fared better.

King's Cross did not escape the impact of enemy action. Two 1,000lb bombs, chained together, fell on the west side during the Blitz early on Sunday 11 May 1941, destroying much of the general offices, the grill room and bar, and wrecking the booking hall, killing twelve men. Fortunately, the station was quiet at the time. Temporary booking and refreshment facilities were organised quickly, and no trains were cancelled. On the London Transport Metropolitan line, bombing meant that services to Moorgate were suspended from 30 December 1940, and not reinstated until after the war.

All too often the King's Cross long distance trains carried as many as 2,000 passengers, and were often as long as twenty or more carriages. Locomotives would pull one portion out of the platform, and then reverse on to the second portion. This imposed risks of its own. On 4 February 1945, the 6 pm to Leeds stalled in the tunnel and then ran backwards into the front of the 7 pm 'Aberdonian' standing in platform 10. Despite the low speed, the moving carriages rose into the air and demolished the signal gantry, while two passengers were killed. It took two weeks before a new gantry could be installed, causing the termination of all up suburban services at Finsbury Park.

Across the road from King's Cross, the Second World War saw St Pancras suffer bombs and land mines, but the station's structure, despite being built over cellars and vaults, as at Waterloo, proved resilient. During the night of 15/16 October 1940, at the height of the Blitz, a land mine wrecked much of the train shed roof, closing the station for five days. As the Blitz drew to a close, on the night of 10/11 May 1941, the station had to be closed for eight days after a bomb passed through the station floor at the inner end of platform 3, and while no serious structural damage occurred, there was considerable damage to trains.

At Paddington, wartime enforced many changes, and through working of trains to and from the Metropolitan ended on 16 September 1939, by which time emergency cuts were being made to timetables. Paddington did not escape its share of wartime wounds, with a parachute mine demolishing part of the departure side building in 1941, while in 1944 a V-1 flying bomb damaged the roof and platforms 6 and 7. But traffic was not disrupted for long.

Despite the restricted train service, commuter traffic actually increased as many moved to the outer suburbs or even further out to escape the worst of the bombing. For holidays and for evacuees the West of England and Wales were seen as the best options, not least because most of the South Coast was taken over for military purposes with beaches cordoned off behind barbed wire, and during the period before the Normandy invasion in 1944, only residents and those with special business were allowed near the South Coast. On the morning of 29 July 1944, a summer Saturday, Paddington was closed for three hours, and no underground tickets were sold to Paddington, because the main concourse and platforms were blocked solid with people waiting to catch trains. The problems of wartime had been compounded by government restrictions on extra trains and even on extra carriages on existing trains, added to the much reduced frequencies and extended journey times. It took three telephone calls by the general manager, Sir James Milne, to the Ministry of War Transport, and the threat of a visit to Downing Street, before a man from the ministry arrived and authorised the use of the locomotives and carriages that were standing idle at Old Oak Common depot. The restrictions were eased somewhat after this, but even so, at August bank holiday weekend, then taken early in August and not at the end as today, mounted police had to be called in and the queues snaked along Eastbourne terrace, which did at least have the advantage of allowing passengers to get to and from the trains.

There was disruption of a different kind on 16 October 1944. The locomotive of a down empty carriage train was derailed outside Paddington close to the parcels depot. This was soon followed by two coaches of the down *Cornish Riviera* express being derailed at the same point, and although there were no casualties, the line was blocked and normal working could not resume until morning of the next day.

At Victoria, the Second World War brought about major restrictions with train services cut back and, of course, not only did the Continental traffic end on the outbreak of war, but trains carrying service personnel to Europe also disappeared with the fall of France. The heavy air raids during the Blitz of 1940 and 1941 saw Victoria closed at times as bombs and parachute mines closed the approaches, but the station itself was spared serious damage, despite a Dornier Do17 crashing onto the Eastern Section on 15 September 1940. Later, a flying bomb hit the Eastern Section on 27 June 1944, destroying offices and also damaging the booking office.

The invasion of France soon brought back the daily leave trains, and a limited service for civilian traffic to Europe started after German surrender, but a more complete service did not follow until 15 April 1946.

Chapter 15

Austerity and Nationalisation

...an eloquent tribute, to their efficiency, standard of maintenance, and on the high factor of safety attained, all of which reflects the greatest credit on every railwayman and woman for the part they played in this historic year.
Sir Alan Mount, Chief Inspecting Officer of Railways

The return of peace brought no ease to the railways, or indeed any transport operator, war battered, short of skilled maintenance staff and the necessary spares or replacements. The railways suffered badly enough, but so too did the bus operators. While the military required far fewer locomotives and other rolling stock than they had during the First World War, bus operators had seen vehicles requisitioned if they were in a 'safe' area, sometimes for military use but more often to support operators whose normal traffic had been expanded by military bases or shadow factories on war work in their area.

London Transport had 'borrowed' buses from other operators, and its own once smart fleet was showing its age. Early in the war, buses built for export customers had been frozen and then manufacturers had been allowed to complete them for allocation to home operators. London Transport's most interesting vehicles were trolleybuses originally destined for South Africa: they never got there. These were easily distinguishable by having the upper halves of their windows in tinted glass, which was never changed. Others had a lower-deck forward exit door, which was never used and eventually had a double-seat placed across it.

Much of the pre-war fleet was in a poor condition, with some buses even sagging in the middle. New bus bodies seemed to arrive more quickly than new chassis and engines, so some new bodies started their service with London Transport on old chassis until new chassis arrived. London Transport also had to accept very non-standard utility vehicles, mainly of

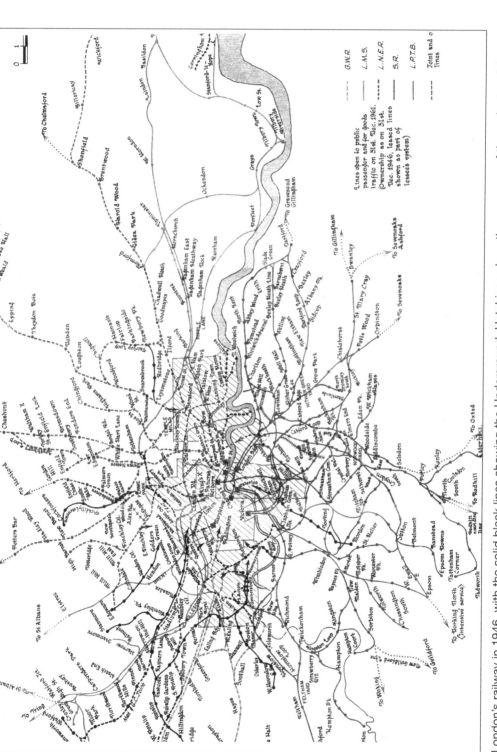

London's railway in 1946, with the solid black lines showing the Underground. Hatchings show the coverage of the major termini.

Guy manufacture, which it got rid off as quickly as possible. The shortage of vehicles, and of fuel, especially once the balance of payments crisis hit hard after the Americans ended 'Lend-Lease' in autumn 1945, was aggravated by the determination of many London bus conductors not to allow standing passengers outside the peak periods.

The Southern suffered from the severe disadvantage that of all the 'Big Four', it was the one closest to the enemy's airfields and operating in what was regarded as a prime invasion area. Between 24 August 1940 and 10 May 1941, there were raids on some part of the Southern network for 250 out of the 252 days. Although spared the massive industrial conurbations of the Midlands and the North of England, or Central Scotland, it did have three major naval bases at Chatham, Portsmouth and Plymouth, as well as a less important one at Portland, the ports of London and Southampton, and a substantial proportion of the RAF's fighter stations within its area, as well as being more heavily exposed to the plight of the capital than any other railway. It also served the area chosen for the massive build-up of men, equipment and supplies for the Normandy landings.

The worst affected of its lines were, naturally enough, all on the approaches to the London termini, and of these the most bombs and parachute mines per route mile were on the 2¼ miles between Waterloo and Queen's Road, with no less than 92 'incidents' as the authorities rather coyly described them. Charing Cross and Cannon Street to New Cross and New Cross gate, 5½ route miles, recorded 123 incidents, while the 4½ route miles from Holborn Viaduct to Herne Hill suffered sixty-two incidents.

All in all, the Southern alone had seen fourteen bridges demolished, another forty-two seriously damaged and 143 less seriously damaged. Incidents per 100 route miles on the Southern tell the story, with 170 incidents per 100 route miles compared to thirty-three on the GWR, twenty-nine on the LMS and just twenty-eight on the LNER, despite the latter's lines in Essex and East Anglia, and up the East Coast. There were 3,637 incidents on the Southern's 2,135 route miles, whereas the LMS had 1,939 incidents on 6,672 route miles.

There were severe wartime production controls to minimise waste and also to allow full use of materials and manufacturing resources for the war effort. Initially, the only new transport equipment authorised for civilian use was for equipment already under construction, which could be completed. In this way, the Southern Railway completed some additional electric multiple units. It also received another two in the winter and spring of 1940. Even before the outbreak of war, continued strong growth in rush hour traffic was causing the Southern to evaluate new trains, and also to see if better use could be made of space. At Eastleigh works, investigation into the use of welding to reduce the thickness of the sidewalls and the use of curved sides, led to the conclusion that up to six passengers could be seated abreast in reasonable comfort on short suburban journeys. Towards the end of the war, these experiments provided the basis for a utility design which crammed as many as eleven compartments into a vehicle really designed for ten, but interestingly, there were also carriages with fewer compartments, anticipating the post-war return of first class suburban services, which never happened.

Post-war, the GWR started to convert steam locomotives to oil-firing as an economy measure, but this was soon banned and the locomotives converted back to coal-firing as the balance of payments problems meant that there was insufficient foreign currency to pay for imported oil.

'A hell of a mess'

When referring to the wartime record of the railways in 1944, Sir Alan Mount, the Chief Inspecting Officer of Railways, was able to say that it represented 'an eloquent tribute, to their efficiency, standard of maintenance, and on the high factor of safety attained, all of which reflects the greatest credit on every railwayman and woman for the part they played in this historic year'. These comments late in the war by an impartial public servant were ignored by the politicians.

It is hard to judge just how much railway passenger traffic was affected by the war since the available statistics do not show the average length of journey, which was likely to have increased considerably. The number of originating passenger journeys on the GWR in 1938 was 129 million, but by 1944 this had increased to 190 million. On the LMS the figures showed a smaller rate of increase, from 421 million to 456 million, itself down two million on 1943, but static on the LNER at 281 million, but again down on 1943. The big exception was on the Southern, where passenger journeys fell from 361 million to 347 million, due in no small part to the loss of the holiday and excursion traffic. For all of the railway companies, the number of coaching train miles fell between 1938 and 1944, including empty stock workings. These figures tell little of the reality of wartime railway travel, as the number of passengers per train mile increased substantially between 1939 and 1943, without taking any account of the length of journey made, which seems to have increased substantially, still less the amount of time spent aboard the train. On the Great Western, passengers per train mile rose from 3 to 5.6; on the LMS from 4.1 to 6.5, the LNER from 3.8 to 5.4, and on the Southern from 5.6 to 7.6.

The statistics are inadequate since they consist of totals provided by each company, not by the Railway Executive Committee, so that, for example, a train from, say, Portsmouth to Rosyth could count as four trains, running over the Southern, GWR, LMS and finally the LNER. Nevertheless, passenger specials for the government rose from 24,241 in 1940, doubtless boosted by the Dunkirk evacuation, and after a drop in 1941, to 47,381 in 1943. Freight specials showed a steady increase, from 20,888 in 1940 to 45,583 in 1943.

In 1943, at the annual general meeting of the Great Western Railway, shareholders were told that the arrears in repairs and maintenance had reached £8.5 million, about a third more than the Great Western's guaranteed annual compensation for the use of its track and trains. The growth in arrears did not represent negligence on the part of the company, but was a reflection of the shortage of materials and skilled manpower.

When it came, the end of the war was a relief, long expected after the invasion of France and seemingly often delayed. Unfortunately, the travelling public expected the service to return to normal almost immediately, despite the damage and the arrears of maintenance and renewals which by this time on the Great Western alone had reached no less than £18 million, equal to some £540 million at today's prices. This sum was almost three times the annual compensation still being paid to the company. The annual compensation arrangement was intended to continue for at least a year after the cessation of hostilities. Nowhere was the continuing impact of the war more obvious than with the ferries, for as 1945 dawned, there was just one GWR ship not in government service.

Perhaps the easiest way to describe the impact of the war years on the travelling public post-war was that the trains simply did not just look neglected and war-stained, even battered, but reliability had also suffered badly. The Great Western maintained that pre-war it had suffered a locomotive failure once every 126,000 miles, but in the immediate aftermath of the war, it suffered a failure every 40,000 miles. These figures are interesting, as a modern electric or diesel multiple unit with even 40,000 miles between failures would be regarded as outstanding.

Unfortunately, the Great Western's management was soon to discover that the company would not receive even the normal peacetime allocation of materials, let alone that regarded as essential to make good war damage and catch up on maintenance and renewals. A good example was that in 1938, the permanent way teams had used around 19,000 cast iron rail chairs, yet in 1946, the Great Western was allocated just 12,500 rail chairs by the Ministry of Supply. This was despite the GWR estimating that

25,000 rail chairs a year would be needed for three years to bring the track back to the pre-war standard. The rolling stock situation was also grim. In 1938, the Great Western had a total stock of 6,168 carriages, and of these 5,819 were available for service every day, but by 1946, the total stock had dropped to 5,738 carriages, and of these just 4,441 were available for service due to the backlog of repairs. This meant that the company had gone from 94.3 per cent passenger rolling stock availability to just 77.4 per cent of a much lower total. The carriages that were left were also much older as the average age had risen from eighteen years to twenty-two years. Not surprisingly, many regarded the grey days of the post-war austerity period as being worse than the war itself. For the unfortunate traveller by bus or by train, journeys were often uncomfortable with trains in particular being overcrowded.

The Great Western's experience was typical of every railway operator, even the nationalised London Transport, although only a relatively small proportion of the country's population used its services regularly. On the Southern Railway, the winter period had seen many trains heavily overcrowded, and punctuality fell far short of the pre-war standard, forcing the Southern to resort to a poster campaign and press advertisements to explain its position. A good example of the impact of wartime was that in January 1946, the 2¼ route miles between Waterloo and Queens Road, identified by the railway as its most bombed stretch of track, had no less than four severe speed restrictions, three to 15 mph and one to just 10 mph. Needless to say, the state of the track was also reflected in the poor state of the rolling stock, with frequent breakdowns, while on the Eastern Section at Victoria, the number and lack of regularity of military leave specials had an impact on the normal services. In December 1945, the electric trains, at one time noted for their punctuality, had an average delay of five minutes.

The chairman raised these matters at the 1946 Annual General Meeting, held in March. He told the shareholders that the restoration of normal services could not be done quickly, due to the shortage of materials and of men, with only a quarter of the Southern personnel serving with the armed forces having been released by that time. The railway was still running 570 special trains for the government every week, and long distance traffic was up 480 per cent compared with 1939, yet the quantity of electric rolling stock available was down by 3½ per cent. While a considerable mileage of track had been renewed in 1945, in 1946 it was also hoped to renew damaged bridges and stations. On a more hopeful note, the chairman also talked of further electrification and explained that the 1935 loans from the government for electrification could be repaid, even though repayment was not due until 1952.

However, the Southern seemed better able than some to cope with its problems. Its management, many of them soldiering on beyond their usual retirement age while they waited for colleagues to be released from military service, turned its attention to improving the railway as it was, and by July 1946, electric trains were suffering an average delay of just one minute.

The railways post-war were in the position of trying to do more with considerably less resources than they had employed pre-war. If 1938 had been a poor year for the railways, 1946 and 1947 brought an embarrassment of traffic. On the LMS, the average train was carrying 140 per cent of its pre-war loading, with passenger miles up 70 per cent while train miles were down by 30 per cent. Engines, carriages, stations, track, signals and bridges were all worn out, crying out for attention while the workshops that had given them regular overhauls had been committed to building tanks, guns, invasion barges and aircraft. All of this was aggravated by poor quality coal and frequent cuts in the volume of coal allowed even the railways, on whose performance other industries depended.

Probably what counted more was the experience of those on some of the London, Midland & Scottish Railway's branch lines, where intending passengers had to open compartment doors and look inside to see whether there was room for them as the windows were so filthy. An acute shortage of labour had meant that even such basics as cleaning carriages and locomotives were neglected, and in any case many carriages needed what is sometimes described as a 'deep clean'. Many recall the LMS locomotives in particular being so dirty that often engine numbers had to be chalked on to aid identification. Not for nothing did one wit scribble the graffito: 'LMS – a hell of a mess'. Schoolboys used to take a delight in swinging their satchels through the air and against seats to send a cloud of soot and dust into the air of an already murky compartment.

The allure of the suburbs

Wartime had not only interrupted railway modernisation, and especially electrification, it had also stopped housing development, whether it was the private estates built by developers or the slum clearance public or council housing planned by local authorities. While the London County Council had built new estates at places such as Streatham, the supply of building land within its area was already scarce during the 1930s and so it had started to build 'out-county' estates, with those at Becontree, St Helier and Downham becoming three of the largest public housing estates in the world by the outbreak of war in 1939. Faced with large numbers of homeless families who had been bombed out of their homes, the need for new housing post-war was even more acute, and for a while slum clearance was put on hold while the dispossessed were housed. So, during the late 1940s, the LCC built more estates outside its area, notably at Harold Hill, which was the largest, as well as Aveley, South Oxhey, Borehamwood, Debden, St Paul's Cray and Hainault. An idea of the urgency of this work was that much of it took place on green belt land which the LCC had pledged itself to protect. Thus, London became even bigger, and the growth was to be a factor in the later decision to create a Greater London Council which absorbed much of its neighbours' territory, including all of Middlesex.

Such developments clearly put more strain on the already overstretched railways, which included the Underground with the Central Line eastwards expansion hastily completed towards Hainault.

Not all of such developments were intended to create additional commuter traffic. There was also a new towns movement, with the intention being that the new towns would be self-sufficient communities with opportunities for employment, shopping and leisure pursuits as well as housing. Intentions were all very well, but a family without a roof over its head is far easier to relocate than a manufacturing or commercial enterprise with its equipment and easy access to markets. New towns in what we can now consider the commuter belt included Crawley in West Sussex, Basildon and Harlow in Essex, Stevenage, Hatfield and Letchworth in Hertfordshire, and Bracknell in Berkshire.

The stimulus for these new towns was the urgent need for re-housing, while the Ministry of Supply, the same department of state that denied the war-battered railways adequate materials to restore their services, ensured that council house building was accorded materials while private house builders went short. It was not just not the railways that were being nationalised, the public were finding that housing was being municipalised.

There was a growing gap between the aspirations of the planners and those of the ordinary citizen. The planners viewed suburban development with contempt, while a survey of the public conducted for housing managers found that 'an overwhelming majority plumped for a suburban house'.

The lesson was clear. Suburban development was to continue on a scale not seen even during the late 1930s, and many towns in the southern and eastern counties were to become dormitory towns. This started with the new towns and the 'out of county' housing estates of the LCC, but as the 1950s progressed, it was suburban development of private housing around many of the towns in the commuter belt that boosted peak period traffic.

The weather takes a hand

It almost seemed as if the fates were ganging upon the railways in the two years after the end of the war. One of the worst winters on record came in early 1947. It was inevitable that services were affected both by the bad weather and by the looming shortage of coal. Bad weather kept miners away from work, and the coal that was brought to the surface was often frozen at the pit head and difficult to load. For those railways operating steam locomotives, water was also a problem, as the water troughs were rendered useless by the low temperatures, forcing longer-distance trains to make additional calls to take on water, itself a hazardous task requiring locomotive firemen to climb on top of tenders in freezing conditions and in strong winds. In early February, the Government introduced curbs on the use of electricity by industry, and this extended to the railways, so that starting on 5 February, cuts were enforced on many suburban services, followed within a week, on 11 February by yet a further round of cuts, while still more followed on 15 February. The massive freeze continued until 8 March, when a thaw started, augmented by heavy rain on 10 March that resulted in flooding of many low-lying stretches of line.

The bad weather had started in January. Heavy snowfalls were accompanied by strong gales and, in between, the periods of calm were marked by freezing fog. The Southern's third rail electrified lines were especially prone to disruption in such conditions and the company responded by introducing de-icing trains, with elderly trailer carriages modified to spread a thin film of warm oil on the third rail sent on a tour of the electrified lines, and this worked up to a point in keeping lines open, provided that the intervals between trains was not too long. By early February, the Southern had enough coal for just one week, including coal for its own power station, and the Government was forced to act, introducing curbs on the use of electricity by industry.

Worse was to follow. In the severe gale of 4 March, heavy rain washed off the de-icing oil from the third rail, then turned to a blizzard, and the resulting precipitation froze, causing massive disruption. The 16.25 non-stop from Brighton to Victoria instead of taking just an hour to reach the capital, took more than eight hours. Throughout the country, many train drivers stopped their trains at stations while waiting for the weather to improve.

If these severe conditions were not bad enough, the massive freeze continued until 8 March, when a thaw started, augmented by heavy rain on 10 March. The Portsmouth Direct, notoriously prone to be blocked by earth slips, was hit between Petersfield and Rowlands Castle, and the section was reduced to single-line working. The line to Sidcup flooded at

Mottingham. The Brighton line was also badly affected as heavy rain caused chalk falls on the approaches to both the Quarry and Merstham tunnels early on 13 March, blocking the former line and leaving the other with just one line clear. The hard pressed control staff had to introduce widespread cancellations and diversions, including the substitution of a steam train via Oxted for the busy 17.45 from London Bridge to Eastbourne. It took until 17 March to clear the mess, by which time the heavy rain had caused the fallen chalk to become sticky, damaging the track and the ballast, and its removal had to be followed by extensive reballasting. Elsewhere, the line between Windsor and Staines was flooded, and the line between Eynesford and Shoreham (Kent) was also closed by chalk falls. It took until the end of March before trains could operate normally, and even then, the service was still massively reduced by the fuel shortages.

Accidents mar the end of the groups

An all too brief period existed between the end of the war in Europe in May 1945 and nationalisation of the railways at midnight on 31 December 1947. The final two-and-a-half years were marred by a number of accidents, with the Southern Railway by far the worst affected.

The first of these was on 24 October 1947, the 07.33 from Haywards Heath to London Bridge was held up by signals at Purley Oaks in thick fog for around eight minutes, before continuing its journey running at between 15 and 20 mph. As the train approached South Croydon Junction at around 08.37, the 08.04 from Tattenham Corner, running at 40 mph, ran into the back of it, causing severe damage to the rear coach of the 07.33 and so damaging its own front coach that accident investigators could not discover whether the motorman had been able to apply the brake or not. The disruption to services caused by the thick fog meant that both trains were packed, with about 800 passengers on the first train and 1,000 on the second. The driver of the second train and thirty-one passengers were killed, with another fifty-eight people injured.

The porter signalman at Purley Oaks admitted responsibility for the accident. This was the first time he had worked the box in thick fog and he could not see the 07.33 standing in the station, and advised Purley North signal box that it was 'out of section' when the signalman there telephoned. The Inspecting Officer felt that the accident was caused by the porter signalman's inexperience and his ready acceptance of irregular working. This was an accident that could have been prevented had colour light signalling been in use of this stretch of track.

On 6 November, again in thick fog, two accidents occurred on the same day. The first was at Motspur Park where the 16.45 from Holmwood to Waterloo ran into the second coach of the 17.16 from Waterloo to Chessington South as it crossed to the Chessington branch, killing four passengers and injuring another twelve, as well as the motorman of the 16.45. At the Inquiry, the 17.16 motorman maintained that the Motspur Park outer and inner distant signals were at caution, he approached the outer home signal slowly, but he saw a fogman showing a green light. The fogman admitted that he had not gone up the signal to check its position, but had instead relied on the sound of it rising or falling as an indication of whether he should put down or take up his detonators. The inspector laid the blame fully on the fogman, but observed that the accident might have been avoided had there been a ground-based repeater or a co-acting detonator placer.

Just a couple of hours later, the second accident happened at Herne Hill at around 19.30, again in very thick fog with extremely poor visibility. The 17.15 from Ramsgate to Victoria pulled by a 2-6-0 tender locomotive, two vans and nine corridor carriages, was checked by signals at West Dulwich after which it should have stopped at the home signals at Herne Hill to allow the 18.54 from Holborn Viaduct to West Croydon cross its path to take the line to Tulse Hill. Instead, the Ramsgate train failed to stop and struck the electric train, again as it was crossing the junction, badly damaging the first two carriages as it forced them across the up line and to the edge of the viaduct, with one passenger killed and nine injured. The Inquiry heard that visibility was almost nil, but on this occasion the fogman at the home signals did attempt to catch the attention of the enginemen as the locomotive passed, but this particular locomotive had right hand drive and the driver was depending on his fireman, who was inexperienced in main line working in fog, to keep a good lookout, in addition to his other duties. Even so, all might have been well as the guard of the Ramsgate train saw the fogman, but only made a partial brake application when a full application would have stopped the train in time.

In his last year of life, his eightieth, Sir Herbert Walker found time to drop a line to his old public relations man, John Elliot, by now running the Southern, offering his sympathy after the last of these accidents. Always supportive and never anything else than realistic, Walker wrote on 7 November from the Devonshire Club:

'My dear John
You have had damnably bad luck! But don't let it worry you. Now that there have been the series of three mishaps, we must all hope there will be no more. These things will happen. Whatever precautions are taken!

Cheer up: give my very best compliments to your wife.'

The only other major accident before nationalisation had been earlier, on 10 February 1946, at Potters Bar on the London & North Eastern Railway, and was largely due to driver error when a passenger train hit the buffers at the station, and derailed. The derailed carriages fouled the main line, where they were hit by an express train and the resulting wreckage was struck by a second express, with the result that two people were killed and another seventeen injured.

Nationalisation

Nationalisation was not a new concept, and in fact consideration of it had been mooted as far as the railways were concerned since the early days. In part, this was due to the continental model, where railways were already owned by the state or had a state interest. As early as 1838 the Duke of Wellington had argued for state intervention to prevent the railway companies exploiting their monopoly power. A plan for state purchase was published as early as 1843 in William Galt's book *Railway Reform*, which led to Gladstone's Regulation Act of 1844, which gave the government the option, from 1865 onwards, to purchase any railway company authorised thereafter. A later edition of Galt's book, published in 1865, continued to press for nationalisation, not on doctrinaire grounds as with the Labour Party and the trade unions, but in the interests of the country. A Royal Commission considered the matter in 1865, but decided that nothing needed to be done. The first British experience of nationalisation came in 1868 with the nationalisation of the hitherto privately-owned and fragmented telegraph system. This was to prove successful and when the benefits of an integrated telegraph system became apparent, it fuelled the pressure for nationalisation of the railways.

While many doubted that nationalisation could be a practical proposition, others had attempted to see how it could work, and politics entered the debate with the trade unions favouring state ownership as early as 1894, while early in the new century this became official Labour Party policy. A Liberal government appointed a Royal Commission to consider the question in 1913, but the First World War intervened before it could conclude its work. Wartime government control of the railways, nevertheless, pointed the way to greater state intervention if not outright control, and this was reflected in the post-war plans to group the railways into four large companies, each with what amounted to a regional monopoly, and with few opportunities for competition. The mainly Conservative governments of the inter-war years managed to bury the question, although the London Passenger Transport Board was a further step towards state control of public transport in 1933, as in some ways had been the restrictions on the road transport sector first introduced in the Transport Act 1930. It could be argued that it would have been better to have removed many of the conditions imposed by Parliament on the railways.

The Railway Companies Association mounted a fierce defence of its members' interests, but to no avail. Labour had an overwhelming majority and was committed to nationalisation.

Labour in 1945 was determined to nationalise almost all transport, including bus companies, canals, road haulage and airlines, although shipping seemed to slip the net, and like ports were only included if owned by the railways. Ports were excluded because many of the non-railway ports were either owned by the local authority or by independent trusts or boards, often with a strong local authority representation. In the case of the railways, shareholders were granted British Transport Stock in return for their shares, with the value of the latter being assessed as the average value of railway shares over the six months prior to the general election or the price immediately before the publication of the Transport Bill, whichever was the higher, with the value of the shares and interest at 3 per cent guaranteed by the Treasury. The interest was to be a charge on the revenues of the new British Transport Commission, which would operate the railways through a management team known as the Railways Executive.

Naturally, the threat of nationalisation was the main point to be made by the Southern Railway's Chairman, Colonel Gore-Browne, at the 1946 AGM.

'Do they think that the public will have a better and a cheaper service?' he asked those present. 'Do they think that the wage earning and the salaried staffs of the Main Line Railway Companies will be better off ? ...I challenge the nationalisers to prove their case. I accept the challenge to prove that public interest can best be served by private ownership of the Southern Railway.'

But, logic had no place in the argument. Ignoring the evidence of the extensive pre-war modernisation and the heavy investment in electrification, amongst other things, the Chancellor of the Exchequer had the nerve to describe the railways as a 'very poor bag of physical assets'. This hurtful insult was disproved in debate. The railways were war battered, but so too was the rest of the country. But the battle was lost and defeat was clear by the time of the 1947 AGM.

The Southern's directors and senior management had continued to plan as if nothing was going to change, and some angry shareholders wanted to know why. After all, every penny spent on modernisation was money that could have been paid in dividends and a gift to the future owner of the railways. They got their answer from the chairman.

'Now may I turn to the record of last year and to the plans which we have in view. Some…have asked "Why as things are now, have you made any plans? Is not your only duty to protect your stockholders' interests?" We feel it necessary to take a wider view. We have always regarded your undertaking as a service to the public…the Chancellor of the Exchequer who described the railways as "a very poor bag of physical assets" will in our case be agreeably surprised.'

Such a poor bag of assets indeed that the Isle of Wight continued to operate Victorian locomotives and rolling stock right up to 1966, and then these were replaced by elderly rolling stock dating from the 1930s and withdrawn from the London Underground, themselves to be replaced by 1938 tube stock that still runs today, every day, in the twenty-first century.

Chapter 16

Rationalising the Railway

In 1963, the Western Region general manager, Gerald Fiennes,
watched in apoplexy when an express from South Wales to Paddington
arrived on time, and was then delayed while first-class passengers off
the Newbury connection walked slowly up the platform to the first-class
seats. Exasperated - the train having lost six minutes - he said to the
up platform inspector: 'Blow your whistle at them.' The unanswerable
reply was: 'Sir, you do not blow whistles at passengers from Newbury.'

The Daily Telegraph

The way in which the state viewed transport was made clear on nationalisation. A massive new body, the British Transport Commission, was formed, under the chairmanship of Sir Cyril Hurcomb, a civil servant. The five full-time board members also included John Benstead of the National Union of Railwaymen and Lord Rusholme from the Co-operative Movement, although Lord Ashfield, who had been chairman of the Underground Group and then of London Transport had considerable experience of urban and suburban road and rail transport, as did Sir William Wood, who had considerable experience of railways in Ireland and with the LMS, before working on the Railway Executive Committee during the Second World War. Lord Ashfield died shortly after taking up office in 1948.

The BTC remit included the coordination of transport and it had powers to influence traffic movement through charging schemes to allow the different costs of the individual modes of transport to be used to direct freight and passenger traffic to the most economic and efficient mode for the particular traffic. The environment was ignored. Bus services were intended to be integrated through a series of area schemes that emphasised local monopolies, and which allowed the newly nationalised bus companies to make local acquisitions to strengthen their hold on the network. Even so, there were many local pockets of resistance in towns such as Winchester.

The BTC in effect became a massive interfering bureaucracy sitting between the Ministry of Transport, which was responsible for government policy on transport and for its regulation, including the operation of the traffic commissioners for road passenger transport and the licensing authorities for road freight transport, and the individual modes of transport, which were in turn administered by 'executives', of which the Railway Executive, commonly known as British Railways, and the London Transport Executive, were but two. The title 'British Railways' had originally been coined during the 1930s to promote Britain's railways abroad, but then revived during the war years and used in publicity then and immediately afterwards, usually to discourage the public from travelling at holiday periods.

Squeezed between the operators and the ministry, the BTC was unpopular. For its part, the BTC saw the different executives as unwilling to modernise and embrace new ideas. The executives saw the BTC as including not just bureaucrats, but often politically-motivated idealists wishing to test their new ideas on the businesses.

From the start, despite being run by a civil servant, it was the intention that the BTC should pay its own way as a business.

The new British Railways started life on 1 January 1948, with 19,639 route miles of track, a small fall in route mileage since 1930 partly due to some minor pre-war trimming of the network and wartime closures of unnecessary routes. It inherited 20,023 steam locomotives, 36,033 passenger carriages, and a further 4,184 carriages contained within electric multiple units. There were small numbers of diesel railcars and shunting engines. The executive was to be criticised for foot dragging and a reluctance to modernise, but it was also subject to direction by the BTC, which can hardly have encouraged initiative. Enterprise must also have been inhibited by the very scale of the undertaking.

The continuing shortage of materials after the war limited what the companies could do before nationalisation. BR also had to standardise the operating practices of the former railway companies. Although it included the Irish Sea ferries operated by the old LMS and GWR, it did not have control of railway services in Northern Ireland: apart from the LMS-owned Northern Counties Committee. Nationalisation was delayed on the other side of the Irish Sea because three out of the five railway companies operating within Northern Ireland had cross-border operations, and it was not worth nationalising the small Belfast & County Down Railway, the other purely 'internal' operator, on its own.

Initially, the boundaries of the old Southern Railway and the Great

Western approximated to those of the new Southern Region and the Western Region. There was some tidying up, with Fenchurch Street transferred to the new Eastern Region, while joint lines were each allocated to the most appropriate region. The LNER was divided between the Eastern, North Eastern and Scottish regions, and the LMS between the London Midland and Scottish regions, almost reverting to a pre-grouping structure. On the Southern Region, the old pre-grouping structure continued in the three divisions, Eastern, Central and Western, that perpetuated the areas of the South Eastern & Chatham, London Brighton & South Coast and London & South Western Railways.

After his opposite number at the Great Western turned the job down, Sir Eustace Missenden, the last general manager of the Southern Railway, chaired the British Railways executive. It was to be an unhappy end to his career on the railways and he soon understood why the job had been turned down by his counterpart on the GWR.

Early priorities included a new corporate identity. Members of the executive stood and watched as a succession of steam locomotives, each wearing different liveries, steamed slowly past, each with railway carriages again displaying different liveries. In the end, blue was selected for express locomotives and black for goods and mixed traffic, while carmine and cream became the new passenger rolling stock livery, variously known as 'strawberries and cream' or, to the cynics, as 'blood and custard'. Exceptions were the Southern electric multiple units with a simplified green livery, Pullmans retaining their traditional brown and cream, and, of course, the *Night Ferry* 'Wagons Lits' remained blue. Later, all over red was used for local and suburban stock outside the Southern region, while diesel and electric multiple units were painted green.

A new standard British Railways carriage appeared as the Mark 1, available as a corridor carriage for main line use, with the option of open carriages, and as non-gangway carriage for suburban and other services. There were kitchen, buffet and restaurant car variants, as well as overnight sleepers and a variant for parcels use that could double up as a guard's vehicle, although second-class and composite brakes were also available. Later, the Mk1 design was also made available for both diesel and electric multiple units, and both suburban and mainline versions were available with corridors or as open stock with gangways. It is worth noting, however, that Southern independence asserted itself with the first versions of new suburban electric multiple units retaining the old Bulleid 'wide-bodied' design, but later conformity was all and eventually the standard carriage held sway, indeed, it remained in production for Southern use well after the Mk2 design had been adopted elsewhere. The standard designs were generally pleasing in appearance, and the use of special wood, to which the attention of the passenger was drawn by a descriptive label, in first class, ended utility. The mainline Mk1's large windows were an attractive feature, especially appreciated by small children who could have a good view from the window seat, not possible with the high sills of later rolling stock.

The selection of a standard design did not mean any great rationalisation of railway manufacturing and production plant, while construction of new steam locomotives continued despite BTC objections. Initially, just one major electrification programme was put in hand by the new British Railways, the Manchester-Sheffield-Wath line across the Pennines, completed in 1954. Exactly why steam locomotive construction continued until 1960 is something of a mystery, as by this time diesel traction was already predominant on many routes and electrification had resumed. The stupidity was all too apparent in 1968, when steam finally disappeared from Britain's railways, just eight years after production ceased. Indeed, at the end of steam, many pre-grouping locomotives were still in service.

A new Conservative government passed the Transport Act 1953, abolishing the Railway Executive and establishing area boards under the British Transport Commission, with the new chairman of the BTC, General Sir Brian Robertson, becoming chief executive of the railways. This was a way of removing one layer of management and of control, but it is questionable whether it was the right layer. The other executives survived, including the LTE, and it would have seemed wiser to have disbanded the BTC itself and given the executives greater freedom, reporting direct to the relative departments of the Ministry of Transport. Many layers of control remained, with the British Railways regions including divisions and in their turn beneath them came the section and then the area.

The newly nationalised railways had an operating surplus of £19 million (£356 million today) in 1948, small enough given the size and turnover of the undertaking, but by 1955 this had become a deficit of £17 million (around £238 million today). The deterioration was blamed on rising costs and renewed road competition as well as an industrial dispute that seriously affected the railways throughout a substantial part of 1955, and doubtless gave a shot in the arm both to road competition and to the expanding internal air services.

With the railways firmly in its control, the British Transport Commission acted decisively. In 1955, a Modernisation Plan was published.

Subsidies

The question of losses became one of the major issues from the mid-1950s onwards. The solution was to be a combination of writing off losses and subsidy, of cutting the number of lines and of removing duplication, while looking for other ways of cutting costs, such as unstaffed stations or removing ticket inspections.

The question of state subsidies dates from as early as 1817, when the Exchequer Loan Commission was established to provide low cost loans for major public works. Initially it was intended to support town councils, but between 1830 and 1844, five English railway companies, including the Liverpool & Manchester, and four Irish companies benefited from loans provided by the Commission. These could have been seen as an early form of pump priming, for afterwards, few English railway companies were in need of state support as money for their construction flowed in from anxious investors, eager to share in the great boom.

Even when £1 million was set aside for the construction of light railways under the terms of the Light Railways Act 1896, only a fifth of the sum was actually used.

The two significant exceptions to subsidy came in the later years of the railway age, and reflected the need to ensure that some of the remoter parts of Scotland were served.

A more generous approach to providing low cost loans had been the spur to modernisation and employment creation of the Guarantees and Loans Act 1934.

Safety

Just as the change from individual companies to four large groups did not provide any guarantee of safety, neither did nationalisation. At Harrow, a station shared by London Transport and the London Midland Region of British Railways, on a misty 8 October 1952, at the height of the morning rush hour the up-Perth sleeping car express was running late while the low-sun made it difficult for the driver and fireman to see the signals, which they overran at speed and collided with a local train sitting in the station. A down Euston to Manchester and Liverpool express ran into the wreckage, knocking down a footbridge and scattering carriages over a platform on which people were waiting for a Bakerloo tube train. At least 122 persons were killed.

There was a further accident a little more than five years' later at Lewisham on 4 December 1957. Steam was still in use on the Kent coast services and when the driver of a Cannon Street to Ramsgate express became concerned about the steaming of his locomotive he overran two caution signals at full speed and did not brake until he had passed a red, crashing into the back of an electric multiple unit suburban train stopped at a signal under the flyover carrying the Nunhead line. The steam locomotive then struck the columns of the flyover, which collapsed on top of the wreckage, contributing to the ninety lives lost.

Modernisation did not stop the toll of accidents either, for by 1967, almost all of the lines in the South East were electrified, and for the few that were not, there were diesel multiple units. At Hither Green, on the evening of 5 November 1967, a diesel multiple unit fast train from Charing Cross to Hastings was derailed by a broken rail, killing forty-nine people and injuring another seventy-eight. The casualty figures would have been far higher but for it being a Sunday evening on what was normally a busy commuter line.

In these accidents, the cause was soon established, but that at Moorgate, then the end of a branch of the London Transport Northern Line, on 28 February 1975, has never been found. An early morning Northern Line tube train on the City & Northern Branch ran into the station at full speed, overshot and went into the sand drag at the end and, still in tunnel, hit the cul-de-sac wall; and the first two carriages concertinaed. There were forty-three persons killed and another seventy-four injured.

Travellers themselves can be a source of danger to those around them, and this was the case in a fire at the underground station at King's Cross on 18 November 1987. A small fire, possibly from a smouldering cigarette end burning amongst rubbish under an up escalator from the Piccadilly Line platforms, developed gradually over fifteen minutes until there was a sudden flash-over and a fireball swept up the escalator and into the booking hall which was below street level. The complex nature of the underground station meant that trains continued to arrive and disgorge passengers for some minutes after the fire started. In the inferno, thirty-one people died. A smoking ban was introduced on all London Underground trains and stations as a result.

The next major accident on the nationalised commuter railway followed resignalling at Clapham Junction on the busy lines of BR's Southern Region South-Western Division between Woking at Waterloo on 12 December 1988. An up-train had been brought to a stand on a stretch of line recently re-signalled while the signal behind the train continued to show clear. The stretch of track had a tight curve and the driver of the following up train from Bournemouth could not see the stopped train, and ran into it at high speed. This very busy section of line had quadruple tracks, arranged fast up, on which the accident occurred, fast down, slow up and slow down, and wreckage was scattered across adjoining tracks from the accident on the fast up, with a fast down train running into it, while a slow train from Waterloo to Portsmouth only just missed being hit. The cause was found to be a loose wire in the signal. The accident cost thirty-five lives and another seventy passengers were injured.

Modernisation

The 1955 Modernisation Plan was the most ambitious programme ever prepared for Britain's railways. The initial plan called for investment of £1,240 million (around £14,880 million today) but this was later increased to £1,500 million, which was, ignoring inflation, three times the cost to the British taxpayer of the Concorde supersonic airliner project in the early 1970s, and rather more if the inflation-prone 1950s, 60s and 70s were included.

The plan was the scheme that should have been introduced immediately following nationalisation, and was the brainchild of a Conservative government. It was meant to dispense with the Victorian and Edwardian railway, of which so much was still in evidence, and create a truly modern railway.

Electrification not only embraced the Southern Region, where the lines to the Kent coast, but not that to Hastings, were to be electrified, but other regions as well. The suburban lines from Liverpool Street and King's Cross were to be electrified, at last, while the other Eastern Region electrification was to be between King's Cross and Leeds, and possibly to York as well. On the London Midland Region, the lines from Euston to Birmingham, Liverpool and Manchester were also to be electrified.

Rationalisation was to accompany the Modernisation Plan as an almost inevitable *quid pro quo* for its implementation. British Railways had already started a number of line closures by this time.

The plan meant the end of inter-regional competition, which did not always provide the savings expected. Birmingham was no longer to be served from both Paddington and Euston, and with electrification in mind for the main lines out of the latter, Paddington lost out. Electrification showed that the railway's technical resources were wholly inadequate for the full extent of the plan, so that only the Euston schemes could be progressed and plans for electrification out of King's Cross had to be delayed. This led to the next mistake for the cost-conscious railway management, the failure to create a long-term rolling programme in which skilled personnel moved on from one to the next, maintaining the most cost-effective pace rather than a series of stop-start schemes.

Meanwhile, diesel traction was not simply to be for those lines deemed uneconomic for electrification, but it was seen as a stop–gap measure for the routes being electrified out of Euston and, later, King's Cross, although, strangely enough, such an interim traction package was not considered for the lines from Victoria, Charing Cross and Cannon Street to the Kent coast on which a straight steam to electric switch occurred.

To replace steam on every branch line, a whole series of diesel multiple units, diesel railcars and even diminutive diesel rail buses derided as being 'too small, too underpowered and too late', were ordered from several manufacturers. The lack of experience on what might be described as 'dieselisation' led to too many different types of locomotive being ordered, usually without prototypes being built and tested, and not surprisingly many of them were found to be unsatisfactory. As they were introduced, the new locomotives did not follow the Southern Railway's pre-war practice with its new electric trains and run from the factory to a purpose-built depot, but instead at first lodged alongside steam locomotives and were serviced in steam engine sheds, with all of the attendant dirt and filth that was the unfortunate weakness of the steam age, and again, once this found itself into the more delicate parts of the diesel locomotive, reliability fell still further. All of these problems were compounded by the failure to realise that, unlike the steam locomotive or the electric engine, a diesel could not be worked beyond its maximum power output without incurring mechanical damage.

Too many classes, too little standardisation, too little preparation and too little experiment but with too much haste were all problems with the diesels, but then, the bill was being picked up by the taxpayer, not the shareholder.

Between the wars, much had been made of conversion of relatively new steam-hauled rolling stock to electric operation, especially when the steam hauled stock had already been made up into pre-formed sets for standardisation of train formations and ease of marshalling. The modernisation plan usually ignored such possibilities. Bulleid mainline rolling stock on the Southern was scrapped, all of it within twenty years of construction, while older electric trains soldiered on for almost twice as long. The best of the old LMS carriages were not retained or converted. Even with the BR standard Mk1 carriages, the only time these were converted for an electrification scheme was with the Bournemouth electrification of 1967/68, and to some extent this may have been because the scheme itself was cut price, with electrification running just beyond Bournemouth to the depot, and trains being operated on a 'pull-push' basis, with a single four-car powered electric multiple unit pushing one or two unpowered sets as far as Bournemouth, where they were taken on to Weymouth by diesel electric traction.

The other major problem arose with single manning. The new electric and diesel traction did not need a fireman, but these were retained as driver's assistants, another advantage of the new forms of motive power lost, leaving the railways to negotiate this as a separate productivity deal, a completely new and unnecessary extra cost and source of industrial conflict. When the Southern Railway had switched services from steam to electric, no one even dreamt of having a second man in the cab.

The so-called 'sparks effect' showed that electrification in particular was popular, but mostly with commuters. The spread of private car ownership has been blamed for the decline in the importance of public transport and for its worsened financial situation, but in 1959, the number of car owners was a sixth of that in 1999. The real culprit was television, ending theatre and cinema trips in the evening. On Sundays, coach trips to the seaside were cheaper and often more convenient than travel by railway. As the working week shortened and the peak period became compressed, the growing gap between peak and off-peak loadings contributed to the worsening financial situation on the railways.

Eventually, the penny dropped. It was no use tinkering around with the executives under the British Transport Commission; it was the BTC itself that was to blame. It had criticised the executives and especially British Railways, for being insufficiently forward looking, but it was itself large and unwieldy, with too few people of any relevant experience at the top. The BTC was by the late 1950s being criticised both for its size and its lack of any commercial sense. It only managed to see through the electrification of the two Southern Region lines to the Kent coast in 1959 and 1961, leaving the residents of Hastings to be served by a distinctly ugly, noisy and rough riding batch of diesel multiple units, costly because they were built exclusively for this line and none of the synergies of using depots and crews for the electrified network could be realised.

Enter Lord Beeching

Mounting railway losses could not continue. The Ministry of Transport had commissioned two reports on the future of the British Transport Commission, one of which was for public consumption, the other for its own internal use. Even so, it was not until the Transport Act 1962 that the ministry grasped the nettle and broke up the BTC into its component parts, establishing the British Railways and London Transport Boards, as well as a holding company for the nationalised bus companies.

The 1962 Act ended the obligation to provide third-class accommodation, it allowed the railways to 'upgrade' this by renaming it second class, later changing this to standard class.

Later, other changes to the charging structure followed. Pre-nationalisation, first-class fares had been around 60 per cent higher than those of third class, but the nationalised railway closed the gap to around 50 per cent. Originally, any third-class (or later, second-class) fare was available as first class provided that accommodation was available, but in order to boost revenues, British Rail abolished first-class day returns. It had the reverse effect, driving people to their cars or to second class, while the under-used off-peak first-class accommodation became the resort for vandals, discouraging season ticket holders and business travellers. First class on many routes was used not only by season ticket holders, but MPs and senior civil servants, as well as railway management and, at one time, members of the National Union of Journalists! The weakness of the measure was soon exposed on many services where the shortage of first-class travellers off-peak was countered by the concept of 'Weekend First' for which standard-class ticket holders paid a supplement, and which required the railways to differentiate between 'first class' and 'weekend first class' accommodation.

Traditionally and in most countries, railway fares were set by the mile, although on some urban railways, so-called 'scheme' or zonal fares would group several stations together for the same fare. This was first applied in the British Isles on the Bakerloo Line in 1911. British Rail, as it had become, decided to try to manage its traffic better by increasing peak period fares and reducing off-peak fares, a system sometimes referred to as yield management and practised by low-fare airlines. Of course, a railway is not an airline and the system did not ensure even loadings throughout the day or throughout the week. In the late 1960s, it was also decided to impose higher fare increases on lines with more modern rolling stock or a better service, with one of the lines treated in this way being that between London and Brighton. The new fares structure simply meant that optional travel, filling trains in the off-peak, was much reduced.

For the railways, there was a new chairman from the private sector, Dr (later Sir) Richard Beeching. He had arrived at the BTC in 1961 before which he had been technical director of Imperial Chemical Industries (ICI), at that time regarded by economic historians as being one of the two truly internationally competitive British companies (the other was Rolls-Royce). ICI itself had been the creation of a kind of grouping of its own in the early 1920s, creating a new unified force in the chemicals industry.

Beeching felt that the new British Railways Board required a much simpler structure, and he also felt that it would benefit from an influx of senior managers from other industries whom he felt would be more familiar with developments in management techniques, and would also have a stronger market focus. Few of them stayed for more than a few years, either because they had difficulty in adapting to the realities of transport operation or they found life in a nationalised industry suffocating. They certainly were to get a difficult ride from some of the old school in the railway world, such as Gerald Fiennes, an ex-LNER man running the Western Region, who eventually resigned after writing a book, *I Tried to Run a Railway*, in which he argued that branch lines should be run more cheaply rather than closed. Many believed Fiennes had a point.

Beeching was expected by the government to at least reduce the growing railway losses, and ideally eliminate these altogether. In fact, his instinctive reaction was that of an accountant rather than a scientist, requiring, and getting, extensive statistics that showed just how much each section of line and each railway service earned, and how much each cost. He came to the conclusion that many lines could be closed and so too could many stations which showed very poor receipts. There was also abundant evidence of poor utilisation of rolling stock, especially for trains such as summer holiday specials that spent most of the year rusting away in sidings. He published his findings in a report, *The Re-Shaping of British Railways*, proposing to close some 2,000 stations and end 250 train services. The media presented this as a plan to cut Britain's railway network by a third.

Few have aroused such fierce passions as Beeching. Some would almost have him as the devil incarnate, while others point out that he merely accelerated a process that had already started. It is true that there were cuts well before Beeching. There are those who agreed with Fiennes. One big weaknesses of his method of analysis was that it concentrated too much on receipts from stations along a line and not enough on the earning potential of these stations. A good example of the way in which these figures can differ considerably comes from stations in resort areas, where the local business, and hence receipts, could be very low, but the station would have considerable earning potential because of the large number of often long distance journeys terminating there each summer. The weakness was one of traffic analysis, since the journeys mentioned would have been credited to the station of departure, which would have enjoyed a double boost to its income due to the fact that almost every passenger would have purchased a return ticket. Insufficient attention was also paid to the impact of branch line traffic on the main lines, what airline managers would describe as 'feeder traffic'. Ironically, shortly afterwards one of the London clearing banks produced an advertising campaign with the memorable slogan, 'Our roots are our branches'.

Beeching maintained that main lines could be profitable, but branch lines couldn't. Commuter traffic was unprofitable by this time, but socially and politically necessary.

To suggest that Beeching himself never actually closed a railway line or a single station is treated by some as if one is engaging in holocaust denial, but Beeching, his predecessors and successors, could only ever *recommend* closure. What followed was an inquiry and it was the Minister of Transport at the time who then decided on closure, which could be accompanied by conditions, including augmenting the local bus service.

If Beeching has been too severely criticised for his programme of cuts, he was also insufficiently recognised for the innovations he urged upon the railways, no doubt because the former obscured the latter in the perceptions of the media and politicians, and also of the public. In a further report, now little referred to, Beeching advocated continuing to invest heavily in the trunk routes.

While the innovations went ahead, Beeching started an accelerated programme of closures that saw many rural branch lines cut. Cities such as Oxford, a suitable distance for a modern commuter found their railway service downgraded, and Cheltenham found itself not just without the famous *Cheltenham Flyer*, but with very few direct trains at all. Within the London commuter area, the impact was less, but lines such as those from Guildford to Cranleigh in Surrey, disappeared.

Post-Beeching

Before all of his proposals could be implemented, there was a change of government, with Labour returning to power in 1963 after a long time in the political wilderness, having spent twelve years in opposition. Railway losses continued to rise, and it soon became clear that the closure programme would have to continue. Beeching retired in 1965 after the new government had settled in and was replaced by a railwayman, Stanley (later Sir Stanley) Raymond.

The Conservatives had been alarmed at the direction the railways had been taking, but had given the management a reasonable head, as well as having given the railways their single biggest dose of new investment ever. The new government took a much more interventionist approach, and the new chairman had to suffer the indignity of the Minister of Transport, Barbara Castle, appointing a Joint Steering Group that reported to both of them. This was a recipe for disagreement and friction, as for the first time, a government tried to run the railways directly.

Raymond left office in late 1967, to be replaced by another railwayman, Henry (later Sir Henry) Johnson, who came from the London Midland Region and just overseen the completion of the electrification project.

Having undermined one chairman, Barbara Castle at least helped his successor into office with the welcoming present of the Transport Act 1968, which at a stroke wiped out most of the accumulated deficit and for the first time recognised the existence of socially (and politically) necessary services that could never be remunerative by providing grants for their operation. It was not an entirely open-handed gesture, for some of the gains were balanced by losses.

Chapter 17

Expansion and Contraction

This is the age of the train!
British Rail advertisement

While the railways were at last being placed on a sound financial basis, there was also much else to give grounds for hope for the future. Almost twenty years after nationalisation, a new generation of electrification programmes were finally reaching completion. This meant that electric trains could operate between Euston and Birmingham, Liverpool and Manchester, but third and fourth rail remained in use between London and Watford, without any attempt to standardise on the new overhead system.

Productivity was at last beginning to improve. Belatedly, the management was pressing for single manning of electric and diesel locomotives, while also looking to remove guards, and by definition brake vans, from fully-fitted goods trains. At the end of 1971, the railway network's route mileage had been cut by 41 per cent since nationalisation, while stations had been cut by 67 per cent. The longest line to have escaped passenger station closures completely was that between London Waterloo and Portsmouth Harbour via Guildford, the 'Portsmouth Direct', but even on that line the goods stations have been closed and many of the sidings surfaced to provide much-needed car parking for commuters. The longest stretch of line in the country without a station closure was on the Waterloo to Weymouth line, where for more than eighty miles from London Waterloo stations remained open until one reached the New Forest, to the west of Southampton. Many short spurs had been closed, including Bournemouth Central and the old terminus in Southampton. It was soon no longer possible to use the line through Alton as an alternative if the main line to Southampton was blocked, or to reach Brighton via Uckfield and Lewes if the Brighton line was blocked. Elsewhere, the number of points and cross-overs had been reduced, sometimes compromising flexibility of working during engineering works or following the failure of a train.

In this light, it seems ironic that the new logo for the renamed British Rail was a double arrow symbol, which bore more than a passing resemblance to two lines joined by sets of points. The new name and new logo was matched by a new livery, with all-over blue for suburban and local trains, and blue and grey for mainline services, even replacing the Southern Region green, while elsewhere all-over maroon had earlier replaced carmine and cream.

As further evidence of improved productivity, and especially the improved use of assets, the number of passenger carriages had fallen from more than 40,000 to just 17,000, and the 20,000 steam locomotives inherited on nationalisation had been replaced by 3,633 diesel and 317 electric locomotives. This last statistic can be misleading as many more of the railway carriages were in self-propelled 'multiple unit' trains.

High-speed trains

Of greater potential benefit, work on the Advanced Passenger Train was not being adequately funded by the government, even though this train, with its tilt mechanism, was intended to lift the maximum speed on Britain's railways to 155 mph, and to be able to take curves at speeds of at least 20 per cent and as much as 40 per cent greater than could be managed by existing rolling stock. This meant that the train offered the chance of a high speed railway without the need to build costly new high speed lines, itself not just an economy but a saving of massive disruption and land use in a densely populated country. The APT project was finally scrapped in 1986, by which time British Rail was investing heavily in other rolling stock and on a programme of easing, but never eliminating, curves to achieve higher line speeds.

Failure to persist with the APT cost Britain dearly. It set a British speed record of 163 mph, which still holds on 'historic' track. Once other European railway equipment manufacturers mastered the problem, Virgin Trains had to buy tilting train technology from Italy.

The substitute for the Advanced Passenger Train was the IC125 or HST, High Speed Train, a non-tilting diesel electric train, in effect a long single multiple unit with a driving power car at each end. In what almost amounted to a re-run of trends in the late 1930s, streamlining was back in fashion on Britain's railways. First entering service in 1974, the HST was streamlined with well swept and rounded ends, made possible by the use of glass fibre technology to achieve curves that would have been difficult and expensive to produce using steel or aluminium. The carriages were officially termed as Mk 3, and followed the later versions of the Mk 2 in having air conditioning and sealed windows. Unlike the Mk 2, however, the Mk 3s were a comprehensive spread of carriages, with kitchen and buffet vehicles, whereas passengers had become accustomed to leaving the comfort and smooth riding of the Mk 2s to be served in a noisy and rough riding Mk 1 buffet, while the dining car crew attempted to cook meals in similar conditions. Later, suburban variations of the Mk 3 followed.

For the London commuter, the HST bought cities such as Bath, Bristol and even York and Cardiff into the commuter belt. To describe many of the traditional commuter strongholds as 'dormitory towns' was in any case often inaccurate with Guildford, for example, having more people commute into the town than out of it to London. Many commuter towns were certainly sufficient in themselves, rather than being dormitories for London workers, who in any case, had to be well paid to afford the high cost of a longer distance season ticket while these were not places known for cheap property.

One missed opportunity of the HST was the decision, on grounds of economy, not to include power-operated doors. It was wholly unnecessary since trains built for the Wessex Expresses for the final extension of electrification from Bournemouth to Weymouth some years later used the Mk 3 body shell and had power-operated doors. The omission of power-operated doors was to have one unforeseen consequence. The Mk 3 enjoyed integral construction, what is known as monocoque construction, with the body providing all of the strength needed and no separate underframe, but instead with bogies and anything else attached to the body. This method of construction combined lightness with strength, but what had not been foreseen was that such bodies, in order to survive and avoid metal fatigue, had to flex while running at high speed. A long series of mysterious deaths amongst passengers standing in or passing through the vestibules at the ends of carriages was first attributed to suicides, before finally being traced to doors suddenly flying open at high speed when the draught sucked the hapless passenger out. Power-operated doors would have saved lives.

The HST brought modular construction to railway carriages for the first time, so that the same construction was used for carriages of either class, but only in first class did seats match up with the windows.

The HSTs offered acceleration and an official maximum speed of 125 mph, when track condition was good enough, although on a test run; just over 143 mph was achieved, setting a world record for a diesel which stands to this day. They revolutionised inter-city railway travel, but were often not utilised efficiently.

Nevertheless, the HST was a success. Reliable, long-lasting and

THE LONDON BUS IN MATURITY

After the Second World War, the changes in the London bus fleet were less dramatic than between the wars, with all vehicles having a covered top deck and pneumatic tyres, almost certainly the two features that were most noticed and appreciated by the ordinary passenger with little or no interest in the vehicle itself.

In fact, there were some significant changes. Although a small number of half-cab front-engined single-deck buses entered service shortly after the war, and some non-standard Leyland Titans served with London Transport before being sold off to what was then Yugoslavia, the fleet soon standardised on two basic types, the RT double deck bus and the RF single deck bus. The RT was purely conventional, except for the standardisation on a pre-selective gearbox which made driving in congested city streets much easier. Two variants were the Leyland-built RTL, distinguishable only by a different fleet number and a different radiator, and the RTW, which was 8ft wide as against the RT's 7ft 6in. The RF, or Regal Four, was an underfloor engined single-deck bus seen in red central and green country versions, but also best known in its Greenline version. There were 4,250 RTs, 1,250 RTLs and 250 RTWs, as well as 700 RFs. The oddity in the fleet was the RLH, of which only around 150 were operated, and which looked like a distinctly nondescript provincial bus, and which had a lowbridge body with an offside sunken gangway upstairs. This was awkward to a conductor having to reach across to get the fare from the passenger sitting next to the window. It wasn't much fun for passengers either, as downstairs the offside had limited headroom, and upstairs the passenger sitting next to the window when the bus was full was squashed, while the unfortunate sitting by the gangway held on for dear life with one buttock on the seat cushion and the other swinging over the gangway! There had been lowbridge versions of the STL.

The Routemaster or RM class first appeared in prototype form in 1956 when the RT was still in production. This integral bus without a chassis but using monocoque construction brought the automatic gearbox and power-assisted steering to London, although country and Greenline versions had semi-automatic gearboxes. One reason for choosing the automatic was because this was the trolleybus replacement vehicle, and it made it easier to retrain trolleybus drivers if they did not have to worry about a gearbox. Eventually, the RM and its stretched version, the 30ft-long RML, started to replace the RT family, although later versions were also replaced by standee single deck buses, albeit with more seats than the Red Arrow vehicles, and by front entrance, rear engined double deck buses. For the enthusiast, the change was a cause for deep dismay, but the bus drivers fought a rearguard action against one-man-operation on double-deck buses for many years, and this may well have been another motivating factor in the quest for fare systems such as the Travelcard and the later Oystercard.

As in many cities, most passengers on London's buses are travelling for a relatively short distance, and one reason why London lagged behind other cities in putting platform doors on its rear entrance buses, of which the Routemaster was the last, although forward entrance versions were built for British European Airways (operated by London Transport) and Northern General, and a front entrance rear engined prototype was also built for London Transport. After a rear-engined Leyland Titan was built mainly for London Transport, LT stopped buying specialised buses and started buying the products on general sale. Not all of these stood up to the stresses of London traffic, and the Daimler Fleetlines were especially failure prone. Another bus that had an uncertain introduction to London use was the Mercedes articulated single deck bus or 'Bendybus', which at first seemed prone to catch fire.

In 1985, London Transport started a similar tendering system to that imposed on British Rail's passenger operations, with individual routes or sometimes groups of routes tendered to operators. The system applies only to what would have been the central area as the break-up of the National Bus Company, which had the country area operations of London Transport passed to it, saw these privatised. London Transport also became Transport for London, TFL, awarding tenders, monitoring operator performance and marketing transport within London, including some river services. Whereas operators outside London have the right to operate a service for as long as they want or for as long as they are capable of operating it to the satisfaction of the traffic commissioners, those in London operate only for the period of their tender. The process has been described as unfair as it is generally the operator charging the lowest price that is awarded the tender and operators who have invested heavily and done much to improve a service have often lost it when re-tendering became due. Buses are often passed from one tendered operator to another, and the Routemaster had an extended lease of life in this way, and some of the vehicles were in fact extended or 'stretched' themselves to become even longer, but the Routemaster has gone from London except for 'heritage' services.

Despite Transport for London insisting that buses are predominantly red in colour, to maintain what it regarded as a tradition, the London bus scene is much less full of a unique character than in the past. London buses today are simply red versions of buses operated elsewhere.

comfortable, it brought time for Britain's railways offering attractive scheduling without the need for special track. Single-handedly, it made railway travel fashionable again, with people actually remarking to their acquaintances whenever they had travelled on an HST.

Short of money, electrification went forward in a series of one-off schemes rather than a rolling programme. It also seems that London commuters were penalised while money was spent 'in the regions'. At a time in the late-1960s when the Waterloo–Portsmouth service was making an annual profit of around £750,000 and the service to Bournemouth around £500,000, investment in new rolling stock for the thirty-year-old Portsmouth line original electrification stock was denied until it could be shown that a return of 6 per cent could be achieved. Nevertheless, the King's Cross to Welwyn and Hertford 'Great Northern' electrification scheme was completed in 1976, resurrecting an old pre-grouping title more than half a century after it had disappeared. That same year, authority was obtained for electrification between both St Pancras and the more convenient new City of London terminus at Moorgate, and Bedford, the so-called 'Bedpan Line', but the full introduction of new services on the former was to be delayed until 1983 by an industrial dispute over single manning.

The big success in railway and marketing terms over the period following the introduction of the new 'British Rail' corporate identity had been Inter-City, advertised under the strapline 'Heart to Heart', to drive home the message that railway stations were closer to the centres of urban areas than airports. Yet, on the Southern Region the often very short turn round times, especially during the morning and evening peak periods, meant that the promised seat reservations could not always be provided, especially at the busiest periods when this service was most appreciated and sought after by the traveller. Progressively, the brand was removed from these services, including even the Waterloo–Southampton–Bournemouth–Weymouth service, which over its entire length was considerably longer than London to Birmingham or Bristol.

The period since the end of the Second World War had been marked by a consensus in British politics. This ended at the 1979 general election, when, spurred by a 'winter of discontent' that had seen the worst industrial unrest experienced in the UK since the year of the General Strike, the voters returned a Conservative administration under a new leader, Margaret Thatcher, determined to reverse the tide, with lower taxation, deregulation and denationalisation, although this latter policy was to be given the title of 'privatisation', probably justified by the fact that not only was the state to discard its own business interests, but so too were local authorities. Yet, even Margaret Thatcher, the 'Iron Lady', did not tackle the railways, leaving that to her successor, John Major.

Red Arrow arrives, and Greenline departs

While commuters to London always like to live on a line that has a terminus close to their place of work, for many, there is an onward journey. That is why, for example, Waterloo's isolation was such an issue before it was served by the Underground. London's dependence on deep level tube lines for most of its Underground network, and for all of the lines crossing the central area, means that a substantial amount of time is lost getting to and from the platforms.

As demand rose, and the cost of building new lines or even finding space for them even underground, something new had to be tried. In 1966, London Transport introduced new express central area bus services linking the main termini with the main centres for work and shopping, known as the 'Red Arrow' network. These buses were London's first 'standee' buses. Until then, the rule had been that buses should have no more standing passengers, or standees, than a third of the lower deck capacity subject to a maximum of eight. Trade union objections limited London buses to five standing passengers. The Red Arrow buses, rear-engined AEC Merlin single deck vehicles, with a separate front entrance and centre exit, carried no less than forty-eight standees, with just twenty-five seats, all at a raised level aft of the centre exit. A flat fare of 6d (2.5p) was charged, but instead of having a ticket, the passenger paid the money into a machine that allowed him to go through a turnstile.

The initial trial services linked Victoria Station with Marble Arch during the peak, and did a tour of Oxford Street and Marble Arch shops off-peak.

The cramming of forty-eight passengers into the space between the two doors, less the considerable amount of space required by the two turnstiles, meant that seldom did the buses carry their maximum number of passengers. Buses of similar layout, but without the turnstiles, were allowed to have forty-seven seats with sixteen standees, just ten passengers less than on a Red Arrow, and in fact would probably have made better use of the space as well as being more comfortable. However, London commuters were used to discomfort, and the network expanded, including two routes between Victoria and Waterloo.

When the trials started, the then Minister of Transport, Barbara Castle, a noted left-winger, dismissed press concerns about so many standing passengers by saying that she was sure that a 'gentleman would give up his seat for a lady!'

By contrast, one of the most comfortable options for commuting was the

Greenline Coach, and probably the one that most closely went from doorstep to destination as, while there were fewer stops than on normal red or green London bus services, there were more than on the railways, and the Greenline services served many places off the railway network. While these survived the creation of the National Bus Company, which assumed control of London Transport's country services in 1969, the country services were broken up into manageable units and it no longer became a single operation, even before privatisation of bus services. There was another problem, even before deregulation of bus services outside London, long-distance coach services were deregulated. Around the London commuter area there was an explosion of new express commuter coach services running from outlying districts, and especially those without a railway station, and this also undermined the viability of the Greenline services. London Transport had introduced Routemaster double deck coaches to most of the Greenline services, and then followed these by a variety of mainly AEC single-deck coaches that could be one-man-operated. For the first time, many Greenline services had *real coaches* rather than buses with extra padding on the seats, but the service was proving too costly, and with different operators at each end of a route, control was weakened, especially when relief vehicles were required. Gradually, the Greenline network contracted, and today just a few isolated routes survive, running into the centre of London, operated by privatised bus companies.

All change at London Transport

This is to jump forward many years for much had happened in London in the meantime. The London County Council had become increasingly a Labour Party stronghold as it consisted of inner London, with the more affluent leaving the rundown districts in the centre (albeit many returned later when gentrification became fashionable) for the outer suburbs and the older dormitory towns. In 1965, the LCC was abolished entirely and replaced by the Greater London Council, which absorbed much of Surrey, to the extent that the county's offices were left in Kingston, part of GLC territory, all of Middlesex, and parts of Berkshire, Bedfordshire, Hertfordshire, Essex and Kent. This recognised that one had to go beyond Surbiton or Slough to find open countryside. The GLC itself was abolished in 1985.

London Transport, which had become the London Transport Board on the winding up of the British Transport Commission, became the London Transport Authority in 1970, before becoming London Regional Transport in 1985, but remained state-owned.

Chapter 18

Sectorisation and Privatisation

Privatisation is a poll tax on wheels.
Conservative MP

By 1992, privatisation was finally on the political agenda, and mentioned in the Queen's Speech early in May, but while this had been delayed by Margaret Thatcher, for some time the ground had been prepared inadvertently by railway management by introducing the concept of 'Sectorisation'. This gradually, and sometimes unhappily, replaced the regions with a period of overlap. The change was accompanied by a method of charging known as the 'prime user' concept, which meant, for example, that if freight was the main user, it would meet most of the costs of that stretch of line, but the downside was that the line was only maintained to freight standards, and unlikely to be suitable for high-speed passenger traffic.

The big success of sectorisation was in the London commuter area, put under the management of one Chris Green, who created what he termed a 'single railway for the South-East', none other than Network South-East, which replaced all of the Southern Region and took over the commuter services and stations of the other regions. London commuters could see Network South-East maps at railway stations, although under Ken Livingstone as mayor of London, when the concept of a powerful US-style city mayor was introduced some years after the disbandment of the GLC, an attempt was made to hi-jack this network under the name of the 'Overground'. Many commentators feel that breaking up Network South-East into three companies to replace what had been the old Southern Railway and Southern Region, with further companies for services from Paddington, Marylebone, Euston, St Pancras, King's Cross, Liverpool Street and Fenchurch Street, was a major weakness of the privatised railway.

Privatisation finally surfaced in a White Paper published in July 1992.
The main points were:

(1) Rail freight and parcels should be transferred entirely to the
private sector.
(2) Passenger services should be operated as franchises by private
companies, who would be subjected to providing a certain pre-
determined minimum standard of frequency and service, and would
receive grants for uneconomic services, while paying for the right to
operate profitable services.
(3) All passenger and freight operators should have the right of access
to all parts of the railway network.
(4) The rump of British Rail should survive as the new track and
infrastructure authority with a new name, Railtrack, and that eventually
this too should be privatised.
(5) The railway maintenance and other technical facilities should also be
privatised.

A number of public appointments were to be essential for the operation of
the new railway, including the Director of Franchising, the Office of the
Rail Regulator and a new Quango, the Strategic Rail Authority, which took
over control of the British Transport Police.

The privatisation proposals were subjected to considerable public
criticism as well as to political opposition, with the Labour Party
threatening to reverse the process on being returned to power. Accustomed
to intense interest in each successive privatisation, the government was
disappointed to find that this was distinctly lacking in the case of the
railways. As the legislation was passing through Parliament, a number of
changes were made, of which the most important was that rolling stock and
motive power would be sold to companies set up for this purpose and leased
to the franchisees, with the entire British Rail 'fleet' divided amongst three
rolling stock leasing companies, or ROSCOs. This was just part of the
alphabet soup cooked up by privatisation, with other acronyms including
TOCs, train operating companies, and TESCOs, technical service
companies.

Not all of the criticism was aimed at the principle of privatisation as
such, but at the fragmentation and division of the railway. The romantics
wanted to see the recreation of the old companies, including some, who
would have been too young to remember the 'old' railway, even wanting a
return to the pre-grouping days. One prominent journalist yearned for the
return of the old London & South Western Railway, and wondered just

what colour the carriages would have been. A trip to a decent public library would have answered his question, while he might have discovered that it hadn't been the best of railways.

There were also those who pointed out that the levels of subsidy being offered at the start of the process was far higher than that given to British Rail, and inevitably questioned the wisdom of this and speculated on just what BR might have achieved with such sums. A glance at some of the poor decisions taken during the years of the Modernisation Plan might have provided some clues. Supporters of privatisation pointed out that the level of subsidy would decline over the period of the franchises, with many lines expected to move into profit and then make a contribution to the state. Government ministers talked up the prospects for the future, with one minister talking of 'comfortable services for the businessman and cheap and cheerful services for the secretary'.

As a sop to the travelling public and an incentive to the train operating companies to keep costs to the minimum, as the first franchises were being let, fares were classified into different categories as 'regulated' and 'unregulated'. On the latter, the TOCs could more or less charge what they wanted, but on the former, mainly covering season tickets and standard tickets, annual fare increases were to be one percentage point below the level of inflation, while a TOC that did not operate satisfactorily could find that certain fares, including season tickets, might even be cut as a form of compensation to the regular customer. The decision to cap season increases in some ways was understandable, as a throw back to the concept of the 'workman's ticket', although it did mean that the discount given to season ticket holders as a percentage of the standard single or return fare was to grow, creating hopelessly uneconomic peak periods. Commuter traffic created massive problems for the railways. For example, in 2003, the Strategic Rail Authority estimated that it could cost as much as £1,500 per passenger per annum to provide an extra rush hour train, but that the average season ticket fare per passenger per annum would be just £560! Far less understandable was the decision to cap some long distance 'saver' tickets. This risked not simply continuing but worsening an anomaly on some routes where the off-peak return fare was less than that of the single fare, so that conscientious booking clerks would recommend that the would-be purchaser of a single ticket bought an off-peak return instead. In theory it would be worthwhile for anyone wanting a single ticket to wait at the barrier to see if any passengers would throw away their unwanted returns.

It certainly seemed odd that one company would be allowed to buy the entire infrastructure, others the rolling stock and motive power or the freight services, but that the passenger services, which were the public's point of contact with the railway and which would have the most individual customers, were simply to be franchised off, with the term of seven years being set at the beginning. Seven years was hardly long enough to encourage investment in an industry in which the average life of rolling stock was four or five times as long. In theory, the rolling stock leasing companies could always lease the carriages and motive power to the next franchisee, but what if the next one had other ideas? Even on the old nationalised railway, cascading rolling stock on to other services was sometimes impractical. There were three traction systems available, diesel, overhead electric and third rail electric. Even within these divisions, there were differences in loading gauge. Traffic patterns also varied. When, for example, it was decided that the first generation of electric multiple units with power-operated doors should be transferred from the Southern Region's Western Division to Merseyside, these four car units had to be cut down to just three cars: the fourth carriage in each case was retained and inserted into a new build of emus of different design, leaving many of the inner suburban services from Waterloo worked by trains with a distinctly odd and uneven roof line.

On 5 November, the Railways Act 1993 received the Royal Assent and passed into law. There was a short period of calm before a major restructuring of British Rail occurred the following 1 April, ready for privatisation to start. Although intended to be sold in its entirety, Railtrack was organised into ten regional zones, although this was reduced to eight in 1995, few of which related directly to a franchise area except in Scotland where there was a perfect match. Only on the Isle of Wight, would the franchisee would also be responsible for track maintenance. British Rail's passenger services were organised into twenty-five companies ready for the franchising process to start, each with a subsidy profile and some of them also having funding from local passenger transport executives as well as from central government.

The original franchises were:

Anglia Railways	Great Western
Cardiff Railway	Inter City Cross Country
Central Trains	Inter City West Coast
Chiltern Trains	Island Line (Isle of Wight)
Gatwick Express	LTS Rail (London Tilbury &
Great Eastern	Southern)
Great North Eastern Railway	Merseyrail Electrics

Midland Main Line	South Central
North London Railways	South Eastern
North West RR (Regional	South Wales & West
Railways)	South Western
RR North East (Regional	Thames Trains
Railways)	Thameslink
ScotRail	West Anglia Great Northern

The first franchises were let in time for operations to start early in 1996. Many of the names changed, especially when franchises were re-let. North London Railways became Silverlink and then London Midland, while LTS became C2C, to the bewilderment of many, and South Central eventually renamed itself as the Southern Railway, showing scant regard for accuracy.

Tube expansion and the docklands

While the surface railway was under threat in many areas, the London Underground had completed its planned pre-war extension of the Piccadilly and Central Lines, and had eventually electrified the entire length of the Metropolitan Line. Nevertheless, it was becoming clear that much more needed to be done, and that the limits to any intensification of the service on most of the existing lines had arrived, so that only new underground lines could solve problem. Although London did get two new tube lines, it also obtained its first light railway, in docklands, using much abandoned track bed but with its own extensions, including a tunnel to the Bank.

Authorised in 1955, the Victoria Line was the first new tube railway in central London since 1907, and when opened in 1968-69, provided the capital with its first fully automated passenger trains. It provided interchanges with all of the other underground lines and initially ran from Walthamstow via King's Cross, St Pancras and Euston to Victoria, but an extension to Brixton opened in 1971, giving a route mileage of fourteen miles. Construction of a new line through the centre of London caused considerable disruption, and a steel 'umbrella' had to be built over the booking hall at Oxford Circus so that road traffic could continue along the length of Oxford Street and Regent Street. This was the first railway in Great Britain to have driverless trains, with the train controller or guard sitting in the driving cab at the head of the train, not simply to reassure passengers but also so that manual control could be assumed if the automatic control failed.

The pressure at the London end of the Metropolitan and Bakerloo lines also needed to be relieved, by a new line, known initially as the Fleet Line when it was authorised in 1969 to run 2½ miles from Charing Cross to Baker Street to ease pressure on the Bakerloo Line in central London, and then take over the Stanmore branch. In 1972, an extension was authorised along the line of Fleet Street through the City of London and south to Lewisham. It was renamed the Jubilee Line in 1977 by the then Greater London Council, after opening in 1979 between Stanmore and Charing Cross, the eventual extension ran to Waterloo, then to the new developments in London's docklands, and finally north to Stratford.

Originally planned to have moving block signalling, this was found to be impractical and conventional signalling was used initially. On the new stretches of line, it became the first London tube line to have platform doors. Moving block signalling would have been another significant first for London, not only eliminating line side signals, but also ensuring that the distance between trains increased as speed rose. That it couldn't work on the Jubilee indicates that the system is very difficult to install as the line, with no branches and with all trains having the same stopping pattern, should have been ideal. The line has been very popular and in 2007 started to receive additional trains while the existing trains were lengthened by having an extra carriage inserted: something that took a working day for each train as the train's computers had to be reset.

During this time of change, the London Transport Authority was replaced in 1984 by London Regional Transport and, later, by the present Transport for London.

Although London did not actually get an overhead railway as proposed by Paxton, it did get a railway with much of its route elevated above the ground on arches. The Docklands Light Railway gave full rein to all of those commuters who knew how a modern railway should be run, rather than risk leaving it to the professionals. No railway has ever had so many years of wide speculation over the best form of railway for regeneration of the London docklands, with monorail and trains with pneumatic tyres, as in some lines in Paris and Toronto, being amongst the proposals. Eventually, the steel wheel on steel rail won, and the Docklands Light Railway was authorised in 1985 to run from the Minories, with the station named Tower Gateway, to Island Gardens in North Greenwich and from Poplar to Stratford, giving 7½ route miles initially. Although London Transport originally acted as a consultant, the line was independent until later absorbed by Transport for London, and while using standard gauge track, used third rail electrification in contrast to the third and fourth rail of the London Underground network. It used part of the infrastructure built for the London & Blackwall Railway.

Meanwhile, accommodation in the City of London was scarce for offices and for those wishing to live there. The most upstream docks soon found their warehouses converted into flats, while those further downstream were rebuilt to provide Canary Wharf and the rest of the Docklands development, including the City Airport. Without these developments, many foreign banks and other financial institutions that had wanted a foothold in the London market could not have been accommodated. Yet, transport links at first were poor, hence the importance of the Docklands Light Railway and the more traditional Jubilee Line extension.

Built as a light railway with two-car multiple units often working in pairs, the DLR offers fine views over the former docklands and Canary Wharf, but suffers from tight curves. The trains are completely automatic, but an attendant can take control if necessary. Initially, the line proved both unreliable and inadequate for peak period loads, and substantial rebuilding proved necessary. The line was extended to Bank, with transfers to the tube lines, in 1991, and later to serve the City Airport. It now runs under the Thames to serve Lewisham and platforms have been lengthened and the trains to converted to three-car units while additional new trains have also been introduced. The views from the line make the journey worthwhile and welcome change from the tunnel walls of the deep level tubes, but the ride is very poor and speeds are low, while the short carriages give the impression of always being crowded.

Privatisation of Britain's railways saw the British Rail network divided up amongst a large number of train operating companies, one of which, North London Railways, gradually evolved into Silverlink and then subdivided itself into Silverlink County and Silverlink Metro, with the latter running services along the old North London Railway's lines, including the North London Line itself and the West London Line. In 2007, Transport for London took over the franchise for these lines and added the East London Railway, originally authorised in 1863 to connect all of the lines running into London from the north, east and south. Although still theoretically a franchise, the franchising authority became Transport for London, following a precedent set for MerseyRail. For this collection of lines, TfL revived an old name, Overground, originally created for buses operated by the Dangerfield group of companies, operating around Enfield, until they were acquired by the LGOC in 1927. The line is operated on behalf of TfL by London Overground Rail Operations Ltd, or LOROL. Silverlink County later became London Midland.

The East London Line utilised the Thames Tunnel built by Sir Marc Brunel between 1825 and 1843. Opened between New Cross and Shoreditch, a distance of 5¼ miles, in 1876, it also provided access to Liverpool Street. At its southern end, it connected with the London Brighton & South Coast, London, Chatham & Dover and South Eastern Railways at New Cross, but failed to provide any substantial link at the northern end. No rolling stock was owned by the ELR, and services were worked by other companies. It was leased in 1882 by a committee of five railways, the LBSCR, LCDR, SER, Metropolitan and Metropolitan District Railways, with the Great Eastern joining in 1885. It was electrified on the third and fourth rail system in 1913, after which the MR operated the trains, but ownership passed to the Southern Railway in 1925.

The line did not pass to London Transport until nationalisation in 1948. The London Overground network is being extended north to Dalston and south to East Dulwich, based on the East London Line, while a further extension to Clapham Junction is envisaged. Much of the Overground track mileage is also used by freight traffic, but it is intended to convert operations to a high frequency metro–style network.

The Overground is probably a big disappointment for TfL as the original idea under a Labour mayor for London, was that TfL should become the London Regional Rail Authority with powers over all railway services operating into the capital. The then mayor, Ken Livingstone, wanted to be able to order the mainline companies to make adjustments to their services, conflicting with the franchising system under which these were operated. A good example was that all trains running to Waterloo, and those on the old LB&SCR line to Victoria, should be made to call at Clapham Junction so that this would become a major interchange and reduce the pressure on Waterloo and Victoria. The idea is not without its attractions, but it would substantially reduce the number of trains on the lines concerned, creating problems of capacity, and also extend journey times, albeit slightly. As it is, Vauxhall Cross has become an interchange between suburban trains bound for Waterloo, the Victoria Line and the London bus network.

Jumping the gun slightly before gaining the necessary powers, Livingstone had maps produced showing the London area mainline and surface suburban network, dubbing these as the 'Overground', well before any prospect of taking over Silverlink Metro was raised. The maps were quietly withdrawn some time later. On the other hand, ensuring that railway travellers, whether Underground, Overground or simply on the surface, know all of the routes and connections available to them, had to be a good idea.

Off to the airport

London's second airport at Gatwick was the first to be served by its own railway station, although the airport site and station actually moved slightly when it re-opened after the Second World War in the mid-1950s. London's main airport was nevertheless without any railway connection of its own until the Hounslow branch was extended in 1977; the first deep level tube link to any airport in the world, and in 1986, a loop was added to serve Terminal 4, followed later by a shuttle to and from Terminal 5.

The tube link with central London was doubtless better than nothing, but paled in comparison with the frequent surface trains of the Gatwick Express and, after it was rebuilt and opened as London's third airport, the fast trains of the Stansted Express. Something better was needed, and this came in the form of a new direct railway from the airport to Paddington, the Heathrow Express. The new service ran from the airport to the mainline into Paddington, and with its overhead electrification it brought electric trains to Paddington for the first time when it began running to the station in 1998. The Heathrow Express was an operation owned by BAA, operators of London Heathrow, and was joined in 2005 by Heathrow Connect, a stopping service to the airport intended for airport workers and others living along the route.

One lesson learnt by railway operators with the Heathrow Express and Stansted express was that airport operators had a far better idea of the ideal train for airport passengers than railwaymen. The higher proportion of passengers with luggage and the often larger quantities of luggage carried meant that extra space and wider doors were essential for a suitable service. The original Gatwick Express trains consisted of converted mainline stock that was unsuitable. Nevertheless, one feature of the Gatwick Express that was appreciated by commuters was the fact that it boarded only at the terminus at each end and ran non-stop every fifteen minutes throughout the day. The better-heeled passengers from intermediate stations on the Brighton line soon found it worthwhile, if costly, to drive to Gatwick and catch the Gatwick Express. Sadly for them, a route utilisation study has decreed that there is no longer sufficient space for a dedicated airport service.

One problem with using Paddington as a terminus for the Heathrow Express and Heathrow Connect, is that the station is the worst placed of all London termini for the City and not that good for the West End. The Stansted Express runs straight into the city at Liverpool Street, and the

Gatwick Express ran into the edge of the West End at Victoria, with other services to London Bridge and to what was Holborn, but is now City Thameslink, with services continuing northwards to King's Cross and Bedford.

While the Docklands Light Railway serves London City Airport, passengers to and from Luton Airport have a service to St Pancras, but with a bus link between Luton Airport Parkway station and the airport terminal building.

The presence of London City Airport has been a boom to the business air traveller, underlined by the fact that it is closed overnight and also during Saturday afternoons and Sunday mornings. The runway has been lengthened since it opened. Initially there were limits on the destinations served as the aircraft using the airport were slower, due to the need to be able to use the short runway, than those using the main airports, even when turbofan aircraft such as the BAe 146 and its derivative, the Avro RJ series, were used. Air Malta, for example, found that its service to the airport did not offer any great time saving over its flights to Gatwick and Heathrow. Nevertheless, British Airways has introduced transatlantic flights to New York using a small fleet of Airbus A318 airliners with premium-class seating, but the catch is that these have to refuel westbound to be able to take-off from London City.

What the airport does mean is that it is now possible to commute daily from, say, Edinburgh or Amsterdam, to London, and home again in the evening. Possible, but expensive, and so those needing to work in London probably find a *pied a terre*, now more usually known as a 'crash pad', less expensive.

While the construction of a third runway at Heathrow has been given official backing, it will need to go through the tortuous British planning process; others are calling for a new airport in the Thames Estuary. Originally it had been intended to locate London's third airport at Foulness, not too far from Shoeburyness on the former London, Tilbury & Southend Railway, but the dangers of unexploded shells from the army firing range at Shoeburyness and the fact that the area was a focal point for migrating birds, which don't mix well with aircraft, and the cost of a high speed connection to London, all went against Foulness and eventually Stansted was chosen. The revised plans are for a Heathrow replacement, with the current mayor of London, Boris Johnson, seeing the site of Heathrow redeveloped as a business park. It would be some business park, and would have to be to justify the continuation of Heathrow's existing railway links and the collapse of property values once the airport goes. The new airport would be further south towards the Kent side of the Thames Estuary, and could possibly use the high speed service to St Pancras of the Channel Tunnel Rail Link, otherwise known in railway circles as High Speed 1, or HS1.

High Speed 1

When the Channel Tunnel opened officially in 1994, the trains ran into Waterloo International, a terminus completed at the northern end of Waterloo Station and using the former Windsor Lines station and the Necropolis Station. The concept of a Channel Tunnel dated from early in the nineteenth century when the French mining engineer, Albert Mathieu-Favier, proposed two tunnels meeting in an artificial island to be constructed on the Varne Bank in mid-Channel. This was meant to be a road tunnel and the island would allow horses to be changed. Much later, one French and two British companies started trial boring on both sides of the Channel, and using compressed-air boring machines they successfully completed a mile-long tunnel that dropped around 160 feet into the chalk beneath the sea. The work stopped because the British Army saw a potential threat to national security.

The concept was not taken seriously again until 1929, when a Royal Commission considered proposals for a broad gauge line from London to Paris, which would have been incompatible with the gauges in use on either side. Nevertheless, it was not until 1955 that it was finally accepted that a tunnel presented little threat to national security.

The original line used largely commuter railway with some new connections to enable trains to get from the Kent coast and into Waterloo, with little scope for true high speed running. A new line was built to St Pancras and the East Midlands Trains services from this grand terminus were displaced to a new and somewhat utilitarian station outside while the Eurostar trains from Paris and Brussels moved into the renovated historic Midland Railway terminus. This left the station somewhat underused, but it was always intended that the costly new line from St Pancras to the Channel Tunnel, High Speed 1, or HS1, should be used to cut commuter journey times from much of Kent, as well as making a significant reduction in the London to Brussels and Paris railway times.

The new service was written into the franchise for Southeastern Trains, which have a new high-speed domestic commuter services operated with Class 395 electric multiple units built by Hitachi in Japan. Commuter services started in December 2009, between Ashford International in Kent and London St Pancras, giving a journey time of thirty-seven minutes, while there are intermediate stations at Stratford International railway station. The trains will start and end their journeys beyond these three stations, reaching destinations such as Margate, Folkestone and Dover, although this involves running on existing lines so the journey time savings will be much less. The new fleet of twenty-nine trains is able to reach speeds of 140 mph, 225 kmph. It is too early to say how successful the new service will be. Existing commuters from Kent to London will usually have their place of work within easy reach of the mainline terminus used by their trains, with as few stops as possible on the Underground, and only a small number would be travelling to North London, for which the new service would be most convenient – but travelling patterns do change once a new service is available. Interestingly, the new service will be standard class only, although with a premium fare for reflect the faster service.

Of course, the reduced journey time between London and Paris or Brussels offers the possibility of international commuting, albeit the time differences between the UK and the Continent mean that the commuting could only really be in the London direction.

Across London North and South-Thameslink

The idea of running railway lines across London is not new. As we saw earlier, there was a plan for a line from Charing Cross to Euston. Such lines were originally conceived with good north-south connections in mind, bringing the Channel ports closer to the Midlands and North West England. They would also have been useful for commuters as not everyone alights from a train to find themselves within walking distance of their place of work. The ultra deep level tube stations built during the Second World War under some of the central London tube stations could also have been used for a limited stop higher speed underground network on the lines of the RER regional expresses across Paris.

Yet, for the most part, railway services across London became fewer as the railways matured. The Great Western services to Victoria must have benefitted some, but not enough to justify their continued existence. There were other lines around London, such the West London and East London, and of course the great connecting link of the North London, which was most useful for goods en route to or from the docks.

The most important line across London, and today the only line to actually cross the centre of London, is that today operated by Capital Connect, formerly known as Thameslink, and indeed this is still the name used for the route of 93 miles, 147 km, from Brighton to Bedford, with onward connections to Leeds. The route is being extensively modernised and will become a vital link in the capital's railway system, although capacity will be limited.

The line dates from 1 January 1866, when the London Chatham & Dover Railway completed its Metropolitan Extension, extending its lines from their temporary terminus at Ludgate Hill to Farringdon Street, having persuaded both the Great Northern and London & South Western Railways to subscribe more than £300,000 apiece towards the cost of the extension with the promise of through running powers, which they soon exercised, along with the Midland Railway, which started running trains through to Victoria in 1875. The LCDR itself sent trains from Herne Hill through to Kings Cross and then as far as Barnet. With the centre of London already congested, the extension was a considerable success, although not used by anything so ambitious as the Brighton-Rugby services of recent years. Unfortunately, a shortage of space meant that Ludgate Hill offered just two island platforms, which soon proved insufficient for the traffic on offer and, as expansion was out of the question given the high cost of property and the LCDR's over-stretched finances, an additional station was built on a spur off the Metropolitan Extension, and it was this that was named St Paul's when it opened on 10 May 1886.

Despite its popularity, passenger services were cut back during the First World War to terminate at Moorgate from the Midland line to the north, and at Holborn Viaduct for what had become the South Eastern & Chatham from the south. One reason for this was that the line was still steam-worked and therefore very unpleasant as much of it was in tunnel, while much of the inner cross-London traffic had been lost to buses and trams. The lines nevertheless proved invaluable for freight, and during the war years even handled ammunition trains! It remained a freight-only line until 1970 when the short section between Farringdon and Holborn Viaduct was closed. There were separate lower level platforms under the main part of Holborn Viaduct station known as the Snow Hill platforms, and these gave the name to the route. A few local trains used Holborn Viaduct, but most were relegated to a low level station with two platforms used by trains running through to Farringdon, and known initially when it opened on 1 August 1874 as Snow Hill, but changed to Holborn Viaduct (Low Level) on 1 May 1912.

It was not until 1988 that the Snow Hill tunnel was re-opened to passenger trains after seventy-two years, with timetabled cross-London services starting on the full Thameslink network in May 1988. By this time, after overhead electrification completed in 1982, the northern section was run as the *Midland City Line* service from Bedford along the Midland Main Line to London St Pancras and the City Widened Lines to Moorgate. From the south, services terminated at Holborn Viaduct. South of the river, it divided into two routes with main line running through London Bridge to East Croydon, Gatwick Airport and Brighton. The other route was a branch line serving the inner suburbs.

Initially, trains went via Bromley to Orpington and Sevenoaks, but this was later changed to run via Elephant & Castle and Streatham to West Croydon. After West Croydon the line ran through Carshalton Beeches to Sutton then to Epsom, Leatherhead, and Effingham Junction, finally terminating at Guildford. However, this route crossed the commuter networks of what were to become several different rail companies and the onset of privatisation made the route increasingly difficult. Around 1994 the second branch was cut back to West Croydon. Then, around 1995, a major overhaul occurred when the route was changed completely. Thameslink no longer served the West Croydon route and instead a new route to Sutton was opened up over existing track through Mitcham Junction with the line then continuing on a loop up to Wimbledon and then rejoining itself south of Streatham. It should be noted, however, that morning peak trains only ran in a clockwise direction around this loop, inconvenient for commuters.

When British Rail was privatised, Thameslink was franchised to a subsidiary of Govia. On 1 April 2006, the franchise passed to First Capital Connect. The branding of most trains, stations, and signs has been changed to reflect the name of the new company, but criticism of the loss of what had been widely regarded as an apt name for these services forced First Capital Connect to refer to it as the 'Thameslink route'.

In the meantime, the importance of the route had been recognised and starting in 1991, British Rail, then Railtrack and finally its successor, Network Rail, started to expand and upgrade Thameslink which was becoming to suffer severe overcrowding at peak hours. Originally called Thameslink 2000, it is now known as the Thameslink Programme. It was left to Network Rail, after the demise of Railtrack, to tackle the main elements of the work once funding was authorised on 24 July 2007. Construction began on 24 October 2007, with Luton Airport Parkway the first station to be extended. The provisional completion date is 2015.

In retrospect, it seems strange that such an important north–south link remained unused by passenger trains for so long, especially when one recalls the Victorian plan for a through line from Charing Cross to Euston.

All change on the Underground

London Regional Transport disappeared in its turn in 2000 to be replaced by yet another new body for the capital's transport, Transport for London, TfL. While the GLC was long gone, a new elected body, the London Assembly, was created and for the first time a directly-elected Mayor of London was instituted. The first of these US-style mayors was Ken Livingstone, regarded as 'far left', even within the Labour Party.

Outright privatisation of the Underground was rejected and would in any case have been politically impossible with Livingstone in power and Labour back in government. Instead, in January 2003, it became a Public-Private Partnership, PPP, with the infrastructure and rolling stock divided between two companies, with one, Metronet, for the sub-surface lines and the other, Tubes Lines, handling the deep level tubes under thirty-year contracts, whilst London Underground Limited remained publicly owned and operated by TfL. As with the main line railways, this was controversial, and the doubters doubtless felt vindicated when Metronet went into administration on 18 July 2007, with its responsibilities passing to TfL. While efforts were made at central government level to find a new operator, at the time of writing TfL seems determined to retain control of the sub-surface lines. Tube Lines seems to be holding steady, but the collapse of Metronet cost the taxpayer some £2 billion, although some of this was offset by payments of £70 million apiece by the five main shareholders in Metronet.

A card for all seasons

The birth of London Transport coincided with a growth in longer distance commuting. Brighton was already a dormitory for the more adventurous, but as faster services spread along the South Coast, other places became important as well. Of course, at first it was the intermediate stations that benefitted most as the non-stop London and Brighton electric trains were no faster than the steam trains that had preceded them, although more consistent, and it was on semi-fast and stopping services that the improvement in journey times was most marked.

Many season ticket holders had an underground journey added to their ticket, saving the need to re-book. While London Transport did issue season tickets for its railway services, it did not do so for bus services. One-day cards for unlimited travel on central buses, the 'Red Rover', country buses, the 'Green Rover', and all buses, including Greenline coaches, and underground, the 'Gold Rover' were available, usually bought at underground stations or travel offices, but the Green Rover had to be bought on the bus, and a lengthy process it was as the ticket had to be punched to mark the date of issue.

A step towards providing an integrated ticketing system was the 'Travelcard' which covered all London Transport, and later Transport for London, services and those of the then British Rail within the London Transport zone. There were five Travelcard Zones initially, and cards were issued for a single zone or any number of zones, including an all-zone Travelcard. Buying a longer distance return ticket on the underground after 9.30 am would mean being issued with an all-zones Travelcard – something which was very useful if one arrived at London Heathrow Airport for example.

Far more ambitious was the Oystercard, an electronic ticket, first issued in 2003, and which card-holders 'top-up' with money to pay for bus and railway fares, with a maximum 'stored value' on the card of £90. An earlier system which effectively acted as a prototype and proved the technology was the Octopus Card, launched in Hong Kong in 1997. Unlike credit cards, Oyster does not actually provide credit and funds have to be added to it. It is valid on the Underground, buses, the Docklands Light Railway (DLR), London Overground, Croydon trams and some main line railway services, although here use is sometimes restricted because of a lack of reader machines at many railway stations. The number of travel zones in London was increased from five to nine with the launch of Oystercard.

The blue, credit-card size Oyster is a stored value smartcard which pays for variety of single tickets, period tickets and travel permits which must be added to the card prior to travel. It can hold up to three season tickets at any one time, so that regular commuters still enjoy the savings of a season ticket as well as the benefits of having an Oystercard. Passengers pass the card over electronic readers when entering and leaving the transport system in order to validate it or deduct funds, except on flat fare services where a single pass on boarding is sufficient. The cards are topped up or recharged at numerous sales points, by credit transfer or by online purchase. Usage has been encouraged by offering substantially cheaper fares on Oyster than payment with cash, so that a £4 minimum fare central zone Underground magnetic card ticket is just £1.60 with Oystercard. On the buses, a flat fare of £2 using a paper ticket is reduced to £1 with Oystercard, with the cost of any number of journeys capped at £3.30 a day. By March 2007 more than 10 million Oyster cards were in circulation, more than the population of Greater London, and more than 80% of all journeys on services run for Transport for London used the Oyster card.

The benefit of the card to Transport for London and its contractors is that it eases accounting and reduces cash transactions. Originally the rights to Oystercard lay with TranSys, the operator, but Transport for London purchased the right to use the name indefinitely in 2008.

In 2005, the Mayor of London, Ken Livingstone, tried to persuade train operating companies to allow Oyster on all of their services within London, but a dispute about ticketing prevented this plan from going ahead. After further negotiations, Transport for London offered to fund the train operating companies with £20m to provide Oyster facilities in London stations; this resulted in an outline agreement to introduce PAYG acceptance across the entire London rail network. The danger is that someone who boards a train and then alights at a station without an Oystercard reader is liable to be charged for a far longer journey than has actually been made. The railway objections are understandable as the system does not really allow for such fares as off-peak day returns, for example.

A variation on the Oystercard is the the free travel pass issued to London residents who are aged over sixty years or are disabled, and which uses the Oystercard. Travel is free at all times on the Underground, Overground, Docklands Light Railway, buses and Croydon Tramlink, and after 9.30 am on some railway routes, while for travel outside these times they need a standard Oystercard or other form of ticket.

The success of the card has been matched by adding new services to it so that it can be used for some non-travel transactions. Plans to introduce an Oystercard for public transport throughout Wales have been mooted, but the geographical limits to the scheme have generated some objections.

The railway companies are introducing their own smart card system, known as the ITSO (standing for Integrated Transport Smartcard Organisation) smartcard. When these are eventually introduced, it will be possible to load one 'stored journey right', or e-ticket for railway travel outside Greater London on to the card at ticket offices or self-service machines. There is not enough space on the card for more information to be stored. Travellers starting their journeys outside London will be able to use Oystercards in certain cases, if they are regarded as 'trusted customers'. The gates or 'validators' will calculate the applicable fare on arrival in London.

It is likely that credit held on ITSO smartcards will be usable for pay as you go journeys, but there may be limitations on fare capping, and combining season tickets and pay as you go usage.

ITSO is being slowly introduced with trial schemes in Yorkshire as the 'Yorcard' and in both Wales, where a principality-wide scheme is proposed, and in parts of Scotland, while the companies supporting this initiative include ticket machine manufacturers such as Almex and many bus and railway operators such as First Group, Arriva and Stagecoach.

Across London east and west - Crossrail

Thameslink used a disused railway line to revive long-lost connections across London and extended these beyond the suburbs. No such route existed running east to west, possibly because in the early days of the railways, river traffic was still significant, but the Metropolitan and District Lines also provided an east-west route, albeit one that was slow and often required a change of trains. Nevertheless, Paddington failed to offer good fast onward connections to the City and to the new development at Canary Wharf, and it eventually became clear that something faster and more direct was needed, especially with the example of Parisian RER regional expresses putting London's railways at a disadvantage. The new project became known as 'Crossrail', and it has become a matter of controversy concerning both the route and even the question of whether the money spent on the Channel Tunnel Rail Link would have been better spent and benefitted more travellers if it had been devoted to Crossrail.

As a new railway, it required parliamentary approval and the Crossrail Act was passed on 22 July 2008. The plan is for the line to be completed by 2017, with 200-metre long ten-car trains running at two–and-a-half minute frequencies on two routes, the first of which will be a tunnel linking Liverpool Street with Paddington, while there should also be a Chelsea-Hackney line. Costing an estimated £16 billion, it was originally intended to be a joint venture between the Department for Transport and Transport for London, but the latter has now assumed full control and the line will be integrated with the London Underground and the national railway network, with Oystercard being valid, and Travelcards will also be used except for journeys to Heathrow, which will continue to have special fares. The trains will run past Paddington to Heathrow and Maidenhead, and beyond Liverpool Street to Shenfield and Abbey Wood, replacing many existing local services. Plans exist to extend the services westwards to Reading and eastwards to Ebbsfleet, with a station at Woolwich. In the centre, there will be a need for underground stations at Paddington, Bon Street, Tottenham Court Road, Farringdon, Liverpool Street, Whitechapel and the Isle of Dogs.

In contrast with the early railways, which landowners and others viewed with concern, if not outright fear, many have viewed their community being left off the Crossrail map as a disaster. Early plans considered routes such as Paddington to Richmond and Kingston-upon-Thames, or to

Aylesbury, High Wycombe and Watford, or in the east a service to Dartford.

One problem is that the original plan anticipated generous contributions being made by property developers who would see the value of their investment rise with the completion of Crossrail. The economic problems which first became apparent in 2008 have placed such contributions in doubt.

In 2009, work began at Tottenham Court Road station, a particularly difficult site where it is expected to take seven years to complete.

The project still attracts controversy, especially from railway goods operators, who see much of the existing spare capacity in the London area being without additional capacity or new connections being made. In contrast with the early days of the railways, it seems that there will be little impact on housing.

Safety on the privatised railway

The separation of infrastructure, track, signals and stations, from the train operating companies, except on the Isle of Wight, has been widely criticised, although to-date nothing has been done about it. However, safety on the privatised railway, while not without its incidents and even some major accidents, seems on balance to be far better than in earlier years. To a great extent, this is due in part to the design of modern rolling stock, which does not concertina, does not have the bodywork swept off a chassis or underframe, and is less likely to ride up over the adjoining carriage. It is also true that in many railway accidents, luck still plays a part. If the train does not hit a lineside structure or another train when it leaves the track, the chances of serious injuries or fatalities are much reduced. On the other hand, there is the tendency amongst many journalists to immediately and instinctively blame the privatised railway for everything. An accident at Great Heck on the East Coast main line was caused by a motorist whose vehicle and trailer ended up on the line in front of an oncoming express train, which was derailed into the path of a freight train travelling in the other direction, and was not the fault of either train operator or the infrastructure owner.

Just a few months separated the first accident to follow that at Clapham Junction, and the railway had still to be privatised. This was at Purley Station, a popular commuter destination, on 4 March 1989, when a train driver missed the distant signal and then over-ran a home signal at danger, hitting the train in front, killing five people and injuring another ninety, leaving part of one of the trains hanging down an embankment.

Driver inattention was a factor in a number of other accidents in the years that followed. On 8 January 1991, two were killed and no less than 240 injured when a train hit the buffers at Cannon Street. One reason for the number of injuries was the practice of London commuters to be standing at the doors, with them open, ready to jump out before the train actually stopped. The accident led to a renewed push to get rid of 'slam door' rolling stock, and also to drivers being forced to crawl into stations rather than brake steadily from the approach speed. Slam door rolling stock had one big advantage, which was that passengers could board and alight from trains quickly, and the change to sliding door rolling stock has seen journey times increase on many routes. The line from Guildford via Cobham to Waterloo now takes longer than in 1929.

Another serious accident was just south of Watford Junction, on Thursday 8 August 1996, when an evening train operated by North London Railways, the predecessor of Silverlink, from Euston passed a red signal and collided with an empty train, killing one person and injuring another sixty-nine. The driver of the train was charged with manslaughter, but later found not guilty when the case reached court.

Even more serious was that at Southall when a Great Western Trains HST running from Swansea to Paddington went through a red light and crashed into a freight train due to driver inattention on 19 September 1997. The accident might have been avoided had the automatic train protection system, APT, been switched on, but the system was troublesome and many drivers preferred to work without it. The leading power car leapfrogged over a heavy goods wagon, but the carriages immediately behind were derailed and six passengers were killed and another 150 injured.

Still more serious was another accident on the lines in and out of Paddington on 5 October 1999, with a head-on collision shortly after 8 am between another London-bound Great Western HST and a Thames Trains diesel multiple unit leaving the station. The first carriage of the DMU was completely destroyed and the driving car of the HST was badly damaged, with fuel vapour from a fractured tank or fuel lines ignited when the driving car struck the overhead wires installed for the Heathrow Express. In the accident and the resulting inferno, thirty-one passengers were killed and another 400 injured; many seriously. The cause of the accident was that driver of the departing train passed a signal at danger, possibly in part due to his inexperience, but also because his view of the signals was found to be obstructed by overhead gantries, for which Railtrack was held responsible

In fact, Railtrack, which was re-nationalised under somewhat controversial procedures shortly after a serious accident at Hatfield, and became Network Rail, was held responsible for a number of serious accidents, and the situation has not improved as quickly as many believe it should since re-nationalisation.

On 17 October 2000, a Great North Eastern Railway InterCity 225 (the reference is to 225 kmph, or 140 mph) from King's Cross to Leeds, was derailed by a broken rail that seems to have been left undetected for some time, and a restaurant car struck the supporting mast for the overhead wires, or catenary. The four fatalities and many of the thirty-five injured were travelling in the restaurant car, and the casualties would have been far worse had it not been for the structural integrity of the Mk 4 carriages. The fault was laid firmly at the door of Railtrack which had been subcontracting maintenance, a system which is being reversed, but slowly, by Network Rail.

The year 2002 was another very bad period for accidents, again caused by track defects. The first of and the worst of the two accidents was on 10 May at Potters Bar when a West Anglia Great Northern electric multiple unit from King's Cross to King's Lynn via Cambridge was running at 97 mph as it approached the station, but as the last carriage passed over a set of points, these failed and the carriage was diverted onto the adjoining line and then derailed, flying into the air and onto the station platform, sliding along it. The first three carriages came to a stand just to the north of the station, having passed through it. Six of the seven people killed in the accident were in the carriage, which had knocked masonry off a bridge onto the street below where the seventh victim was killed. Another seventy people were injured. Despite claims by the maintenance contractor of sabotage, the accident investigation discovered that the bolts holding the stretcher bars had been loosened and gone missing, causing the points to move as the train ran over them. The potential fault had been reported by an employee who was travelling on a train the previous evening when he noticed excessive vibration, but the inspection team had gone to the wrong end of the station.

Later that year, the second accident occurred at Southall East on 24 November, when a high-speed train was derailed due to a broken fishplate (the strip of metal that connects two jointed rails), with ballast being thrown through the windows injuring thirty-one passengers.

Terrorism hits London's transport

While London had experienced terrorist attacks in the past, including those of Irish nationalist groups, the capital's transport had not been specifically targeted. This changed on 7 July 2005, when no less than four Islamic suicide bombers exploded their charges on the Underground and bus network. The day became known as '7/7'. The three bombs exploded on the Underground were all detonated within fifty seconds of one another, at 8.50 am, while the fourth bomb followed almost an hour later, on a double-deck bus as it passed through Tavistock Square. In all, fifty-six people were killed, including the bombers, and another 700 wounded.

The first bomb on the Underground was on a Circle Line Underground train as it travelled west between Edgware Road and Paddington. The second bomb also damaged a passing eastbound train and a wall that later collapsed. The third bomb exploded on a Piccadilly Line tube train as it ran between King's Cross and Russell Square, and damaged the tunnel linings as well as two carriages of the train. The fourth bomb exploded on a No 30 bus, with the bomber sitting upstairs, towards the back, so that most of the victims were also at the rear of the bus on both decks. The bus was running off its normal route as it had been diverted following the other bomb attacks.

Transport for London immediately cancelled all Underground services and withdrew bus services from the centre of London - something that did not happen during the Second World War. The loss of life was considerable, but could have been even worse had all of the bombs been detonated on the deep level tube lines rather than just the third bomb. The lack of space between the trains and the tunnel walls would have meant that the bombs would have been much more lethal than on the sub-surface Circle Line. Some believe that the bus bomber had in fact intended to travel by train, but for reasons not known, had delayed boarding a train and opted for a bus instead.

Chapter 19

The Future of Railways
in London

When a man is tired of London he is tired of life.
Dr Johnson

he shape of London today, built up to beyond Surbiton or
Croydon to the south, and similarly extended to the west, north
and east, would not have been possible without the railways.
London as we know it is a creation of the railways. Only railways can
handle the massive volume of passengers and provide reasonable speeds
safely in a built-up area. This has become more critical as London has
followed the trend set initially in the United States, but now copied almost
worldwide, of building ever taller buildings. Building upwards satisfies the
need for more accommodation, be it residential or business, but it also
imposes massive strains on the infrastructure, and in this context that
means railways. Quite simply, the number of people who need to travel is
vastly increased.

There is another problem, which is the ever deeper foundations
required by higher buildings means that it becomes progressively more
difficult to find routes for underground lines, or for that matter for
electricity, gas, telephone, water and sewerage.

Compared to Paris, London has shown considerable lack of foresight in
not establishing a regional express network along the lines of the French
capital's RER (Reseau Express Regional), that can provide reasonably high-
speed travel over relatively short distances, easing the burden on the
Underground and the suburban services of the mainline companies. The
first RER route opened in 1969. The only British equivalent is
Thameslink, which sets no records for speed, while Crossrail waits some
time in the future. It should be ready in the next decade, but major British
projects have a habit of running late, so if it opens by 2020, that will be an
achievement. Many commentators believe that the twenty-five minutes or
so time saving on services from London to Paris and Brussels by the

Channel Tunnel Rail Link does not justify the cost and that the money would have been better spent on Crossrail. The CTRL has also made life much less convenient for passengers to the East Midlands using St Pancras, who now have a longer walk to what amounts to a satellite station outside the terminus.

There is no excuse for this oversight and delay. The railways are necessary for a major conurbation and its population, including both the resident population and that of workers.

One can argue very convincingly, as Transport Watch would, that many railways would serve the community much better if they were converted into roads, and there is little doubt that there are lines on which the frequency of trains and the proportion of seats occupied are so low that using the better alignment of the railway would often provide a low-cost road improvement. This is not always the case as some railway lines fit very tightly into the surrounding terrain, with narrow cuttings and tunnels.

The bulk of longer distance British inter-city travel, such as that between the main Scottish cities and London, is by air. Until air travel was crippled by over-zealous and untargeted security measures, meaning that short-haul passengers spend most of their time at the departure airport, it was unrivalled, and while it suffered from the airports being too remote from the central business districts, by choosing one's airport at the London end of the journey, one could minimise this. That is one advantage of London having five airports spread around the fringes of the Greater London area, and it also means that the airports are closer to the homes of many London commuters when they need to travel by air. The exception is London City, close to the Docklands and also exceptional in that check-in time is still just fifteen minutes.

The trouble is that the current regulatory regime for all of Britain's railways has also caused the train operating companies to take the easy way out, with journey times extended to ensure absolute punctuality. Today, a train is still theoretically on time if it is five minutes late, before the Second World War it was either on time or it was late. No nonsense!

A rolling programme of electrification has long advocated by the railway press as the only cost-effective means of electrifying the railway. Nevertheless, costly overhead electrification which requires bridges and tunnels to be rebuilt is only necessary and justifiable if one is building very high speed lines. Much more could have been done sooner, cheaper and more quickly had the London suburban network used third rail, which would also have standardised each generation of suburban and short distance mainline rolling stock. The money spent on raising overhead structures could have been saved for those lines on which capacity is now so tight that double deck trains, known in the trade as 'bi-levels', would be the cheapest solution. One advantage of bi-levels over longer trains, which require costly platform lengthening, changes to points and signals and often other works as well, is that they also keep the train within a set length which means that the passengers don't have to spend five minutes walking along the platform getting to the front of the train. For disabled passengers, bi-levels are a practical solution, as the ends of the carriages over the bogies provide a third level that is easily accessible with having to use steps to reach the lower or upper saloon.

So, what is the future for the railways in London? For the next twenty years, Crossrail will be the big step forward, and for much of the rest, what is running today will still be running. The most obvious change will be that at last the Metropolitan Line will have its 'A' stock replaced by a new fleet of what has been dubbed 'S' stock, with variations of this following later for the other sub-surface lines. However, the new 'S' stock will have fewer seats, with the current 2+3 configuration being replaced by 2+2 and also longitudinal seating in the interests of extra standing room. In defence of the new stock, the current Mayor for London, Boris Johnson, has suggested that the three-abreast seats on the 'A' stock are so cramped that they are seldom used efficiently. Others have suggested that those boarding trains at the outermost stations are likely to get a seat, but this ignores their homeward journey!

There has for long been a proposal for a line between Chelsea and Hackney, which some believe could be completed by 2025, but with Crossrail and the mounting deficit in the public finances, this is a project that may remain a dream for many more years.

Within the next twenty years we can expect some move on electrification of the remaining diesel lines, with priority being given to the lines from Paddington, but it remains uncertain whether the projected HS2, the high-speed line that will run, possibly via Heathrow Airport, to the Midlands, Manchester and then possibly to Edinburgh and Glasgow, will be even started during that period. Failure to do so means that the London commuter belt will remain much as it is for now.

The problem is that when money was available, it was spent none too wisely, and now the money isn't available as government borrowing has soared. The previous massive debt, built up to finance two world wars, to cover the years of recession between the wars and post-war reconstruction, was largely eliminated due to North Sea oil revenues, but now we are a net importer of oil, gas and coal. One problem with Crossrail is that a contribution was expected from business, but the recession has made this unlikely, and as for HS2, the estimated cost today is £34 billion, money which the government does not have and is unlikely to have for many years.

Electrification is vital, and to provide reliable supplies for the long term, the only source of this power must be nuclear energy. It is also the only way to get our future energy needs off the balance of payments.

Re-opening railway lines as has been proposed recently is something that will have to be addressed, but re-opening for an hourly two-car diesel multiple unit would be a waste of resources. Few of the closed lines are in the London area, or even the commuter area, but there are some, such as that to Cranleigh and the old Great Central line through Quinton Road – but would these be viable?

Viability is important. The heavy cost of providing an extra train for commuters and the low revenue that would be earned has already been mentioned, and now the country can't afford it. Something has been lost somewhere compared to the Victorian age. Perhaps a political solution is needed, reuniting ownership of trains, infrastructure and the operating companies, should we consider re-creating the old grouped companies, and perhaps just a few more so that East Anglia and the longer distance services to the north-east and Scotland are not lumped together? These new companies should be in private hands so that they can raise capital once again, given absolute tenure to make long-term planning possible and to allow employer-employee and customer loyalty to grow, and, of course, to make them aware of market opportunities.

As for the longer term, beyond twenty years, is it worth making any prophesy? Much can happen in a year, still more in ten, except in railways where rolling stock lasts for more than thirty years.

Appendix I

The Railway Grouping
of 1923

Companies were defined as constituent companies if they were major elements in the grouping, being merged or amalgamated with one another, or subsidiary companies if they were minor companies that could be acquired rather than given the status of being 'merged'. In anticipation of the grouping, there were a number of acquisitions of smaller railways in the year or so before the grouping took effect on 1 January 1923.

The Railways Act 1921 defined the new shape of the railways as consisting of a 'Southern Group', a 'Western Group', a 'North Western, Midland, and West Scottish Group', and a 'North Eastern, Eastern, and East Scottish Group', which, of course, became the Southern, Great Western, London Midland Scottish and London & North Eastern respectively.

This meant that the Great Western Railway had as its constituent companies the original GWR itself, plus the Barry Railway; Cambrian Railway; the Rhymney Railway; the Taff Vale Railway and the Alexandra (Newport and South Wales) Docks & Railway; with, as subsidiary companies, the Brecon & Merthyr Tydfil Junction Railway; Burry Port & Gwendraeth Valley Railway; Cleobury Mortimer & Ditton Priors Light Railway; Didcot Newbury & Southampton Railway; Exeter Railway; Forest of Dean Central Railway; Gwendraeth Valleys Railway; Lampeter Aberayron & New Quay Light Railway; Liskeard & Looe Railway; Llanelly & Mynydd Mawr Railway; Mawddwy Railway; Midland & South Western Junction Railway; Neath & Brecon Railway; Penarth Extension Railway; Penarth Harbour Dock & Railway; Port Talbot Railway & Docks; Princetown Railway; Rhondda & Swansea Bay Railway; Ross & Monmouth Railway; South Wales Mineral Railway; Teign Valley; Van Railway; Welshpool & Llanfair Light Railway; West Somerset Railway, and the Wrexham & Ellesmere Railway.

The London & North Eastern Railway's constituent companies were the Great Central Railway; Great Eastern Railway; Great North of Scotland Railway; Great Northern Railway; Hull & Barnsley Railway; North Eastern Railway and the North British Railway; while as subsidiaries there were the Brackenhill Light Railway; Colne Valley & Halstead Railway; East & West Yorkshire Union Railway; East Lincolnshire Railway; Edinburgh & Bathgate Railway; Forcett Railway; Forth & Clyde Junction Railway; Gifford & Garvald Railway; Great North of England Railway; Clarence & Hartlepool Junction Railway; Horncastle Railway; Humber Commercial Railway & Dock; Kilsyth & Bonnybridge Railway; Lauder Light Railway; London & Blackwall Railway; Mansfield Railway; Mid-Suffolk Light Railway; Newburgh & North Fife Railway; North Lindsey Light Railway; Nottingham & Grantham Railway; Nottingham Joint Station Committee; Nottingham Suburban Railway; Seaforth & Sefton Junction Railway; Stamford & Essendine Railway and the West Riding Railway Committee.

The London Midland Scottish had as its constituent companies the Caledonian Railway; Lancashire & Yorkshire Railway, which had already reached an agreement to be purchased by the London & North Western Railway; Glasgow & South Western Railway; Highland Railway; the Midland Railway; North Staffordshire Railway and the Furness Railway; with subsidiaries including the Arbroath & Forfar Railway; Brechin & Edzell District Railway; Callander & Oban Railway; Cathcart District Railway; Charnwood Forest Railway; Cleator & Workington Junction Railway; Cockermouth Keswick & Penrith Railway; Dearne Valley Railway; Dornoch Light Railway; Dundee & Newtyle Railway; Harborne Railway; Leek & Manifold Valley Light Railway; Maryport & Carlisle Railway; Mold & Denbigh Junction Railway; North & South Western Junction Railway; North London Railway; Portpatrick & Wigtownshore Joint Committee; Shropshire Union Railways & Canal; Solway Junction Railway; Stratford-upon-Avon & Midland Junction Railway; Tottenham & Forest Gate Railway; Wick & Lynster Light Railway; Wirral Railway and the Yorkshire Dales Railway.

As the smallest of the 'Big Four' grouped companies, the Southern Railway consisted of three constituent companies, the London Brighton & South Coast Railway; the London & South Western Railway and the South Eastern & Chatham Railway Companies Managing Committee, itself representing two companies, the South Eastern Railway and the London, Chatham & Dover Railway, that still retained their own assets and shareholders. The subsidiaries were the Bridgwater Railway; Brighton & Dyke Railway; Freshwater, Yarmouth & Newport (Isle of Wight) Railway;

Hayling Railway; Isle of Wight Central Railway; Isle of Wight Railway; Lee-on-Solent Railway; London & Greenwich Railway; Mid Kent Railway; North Cornwall Railway; Plymouth & Dartmoor Railway; Plymouth, Devonport & South Western Junction Railway; Sidmouth Railway and the Victoria Station & Pimlico Railway.

For each of the 'Big Four', many of the minor companies were already operated by or managed by the constituent companies.

Appendix II

Main Transport Operators Absorbed into London Transport, 1933

No less than ninety-two transport undertakings of all kinds were taken over by the London Passenger Transport Board on its formation in 1933. Apart from the four main line or 'grouped' companies, which remained independent, but were forced into a revenue-sharing agreement with the LPTB, the two railway companies absorbed into the London Passenger Transport Board were the Metropolitan Railway and the London Electric Railway. The Metropolitan Railway included a subsidiary, the Great Northern & City Railway. The London Electric Railway's subsidiaries were the District Railway, Bakerloo Line, Piccadilly Line, Hampstead & Highgate Line (now Northern Line Charing Cross branch) and the City & South London Railway (now Northern Line Bank branch), and the Central London Railway. The LPTB's railways consisted of 174 route miles in 1934, excluding operations over the main line railways, and overall it had 3,072 carriages in electric trains, eighty-four locomotive-hauled carriages, fifty-one electric and thirty-eight steam locomotives. The Underground accounted for 315.8 million railway journeys annually, against 525 million suburban journeys on the trains of the 'Big Four' mainline companies.

The tram operators absorbed were the London County Council, with 1,713 tramcars and 167.17 route miles, including tracks owned by the Borough of Leyton with nine route miles and the 0.25 route miles owned by the City of London; Middlesex County Council, with 42.63 route miles, all leased to the Metropolitan Electric Tramways; Metropolitan Electric Tramways, with 316 tramcars and 53.51 route miles, of which 9.38 were owned by the company and 46.23 leased from Middlesex County Council, and 21.5 miles from Hertfordshire County Council; Hertfordshire County Council, with 21.5 miles, leased to the Metropolitan Electric Tramways; Barking Corporation, with just 1.8 route miles operated by Ilford

Corporation, London County Council and East Ham Corporation since 1929; Dartford Urban District Council, a joint undertaking since 1921, with thirty-three tramcars and 10.3 route miles; Croydon Corporation, with fifty-five tramcars and 9.3 route miles; East Ham Corporation, with fifty-six tramcars and 8.34 route miles; Erith Urban District Council, with four route miles; Ilford Corporation, with forty tramcars and 7.13 route miles; Walthamstow Corporation, with sixty-two tramcars and 8.93 miles; West Ham Corporation with 134 tramcars and 16.27 route miles; London United Tramways, with 150 tramcars and 29.05 route miles, as well as sixty-one trolleybuses; and the South Metropolitan Electric Tramways, with fifty-two tramcars and 13.08 route miles.

The London General Omnibus Company, LGOC, provided the bulk of the bus services, including London General Country Services, the Overground, which has originated with the Underground Group, and the bus operations of Tilling and British Automobile Traction which although financially independent were operationally integrated with the LGOC. In 1931, the LGOC had created the first Green Line coach network out of its coach services into London, rearranging these to run across the centre.

Central buses, trolleybuses, underground trains and trams were painted in 'Underground' and 'London General' red and white, country buses in green and white, while all coach services were branded 'Green Line' and painted green and pale green. The fleet name 'London Transport' was adopted for all road transport, but as a sub-title on Greenline, while the railways became 'UndergrounD' a title adopted by the Underground Group in 1909.

Chronology

1634   Sir Richard Dunscombe introduces the sedan chair to London.

1784   Mail coaches introduced.

1801   Surrey Iron Railway authorised by Parliament.

1829   Metropolitan Police Force established.
       George Shillabeer commences the first horse-drawn omnibus service between Paddington Green and the Bank.

1832   First legislation covering buses, Stage Carriage Act 1832, enacted. Railway companies to pay a duty of ½d (0.4p) per mile for every four passengers carried.

1833   London & Greenwich Railway authorised.

1836   London & Greenwich Railway opened between London Bridge and Deptford.
       Commercial Railway authorised, later renamed as the London & Blackwall Railway.

1837   Grand Junction Railway opened throughout.
       First section of Great Western Railway opened.

1838   London & Greenwich Railway completed.
       Further legislation requires buses to display licences and number of passengers allowed prominently, while drivers and conductors working within ten miles of General Post Office licensed with numbered badges. First Registrar of Metropolitan Public Carriages appointed by Home Secretary.
       Paddington and Euston stations opened.

1839   Commercial Railway renamed as London & Blackwall Railway. Extension of L&BR to Fenchurch Street authorised.

1840   London & Blackwall railway opens.
       First legislation on railway safety.
       Board of Trade given powers to regulate the railways.

1841   Christmas Eve, a Great Western train derailed at Sonning, killing eight passengers, forces Parliament to take a closer interest in the railways.

1842   Mileage duty on omnibuses reduced from 3d per mile to 1½d per mile.
       Railway Clearing House starts business.
       HM Queen Victoria makes her first railway journey, travelling between Slough and Paddington.

Midland Railway formed from amalgamation of three smaller companies.

1844   'Gladstone's Act, The Railway Regulation Act 1844, provides for 'Parliamentary Trains' with low fares and also permits nationalisation in the future.
Midland Railway formed on amalgamation of Birmingham & Derby Junction, Midland Counties and North Midland Railways.

1845   Gauge Commission starts work, and in twelve months supports 4 ft 8½ in as standard gauge, but makes exception for Great Western and its associated lines.

1846   London & North Western Railway formed on amalgamation of Grand Junction (which included the Liverpool & Manchester), London & Birmingham and Manchester & Birmingham Railways. *Royal Commission on Railway Termini within or in the immediate vicinity of the Metropolis* appointed.

1847   Collection of duties transferred from the Commissioners of Stamps to the Commissioners of Excise.

1850   Metropolitan Public Carriages Office closed and duties transferred to the Metropolitan Police, with Public Carriage Office opened on 10 April.

1851   1 May to 15 October 1851, Great Exhibition opens at the Crystal Palace in Hyde Park.
London & South Western Railway extended from Nine Elms to Waterloo.
GWR introduces season tickets on London suburban services.

1855   World's first special postal train introduced by the Great Western Railway between London and Bristol: no passengers carried until 1869, when first-class accommodation added.
London General Omnibus Company formed in Paris as the *Compagnie General des Omnibus de Londres*.
The government duty on horse omnibuses reduced from 1½ d a mile to 1d.

1858   Local Government Act limits rating assessments of railway property to a quarter of their net value.
London General Omnibus Company transfers its head office to London.

1862   Chalk Farm: London & North Western Railway lays first standard production steel rails.

1863   Metropolitan Railway opens between Paddington and Farringdon using mixed GWR broad gauge and standard gauge.

1866   Bankers Overend Gurney collapse on 10 May with gross liabilities of £18 million, forcing many railway companies into receivership.
Duty on horse omnibuses reduced from 1d per mile to ¼ d.

1867   Metropolitan Railway changes to standard gauge.

1868   First section of the Metropolitan District Railway, the 'District', opens between South Kensington and Westminster Bridge.
St Pancras Station opens.
Tower Subway Company opens tube tunnel under the River Thames.
Government nationalises telegraph companies, many of which are owned by railway companies.

1869   Duties on horse drawn public transport removed.
Responsibility for horse buses passed to the Metropolitan Police under the Metropolitan Public Carriage Act, which took effect in 1870.

1870   Tramways Act provides statutory basis for street tramways.

1871   Railway Regulation Act imposes duty to report all accidents, not just involving passengers.

1872   Third-class passengers conveyed by all trains on the Midland and Great Eastern Railways.

1873   First-class sleeping cars introduced on services to Scotland from King's Cross. Two months later, Euston follows.

1874   Midland Railway introduces Britain's first Pullman cars.

1875   Bogie coaches appear.
Midland Railway abolishes second-class fares and scraps or upholsters third-class carriages.
First electrical passenger emergency communication introduced on London Brighton & South Coast Railway.

1879   Dining cars introduced by Great Northern Railway between King's Cross and Leeds.

1881   London Brighton & South Coast Railway experiments with electric lighting in Pullman car.

1884   Metropolitan and Metropolitan District Railways complete Inner Circle, the 'Circle', and connection with East London Railway.

1885   First mail train between King's Cross and Aberdeen, but no passenger accommodation.

1888   'Race to the North' between Euston and King's Cross Anglo-Scottish expresses.

1889   Regulation of Railways Act enforces the use of block system, interlocking of signals and points, and continuous fail-safe brakes on passenger trains.

London County Council formed.

1890   City & South London Railway opened, the first underground electric railway.

1892   Great Western Railway introduced corridor carriages, although initially only guards can use corridor connections.

Great Western Railway completes conversion to standard gauge.

1895   Race to Aberdeen with West Coast train covering 541 miles in 8 hrs 32 mins against East Coast train covering 523½ miles in 8 hrs 38 mins.

1896   The Locomotives on Highways Act raises speed limit and removes many restrictions on mechanically-powered roads vehicles.

1898   Waterloo & City Railway opens, ending Waterloo's isolation.

1899   South Eastern & Chatham Railway formed by combining services of London Chatham & Dover and South Eastern railways.

1900   Central London Railway opens.

1902   Underground Electric Railways Group formed by Yerkes.

1904   Great Western *City of Truro* sets unofficial speed record of more than 100 mph.

Great Western Railway inaugurates non-stop running between Paddington and Plymouth.

Motor Car Act 1903 takes effect, requiring drivers to be licensed and vehicles registered.

1905   Inner Circle electrified.

1906   Great Northern Piccadilly & Brompton Railway opens.

Bakerloo Line reaches Waterloo.

1907   Baker Street & Waterloo Railway opens.

Charing Cross Euston & Hampstead Railway or 'Hampstead tube' opens.

Thomas Tilling's sons introduce first longer distance or commuter motor bus service between Sidcup min Kent and Oxford Circus.

LSWR acquires Waterloo & City.

1908   Britain's first all-Pullman train, the *Southern Belle*, introduced between Victoria and   Brighton by London Brighton & South Coast Railway.

1909   Electric train service starts on the LBSCR's South London Line, linking Victoria and London Bridge.

1910   London Electric Railway formed.

1914 First World War begins; Britain's railways pass into government control.

1919 Ministry of Transport formed.

1921 Government control of railways in Great Britain and Ireland ends. Railways Act requires formation of Southern; Western; North Western, Midland and West Scottish; and North Eastern, Eastern and East Scottish 'groups' in Great Britain.

1923 Grouping sees 123 railway companies combined into four, although many joint railways continue.

1928 London & North Eastern Railway introduces world's longest non-stop service between King's Cross and Edinburgh. London & North Eastern Railway introduces first all-steel carriages on the Pullman 'Queen of Scots' between King's Cross, Edinburgh and Glasgow. Third-class sleeping cars introduced by Great Western, London & North Eastern and London Midland & Scottish Railways.

1933 London Passenger Transport Board is formed. Southern Railway completes Britain's first mainline electrification between London (Victoria and London Bridge) and Brighton.

1935 London Passenger Transport Arbitration Tribunal announces the apportioning of receipts within the LPTB area. London & North Eastern Railway introduces Britain's first streamlined train, the *Silver Jubilee*, and on trials runs at average of 100 mph for forty-three miles and reaches 112½ mph twice.

1937 London Midland & Scottish Railway introduced *Coronation Scot* streamlined express between Euston and Glasgow, and on trials reaches 114 mph near Crewe.

1939 Second World War breaks out and railways taken into government control, although serious delays in fixing compensation. Restricted timetables introduced. Catering services cut back.

1941 Ministry of War Transport, includes Ministry of Transport and takes shipping from the Board of Trade. First-class abolished on London suburban services.

1945 Second World War ends. Labour government vows to nationalise transport.

1947 Ministry of War Transport abolished and Ministry of Transport reformed.

Transport Bill enacted setting up British Transport Commission and preparing for nationalisation of railways, canals, railway-owned assets such as ports and bus companies, and for later nationalisation of road haulage.

1948   The 'Big Four' railway companies nationalised, including joint lines, and some other smaller railways. The new British Railways divides itself into six regions.
Non-stop services between King's Cross and Edinburgh reinstated.

1956   British Transport Commission plans most future electrification to be 25kv ac overhead.

1960   Inauguration of electric services between Euston and Manchester via Crewe on the London Midland Region, British Railways.

1963   *Reshaping of British Railways*, the 'Beeching Report' published.
District Line train conducts trials with automatic driving equipment.

1964   Central Line conducts trials with automatic train operation using Woodford-Hainault shuttle.

1966   Electric service introduced from Euston to Manchester and Liverpool.

1974   Electric services inaugurated between Euston and Glasgow.

1991   Electric services inaugurated between King's Cross and Edinburgh.

1994   British Rail restructured ready for privatisation.
First services through Channel Tunnel, running to Waterloo International.

1996   First privatised railway begins operations.

2000   London Regional Transport becomes Transport for London, TfL.

2007   Channel Tunnel trains transferred from Waterloo to St Pancras International.

2009   High-speed domestic railway services from Kent start to use the Channel Rail Link, or High Speed 1, HS1, to St Pancras.

Bibliography

Allen, Cecil J, *Salute to the Southern*, Ian Allan, Shepperton, 1974

Barman, Christian, *The Great Western Railway's Last Look Forward*, David & Charles, Newton Abbot, 1972

Beaumont, Robert, *The Railway King: A Biography of George Hudson, Railway Pioneer and Fraudster*; Review, London, 2002

Bishop, D and Davies, WJK, *Railways and War since 1917*, Blandford, London, 1974

Bonavia, MR, *A History of the LNER*, 3 vols, George Allen & Unwin, London, 1983

Course, Edwin, *The Railways of Southern England: The Main Lines*, Batsford, London, 1973; *The Railways of Southern England: Secondary and Branch Lines*, Batsford, London, 1974

Crump, N, By Rail to Victory: The story of the LNER in Wartime, London & North Eastern Railway, London, 1947

Darwin, Bernard, *War on the Line, The Story of the Southern Railway in War-Time, including D-Day on the Southern*, Southern Railway, London, 1946

Dendy Marshall, CF, *A History of the Southern Railway*, Southern Railway Company, London, 1936

Elliot, Sir John, *On and Off the Rails*, George Allen & Unwin, London, 1982

Glover, J, *London's Underground*, Ian Allan, London, 1999

Gourvish, Terry, *British Railways 1948-73*, Cambridge University Press, 1987; *British Rail 1974-1997*, Oxford University Press, Oxford, 2002

Gritten, Andrew, *Reviving the Railways: A Victorian future?* Centre for Policy Studies, London, 1988

Hamilton Ellis, C, *The Trains We Loved*, Allen & Unwin, London, 1947

Haresnape, Brian, *Maunsell Locomotives*, Ian Allan, Shepperton, 1977; *Bulleid Locomotives*, Ian Allan, Shepperton, 1977

Jackson, Alan A, *London's Termini*, David & Charles, Newton Abbot, 1969

John, E, *Timetable for Victory: A brief and popular account of the railways and railway-owned dockyards of Great Britain and Ireland during the six years' war, 1939-1945*, The British Railways, London, 1946

Kidner, RW, *The Southern Railway*, Oakwood Press, Salisbury, 1958 and 1974

Klapper, Charles F, *Sir Herbert Walker's Southern Railway*, Ian Allan,
   Shepperton, 1973

Moody, GT, *Southern Electric 1909-1979*, Ian Allan, Shepperton, 1979

Nash, GG, *The LMS at War*, London Midland & Scottish Railway,
   London, 1946

Neele, George Potter, *Railway Reminiscences*, 1904

Nock, OS, *A History of the LMS*, 3 vols, George Allen & Unwin,
   London, 1983; *Britain's Railways at War, 1939-1945*, Ian Allan,

Peacock, A J, *The Rise and Fall of the Railway King*, Sutton, Stroud, 1995

Shepperton, 1971; *Sixty Years of Western Express
   Running*, Ian Allan, London, 1973; *The Great Western Railway in the
   Twentieth Century*, Ian Allan, London, 1971

Smullen, Ivor, *Taken for a ride*, Herbert Jenkins, London 1968

Simmons, Jack, and Biddle, Gordon, *The Oxford Companion to British
   Railway History*, Oxford University Press, Oxford, 2000

Sutton, 2006; *Signal Failure – Politics and Britain's Railways*, Sutton,
   2004; *The Southern Railway Handbook 1923-1947*, Sutton, 2003,
   reprinted 2010, Haynes; *The GWR Handbook 1923-1947*, Sutton, 2006

Thomas, John, *A Regional History of the Railways of Great Britain:
   Volume V1-Scotland*, David & Charles, Newton Abbot

White, HP, *Regional History of the Railways of Great Britain, Vol 2,
   Southern England*, David & Charles, Newton Abbot, 1961; *A Regional
   History of the Railways of Great Britain: Volume III- Greater London*,
   David & Charles, Newton Abbot

Williams, Frederick S, *Our Iron Roads*, London, 1884

Wragg, David, *The Great Western Railway Handbook 1923-1947*, Sutton,
   2006, Re-printed 2010, Haynes; *Wartime on the Railways 1939-1945*,

Index